FA CUP
150 YEARS

THE OFFICIAL HISTORY OF THE
FA CUP

Published in 2022 by Welbeck

An Imprint of Welbeck Non-Fiction Limited, part of Welbeck Publishing Group.

Based in London and Sydney.

www.welbeckpublishing.com

A CIP catalogue record for this book is available from the British Library

ISBN 978 1 80279 067 2

Editor: Ross Hamilton
Design: Russell Knowles, Luke Griffin
Picture Research: Paul Langan
Production: Arlene Alexander, Rachel Burgess

Printed in Great Britain by Bell and Bain Ltd, Glasgow

10 9 8 7 6 5 4 3 2 1

FA CUP

150 YEARS

THE OFFICIAL HISTORY OF THE
FA CUP

MIGUEL DELANEY

FOREWORD BY
ARSÈNE WENGER

WELBECK

CONTENTS

FOREWORD

When I led Arsenal out for my first FA Cup Final at Wembley in 1998, I suddenly felt deeply moved. I managed to keep my emotions in check, but maybe my face gives away a little if you watch it back now. It was a thrilling, childlike joy, because I realised this was my perfect idea of football.

There was the sight of that famous stadium, under that brilliant May sunshine. There was the perfect green pitch, inside those pristine white lines. Most of all, there was the atmosphere, one which remains truly unique to the occasion.

There is nothing like that nervous excitement in the moments before a big match, and it is never more exhilarating than before an FA Cup Final. The tradition, the heritage and the sense of occasion are unmatched. You know you are becoming part of history.

Like so many others, some of my first memories of football back in my village, Duttlenheim, were from The FA Cup. That is what gives it a power beyond anything else, as well as a mystique. Some of the first matches I saw on television were FA Cup Finals, the brightness of the ball standing out on the black and white of the screen. These were the pictures that came back to me as I walked out into the glorious colour of the day.

The competition was a major part of why I always wanted to manage in England. It has a rare romance, and there is a simple beauty to it. Anyone can play anyone, and it means anything can happen. This is what makes football so great, and the sport's oldest competition captures this essence like nothing else. It is a spirit unique to English football culture.

That spirit is best illustrated by the crowd on the day of the Final. You walk into a stadium that is split in half, but united by a shared passion. You have your fans on one side, and the fans of your opponent on the other. There is no other match in football with this kind of atmosphere.

Above all, it is a source of deep pride that I am the manager to have won the most FA Cups, and that my Arsenal are the club to have lifted the trophy more than any other. It is a place in history I could barely have imagined when growing up with the game.

Each of my seven victories of course means something a little different. Indeed, they almost tell the story of my time in England.

The win over Newcastle United in 1998 was special because it was my first, and brought a first double. The victory over Chelsea in 2002 confirmed a second double, and the rise of another great team. The 2005 Final came against my great rivals at Manchester United and, in retrospect, perhaps marked the climax of a brilliant Arsenal team. The 2014 victory over Hull City felt the most important because of when it came, and 2017 was my cherished last trophy in England.

All of these, as well as the wins in 2003 and 2015, came between so many other epic FA Cup moments that I look back on fondly. That sometimes even applies to the setbacks, like that famous Semi-final against Manchester United or the manner of my one defeated Final, against Liverpool in 2001. But only sometimes!

All these matches mean something different to me, but their significance derives from the same idea of glory. It may surprise you, but I don't keep any of the medals from my FA Cup wins. There is always someone at the club who didn't get one, or who would appreciate it more.

The memories are enough for me. That's what The FA Cup is really about: that incomparable feeling. It is an honour to have my name associated with this greatest of competitions.

ARSÈNE WENGER

Opposite: Arsène Wenger lifts The FA Cup for a record seventh time as a manager, after his Arsenal side beat Chelsea at Wembley in May 2017.

Previous pages: Thousands of Blackpool and Manchester United supporters make their way towards the twin towers of Wembley Stadium ahead of the 1948 FA Cup Final.

CHAPTER ONE

INTRODUCTION

AS THE LEICESTER CITY SQUAD CELEBRATED THE CLUB'S FIRST EVER FA CUP FINAL WIN IN MAY 2021, SOME WERE EAGER TO GET A PHOTO WITH THE FAMOUS TROPHY. OTHERS SIMPLY WANTED TO STAND THERE ON THE WEMBLEY PITCH, LOOKING OUT, TAKING IT ALL IN. HEEDING THE WORDS OF THOSE WHO HAD GONE BEFORE THEM, THE STAFF HAD TOLD THE PLAYERS TO NOT LET THE OCCASION PASS THEM BY.

Leicester's oldest predecessors, the 1872 Wanderers team that won the very first FA Cup, experienced a rather different occasion. They played nine miles away from Wembley, at the Kennington Oval, and weren't even formally presented with the cup – a very different trophy – until a banquet four weeks later. The only images that exist of the day are sketches.

These completely different pictures still capture the same thing, however – the unique glory that comes from this most communal and democratic of competitions.

That's what the Leicester players were looking out at from the pitch, as their supporters celebrated an achievement for which they'd waited decades – a great coming together that reflects what football is really about, and what The FA Cup represents more than any other sporting event. It's the excitement that comes from rare opportunity. Anyone can meet anyone in this competition. Anyone can beat anyone. There's no seeding, no safety net. It's a totally open draw; one in which amateurs, professionals and everyone in between can still compete.

As The FA Cup reaches its 150th year, this book documents a competition that stretches back further than any other in football history. It is also among the most all-encompassing, featuring clubs from the Premier League all the way down to Step 6 of the FA National League system, involving over 730 teams.

That means it has had very different meanings for different people over the years. Jackie Milburn, Newcastle United's great three-time winner in the 1950s, perhaps put it best: "It means glory, glamour, excitement and – above all – it is instant."

That sudden-death format also leads to immortality.

The FA Cup has been the ultimate prize, the holy grail. It's been part of doubles, trebles and unique feats. It's been the one that got away. It's culture, it's tradition. It involves quirkiness and grandiosity. It's been the coldest winter days in the most rickety of old stadiums. It's been glorious summer sunshine at Wembley.

It's about Alec Stock as much as Arsène Wenger, Tim Buzaglo as much as Didier Drogba, Hereford United as much as Manchester United. The FA Cup has crowned teams, it has saved teams, and it has humiliated them.

The competition brings all of these elements together because it brings the game together. Inherent in the cup's prestige is the precariousness of the Third Round, when the big clubs appear, and its rare opportunity for smaller clubs to go for glory. New storylines get added, as cup runs get going.

There have been seasons when The FA Cup has felt so perfect that it feels like it has been scripted, as with Blackpool's famous, Stanley Matthews-inspired victory in 1953. There have been others when it has felt more unpredictable than any fiction could ever hope to offer, as with Sunderland's shocking upset win in 1973.

Perhaps the greatest glory comes from the knowledge that, when a player steps out onto the pitch for any FA Cup fixture, they are stepping into history. Every moment is imbued with the memory of 150 years of football. Every player performs with the implicit understanding that they can write themselves into this. It's an inspiration that has touched more than 3,200 clubs across those 150 years, over 38,000 matches.

"IT MEANS GLORY, GLAMOUR, EXCITEMENT AND – ABOVE ALL – IT IS INSTANT."

- JACKIE MILBURN -

Opposite top: Leicester City's James Maddison celebrates in front of jubilant supporters during the 2021 Final win over Chelsea at Wembley, the first after the lifting of COVID-19 restrictions.

Opposite bottom: A world-record crowd of over 100,820 people turns up for the 1901 Final between Tottenham Hotspur and Sheffield United at Crystal Palace.

Previous pages: Blackpool's Stanley Matthews meets HRH, King George VI, ahead of his first Final, against Manchester United, at Wembley in 1948.

While the inevitable inclination when celebrating the history of such a competition is to consider the most famous names and games, The FA Cup itself goes way beyond that – another reason it's unique. The early history of the competition is really the history of football and its laws. The FA Cup was where innovations as fundamental to the game as the crossbar and numbered shirts were first implemented, not to mention the very idea of knock-outs and competition itself.

The format was the suggestion of the esteemed Charles Alcock. He was recognised as the first winning captain with Wanderers in 1872, The FA secretary and – most grandiosely – "the father of modern sport", for his foundational work in establishing association football as we know it today. Alcock recognised that the early game was missing form, and remembered from his days at Harrow might suit the sport. For all the images of privilege that conjures, his idea gave birth to the democracy that has made The FA Cup so great.

Rough versions of football – in both meanings of the description – were played all over the world, including the streets and fields of Victorian England. The public-school sons of the privileged classes took it and gave it structure, codifying it and creating competition, only for the working classes to take over and wrest the game back. This involved, among other things, a potentially divisive split over payment, but that only ended up fashioning the sport as we know it. Within 16 years of the 1885 ratification of professionalism – and the game being presented back to the people – Edward VII accepted the role of patron of The FA. This soon meant that monarchs watched working men play, no small thing in the early 20th century. All came together under football. A competition that was initially just a pastime for the privileged became the biggest sporting event the planet had ever see, quickly bringing world-record crowds. By 1901, the Final between Sheffield United and Tottenham Hotspur attracted over 110,000 people. There couldn't be a better demonstration of the game's power than the sight of so many people.

In the cup's first decade, it was exclusively won by the clubs of the so-called "gentleman amateurs". But the original trophy, described as "the little tin idol", had too much of an allure. Geoffrey Green put it best, in the first official history of The FA Cup, back in 1949: "Scarcely 18 inches in height, this was a trophy that set the game alive."

"SCARCELY 18 INCHES IN HEIGHT, THIS WAS A TROPHY THAT SET THE GAME ALIVE."

- GEOFFREY GREEN -

PLAYER'S CIGARETTES

ASSOCIATION CUP WINNERS
BLACKBURN ROVERS, 1885

PLAYER'S CIGARETTES

ASSOCIATION CUP WINNERS
THE OLD CUP

PLAYER'S CIGARETTES

ASSOCIATION CUP WINNERS
SHEFFIELD UNITED, 1899

PLAYER'S CIGARETTES

ASSOCIATION CUP WINNERS
THE MEDALS

The cup also trialled many of the laws of the game, as well as providing the momentum for the creation of the Football League, and the spread of the sport around the globe.

This was all because, more than anything, it captured the imagination. The FA Cup doesn't just bring the game together. It brings communities together. It makes people proud of their towns, and taps into their sense of identity. The competition forms the greatest memories of many people's lives.

Above: Yeovil Town player-manager Alec Stock is carried shoulder high during a dance at the Prince's Ballroom to celebrate the club's Fourth Round win over Sunderland in 1949, having also scored the first goal.

Opposite top: A vintage scene of a draw, as David Wiseman, Chairman of The FA Challenge Cup Committee, and RH Brough, Chairman of The FA, pick out Millwall to host Tottenham Hotspur for the 1966–67 Third Round.

Opposite bottom: A series of FA Cup Vintage Cards, which proved hugely popular in the competition's early history.

One of the most striking things about early reports of the cup is fans travelling en masse for games. For many, it was their first trip to London. But these were still nothing like the scenes that greeted teams when they returned.

When Blackburn Olympic became the first northern and working-class club to win the cup in 1884, they toured a raucous town in "a gaily beflagged wagonette drawn by six spanking greys". Their neighbours, Blackburn Rovers, were greeted by a grand display of coloured lights the following year, for which a special plant had been constructed. In 1885, this was literally dazzling.

The unifying force of the cup changed perspectives. In 1949, the *Bolton Journal* commented how the town's football club – four-time winners Bolton Wanderers – "do more to foster the sense of community" than the local council. FA chairman Amos Brook Hirst wrote in that same year of how The FA Cup has "become as much a part of English life as the hedges around our fields and the slates on the roofs of our industrial towns

and cities". It had become part of the fabric of English life, binding it together.

By 1964, when West Ham United first lifted the trophy, the great Bobby Moore marvelled at how "there must have been a million people out on the streets". "This was what success meant," Moore said. "Not money or glamour, but the satisfaction of knowing you've made your own folk proud of you."

Even a manager as battle-hardened as Don Revie was awed at the sight of 35,000 Leeds United fans greeting the team after winning their only FA Cup in 1972 – and that despite the team squandering the opportunity of a double that same week. "I just didn't believe it would be like this," Revie said.

The life-affirming symptoms of "cup fever" were visible in the

Above: Leeds United manager Don Revie, centre, celebrates the club's first ever FA Cup in 1972 with Jack Charlton, left, and captain Billy Bremner.

Opposite: West Ham United's Bobby Moore lifts the cup with teammates after the club's 3–2 win over Preston North End at Wembley in the 1964 Final.

competition from the earliest days. Journalist J.J. Riley wrote in 1879 of how Darwen had been "affected by a kind of 'Football Mania' and there happens to have been no life in the town, only that caused by football."

As the following pages will make clear, Darwen occupy a crucial place in the history of The FA Cup and the game. This team of local workers may even have been responsible for one of the first giant killings, by eliminating Remnants in 1878–79, though the term "giant killing" hadn't quite entered the footballing vernacular then.

Over time, more seeds were planted and the cup developed new traditions of its own. These are what really enliven the competition, and distinguish it. It's what the great goalkeeper Gordon Banks described as "the charm of football tradition, the ivy-covered venerableness of The FA Cup". It's the careful preparations at small stadiums, such as when Leatherhead hosted Leicester in 1974–75. It's the distinctive atmosphere of a great night at a big ground, like Liverpool's series against Arsenal in 1979–80. It's the pageantry. It's the songs. It's the draw. It's the little customs that teams develop the further they go. In their famous 1953 run, Bolton had their "Cup Drink", a mix of two bottles of sherry and two dozen eggs that was passed around

> ### "THE LITTLE GUY TURNS THE GAME INTO A RIOT WHERE ANYTHING CAN HAPPEN [...] THE BIG FELLOW IS OFTEN FIGHTING AGAINST HIMSELF AS WELL AS THE UPSTARTS."
>
> - DANNY BLANCHFLOWER -

the players on the Friday before every round. The concoction was supposed to bring them luck, but left most feeling unfortunate to have tasted it.

All of these quirks, traditions and superstitions come to the fore at the season's midpoint, and The FA Cup's true centrepiece. The Third Round is an occasion with more lore than almost any other in sport, because the opportunity it offers is almost unparalleled. It's where the game really comes together. It's where Marine – of Northern Premier League Division One North – can meet Premier League Tottenham Hotspur, eight tiers and 161 places between them. So far, this has been the biggest gap between teams The FA Cup has seen. It was a unique moment for Marine in January 2021, at an unprecedented time. That's the luck of the draw.

So many FA Cup heroes, from Terry Venables to Graeme Sharp, talk about gathering around the radio on a Monday afternoon to hear who they would be pitted against. Non-league sides in the Third Round draw are now just as often in a TV studio, awaiting their moment of fame that only The FA Cup can bring. It's where lives can be changed, and even where clubs can be saved.

All dream of doing what Walsall did to Arsenal in 1935, what Colchester United did to Leeds United in 1971, what Hereford United did to Newcastle United in 1972, what Bournemouth did to Manchester United in 1984, what Bradford City did to Chelsea in 2015. It's where the openness of the competition offers its true meaning, where the famous magic is really sprinkled. If the Final is the cup's special day, the upsets are its spirit.

Each upset has its own story but they all have one thing in common: the realisation that "this is on". It is when, in the words of Tottenham's Danny Blanchflower, "The little guy turns the game into a riot where anything can happen," while "the big fellow is often fighting against himself as well as the upstarts." That peril, the danger of humiliation, only amplifies the atmosphere of the cup, along with the enticement of greater glory.

The journey from extreme to extreme offers plot points that create storylines. That's what sport is about after all – it's about stirring emotions. Storylines are what make games and goals truly memorable, affording them a meaning beyond the moment. That could be seen in Darwen's run, in the quest for doubles, in Manchester United recovering after the Munich air disaster, in

Above: Marine and Tottenham Hotspur line up ahead of their Third Round meeting in 2021 amidst the COVID-19 pandemic, a tie that represented the greatest ever gap between two sides in the competition.

Opposite: Blackpool supporters gather in Trafalgar Square before their side's FA Cup Final against Bolton at Wembley, in May 1953.

Following pages: Filipe Morais of Bradford City celebrates after equalising against Chelsea in an FA Cup Fourth Round match at Stamford Bridge in 2015. Bradford shocked their opponents with a 4–2 win.

Paul Gascoigne's agony and ecstasy in 1991 and – most of all – in Stanley Matthews' almost-mythic quest for FA Cup glory.

Then there's the meaning of the cup itself. It isn't just worth celebrating as a piece of silverware. It has long been seen as an equal achievement to the league, with the only distinction being that it tested different qualities. While the title was about being consistent over the course of a full season, The FA Cup was about rising to the day – and then the next day and the next day, until you reach the ultimate goal.

That has a purity all of its own. That is what Milburn meant by it being "instant". Herbert Chapman, the legendary Arsenal manager, spoke of how blind luck can play a much greater role in any one-off game, but that immediate danger of elimination also pushes players and teams to the limits of their abilities.

Alex Ferguson, one of the competition's most successful managers, appreciated this as much as anybody, writing in his first autobiography: "The prospect of battling through a series of sudden-death showdowns to a climax at Wembley has always held a romantic appeal for me."

As much as self-contained storylines, the cup can become a great quest. It has a "holy grail" element, best displayed by Matthews, but also demonstrated by countless other greats. Brian Clough's longing for an FA Cup-winner's medal was one of the last driving ambitions of an otherwise illustrious career. It was a sentiment he shared with one of his rivals. On the

> "IT SHOULD BE REALISED THAT A LEAGUE MATCH AND A CUP-TIE ARE ENTIRELY DIFFERENT PROPOSITIONS [...] IN THE ONE EVERYTHING IS NORMAL; IN THE OTHER EVERYTHING IS EXCEPTIONAL."
>
> - HERBERT CHAPMAN -

Above: Tottenham Hotspur's Paul Gascoigne receives medical treatment after an injury sustained from a tackle on Gary Charles of Nottingham Forest in the 1991 Final. It was later found Gascoigne had suffered a cruciate ligament injury.

Opposite: A Graf Zeppelin sails over Wembley Stadium during the FA Cup Final between Arsenal and Huddersfield Town in 1930.

eve of the 1972 Final, Billy Bremner expressed a lament that so many fellow professionals have sympathised with: "I've won a Championship medal, a European medal and countless Scotland caps, but sometimes I think I'd swap the lot for an FA Cup winner's medal."

Many would settle for the experience of playing in a Final. It's a dream that has been articulated by everyone from George Best to Wayne Rooney, and modern foreign legends like Didier Drogba and Wenger. So many players have spoken of imagining they're at Wembley, playing in The FA Cup Final, when they were a child kicking a ball around on a patch of grass. It was a realisation that struck Wenger in his first Final, in 1998, as he revealed in his autobiography: "I was face to face with my dream and my idea of football: the intensity of the event, the fervour of the supporters, the perfection of the grass pitch, the delicious tension of the players, the white ball – everything embodied to perfection."

Wenger's words emphasise the global fame of the competition.

Like so many other foreign greats to have graced the competition, he didn't just develop an appreciation for this on arriving in England. Wenger was already steeped in it. The Final has long been broadcast all over the world, creating dreams in every corner of the planet.

Before the first Final at the new Wembley in 2007, Drogba made a surprising admission to his Chelsea teammates. He said he was "scared", "nervous", because the name of the stadium was known all over the world, including his native Ivory Coast. It had real heritage. Drogba soon wrote himself into it. Like Matthews before him, who would often vomit before the biggest games, that nervousness evidently gave the Ivorian an edge. He went on to score the only goal in that FA Cup Final, eventually becoming the first player to score in four different Finals – still a record.

But the real distinction of scoring in a Final is not just winning the day but writing yourself into history, as part of a select few, as the world watches. You are with Arthur Kinnaird,

Tommy Barber, Ted Drake, George Robledo, Stan Mortensen, Roy Dwight, Mike Trebilcock, Ian Porterfield, Ricky Villa, Ian Rush, Eric Cantona and so many others.

The FA Cup's list of heroes had mixed careers. Some went on to win everything. Some won nothing else. Some dropped down the divisions, to a level where the First Round proper was seen to be as prestigious as the Final. But all of them helped shape its story. To join that pantheon of FA Cup greats has been an aspiration shared from childhood to adulthood, from non-league to Premier League, from village to metropolis, from working-class heroes to ruling-class officials, from Victorian times to the modern world, from 1871 to now. One trophy has provided all this inspiration and continues to bring the game together today. This is what The FA Cup means above all else.

Above: Manchester United and Chelsea line up ahead of the first Final at the reconstructed Wembley Stadium in 2007.

Right: Ian Rush, the FA Cup's highest scorer in the post-war era, lifts the trophy for the last time in his career in 1992 after Liverpool beat Sunderland 2–0.

Opposite: Nottingham Forest's Brian Clough leads Terry Venables out by the hand ahead of the 1991 Final against Tottenham Hotspur. Clough had never won the competition, and his team was beaten here 2–1.

Following pages: The current FA Cup trophy at Wembley. This is the fifth version of the trophy, and the third of this model.

CHAPTER TWO

ORIGINS

1863–1870

IT WAS IN THE OFFICES OF *THE SPORTSMAN* NEWSPAPER – A FEW MINUTES' WALK FROM ST PAUL'S CATHEDRAL IN CENTRAL LONDON – THAT CHARLES ALCOCK WAS INVIGORATED BY THE POWER OF AN IDEA. IT WAS SOMETHING THAT SEEMS SO ELEMENTARY TO US NOW, SO OBVIOUS, THAT IT'S ACTUALLY HARD TO IMAGINE IT WASN'T ALWAYS THERE AND FULLY FORMED. THAT'S THE REAL POWER OF A GOOD IDEA, AND THIS WAS ONE WAS REVOLUTIONARY.

It changed football, changed sport and consequently changed the world. Its imprint can be seen in almost every sporting competition we watch today, leading Alcock to be known as "the father of modern sport".

His idea was formally proposed on 20 July 1871, at Boy Court just off the bottom of Ludgate Hill. Recalling the knockout tournaments between the houses at Harrow School when he was a pupil there, Alcock felt that a similar format would be well suited to the still-young game of Association Football. His motivation went beyond just creating a competition, the modern version of which could scarcely have been imagined by Alcock and the six other men in the room. As the secretary of the mere eight-year-old Football Association, Alcock felt the whole game needed stimulus.

The sport was in those years rough and ragged, both in form and format. The only fixtures that really existed were one-off games or challenges, and anyone watching with modern eyes wouldn't see football as we know it today. This was even after it was codified, when England's public schoolboys effectively created the version of the game that would take over the world.

A generation before that, a football match would generally take over a town square or a field. Hundreds of people would sometimes gather for contests between villages that would often end in a riot. The only common feature was that a ball would be pushed from one end of an area to another. In some rural areas, the goal was to kick the ball over a fence at the opposing end.

Keith Dewhurst's book, *Underdogs*, quotes an old Etonian named Henry Blake, who in 1833 declared that he "couldn't consider the game at all gentlemanly". The sport had nevertheless become popular in precisely the institutions where these "gentlemen" were brought up. Public schools such as Eton, Harrow, Charterhouse and Winchester realised the value of team games in developing discipline and decorum, and football was perfect for this. It was at this time that the houses of Harrow organised their own tournaments, embedding an idea for Alcock to recall years later.

The game was given more order, but also more potential for a different type of chaos, as each school developed its own style. This became all-too apparent when former pupils mixed at university, with the different slang terms for the game – hacking, piggling, shinning and tagging – causing even more confusion.

The first attempt to properly formalise the laws came with the "Cambridge Rules" of 1848, which proved popular in the south, while "Sheffield Rules" dominated in the north. This was the constant battle in the early stages of the game. "Football" couldn't yet develop in the manner its popularity suggested it should because it wasn't yet clear what football actually was.

This was despite its gloriously enticing simplicity, the source of so much of that popularity. It is no coincidence, despite all this confusion, that early football pioneer J.C. Thring titled his 1862 blueprint for unifying the laws as "The Simplest Game".

The primary split up to that point was between dribblers and handlers – in other words, football and rugby. It was the formation of the Football Association that solved this problem, a suggestion popularly credited to Ebenezer Cobb Morley, a solicitor who was the founder and captain of Barnes Football Club.

Opposite top: The FA's original 1863 minute book, which contains the first agreed, handwritten rules of football.

Opposite: A crowd of people in Ashbourne, Derbyshire, in February 1915, commemorate the ancient Royal Shrovetide football match – an early example of the game which has been played in the town since at least the 12th century.

Previous pages: Charles Alcock (1842–1907), FA Secretary between 1870 and 1895 and a founding father of The FA Cup, as well as the competition's first winning captain, with Wanderers in 1872.

"[ONE] COULDN'T CONSIDER THE GAME AT ALL GENTLEMANLY."

- HENRY BLAKE -

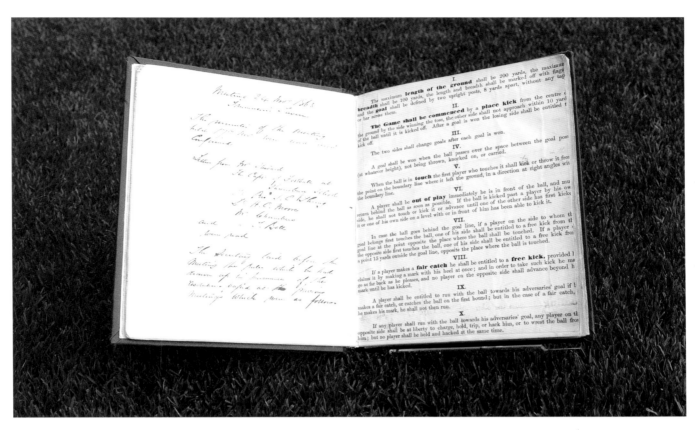

ASHBOURNES. 1915. "MOTTO"
"SHROVE. TIDE FOOTBALL.
AS. USUAL."

An advertisement in the 17 October 1863 edition of *Bell's Life in London and Sporting Chronicle* read as follows:

"PUBLIC MEETING – We are requested by the representatives of several clubs to state that a meeting will be held at the Freemason's Tavern, Queen Street, Lincoln's Inn, on Monday, the 26th Instant, at seven o'clock p.m., for the purpose of promoting the adoption of a general code of rules for football, when the captains of all clubs are requested to attend."

History records that 11 foundation clubs attended, all of them from the London area: Barnes, Civil Service, Crusaders, Forest of Leytonstone, NN (No Name) Club, Crystal Palace, Blackheath, Kensington School, Perceval House, Surbiton and Blackheath Proprietary School. Charterhouse sent a representative, only to realise they played quite a different game, so declined to join. Of the original 11, only Civil Service FC are still in existence and playing football. Forest – who were Alcock's club – eventually became the storied Wanderers, who were later refounded, as were Crystal Palace. Some of those original 11 also quickly left because they favoured the inclusion of body tackling. A further five meetings eventually saw the first rules of Association Football published in December 1863. "Soccer" – which came from an abbreviation of "Association", to distinguish it from rugby – was confirmed as an 11-a-side, non-handling game.

At that point, the game had a rugby-style offside law that required all of a team's players to be behind the ball when it was kicked forwards, but it soon became apparent this was pointless if there was no handling of the ball involved. The FA eventually changed the rule to an early form of the modern offside law, albeit requiring three players to be between the attacker and goal, in 1866. This, exactly a century before England won the World Cup, was a crucial year for English football. It was also when Alcock joined The FA.

It's almost an understatement to describe Alcock as the most important person in football's early history. The description could even be extended to the early history of organised sport as a whole. Among the developments that Alcock can be credited with, or involved with, are England's first cricket Test match (the Ashes), the first rugby union international held in England, and the very idea of competitive international football. As we have seen, there was also The FA Cup's influence on sport as a whole, given the now almost universal use of the sudden-death knockout format.

Born in 1842, Alcock was one of five sons of a wealthy Sunderland ship-broker. He left Harrow in 1859, and founded Forest Football Club – named after his early years spent in Epping

Above: An engraving of the Freemason's Tavern, on Great Queen Street in central London, where the Football Association was founded on 26 October 1863. The meeting probably took place in a hall at the rear.

Opposite: An 1863 photo of Forest of Leytonstone, the London team that would go on to win the first FA Cup under the name Wanderers.

Forest – with his brother and some school friends. Forest became the famous Wanderers in 1863, winning five of the first seven FA Cups, including the first two. Alcock was the team's captain during the first of these victories. Standing 6ft (183cm) tall, he was described as a fine dribbler and scorer, who was difficult to dislodge off the ball.

His influence on the game as a whole was just as certain, direct and creative. Alcock eventually succeeded his brother James on The FA committee in 1869, and became honorary secretary, but it was his vision that really stood out.

Alcock instantly saw that the game needed impetus and a sense of purpose that only a proper competition could foster. The FA had managed to establish a foothold, but its laws and authority were regularly challenged, and its sphere of influence was mostly restricted to the gentlemen of the London area. That constituency ensured it was still at this point an entirely voluntary organisation, since its administrators were affluent men working for the game because they loved it. Alcock wanted it all to be something more. As early as the 1867 annual meeting, he is quoted as stating that "a little more energy was required to establish the game on a sure footing". Alcock could almost be described as a missionary for the game. He quickly realised that the looming matter of professionalism merely reflected the spread and popularity of football, and pointedly arranged the first official international between England and Scotland in Glasgow in November 1872 "to further the interests of the Association in Scotland".

"A LITTLE MORE ENERGY WAS REQUIRED TO ESTABLISH THE GAME ON A SURE FOOTING."

- CHARLES ALCOCK -

It helped that Alcock was a perceptive and persuasive character, known for his diplomacy. When there was some trepidation about the Sheffield Association joining The FA, it was Alcock who suggested they keep their own rules. His calculation that the existing rules would eventually prevail proved correct, and the Association had an important new foothold in the north of England.

It also needed a new competition. Alcock already had his idea and called for the aforementioned meeting to discuss it on 20 July 1871 at the office of *The Sportsman*, which was one of the indications of his immense influence. As a writer for the newspaper, Alcock was an esteemed sports journalist – a pioneer in that field, too. He wrote the first history of football and edited its first annual. The fact that the first Final took place at the Kennington Oval was another indication of his sway, since he was also secretary of the Surrey County Cricket Club.

Alcock made the initial proposal that: "It is desirable that a Challenge Cup should be established in connection with the

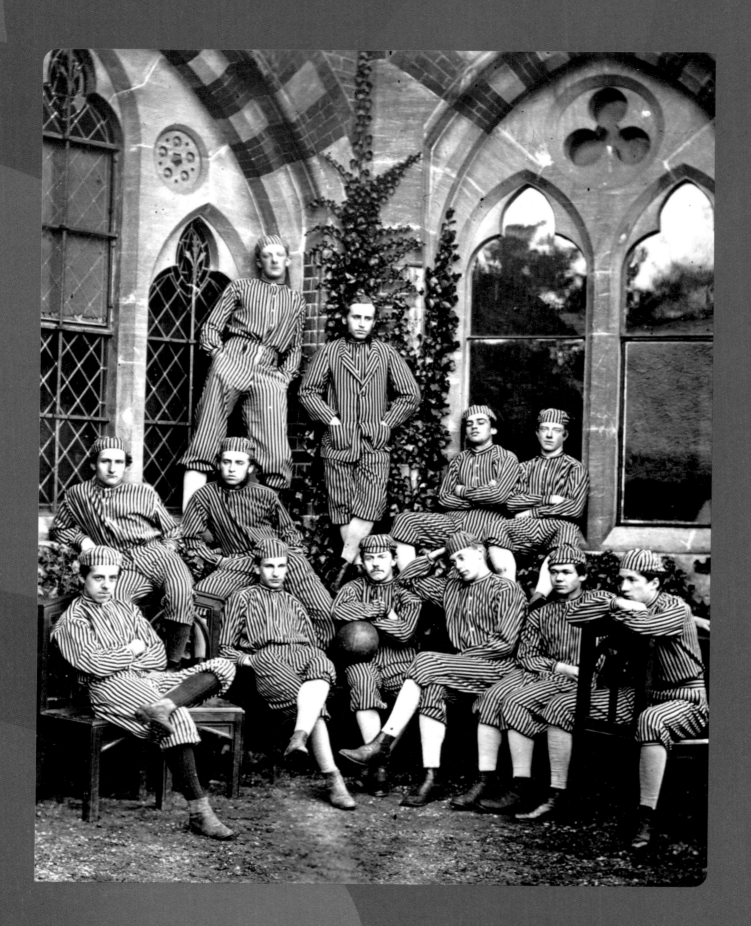

> ## "IT IS DESIRABLE THAT A CHALLENGE CUP SHOULD BE ESTABLISHED IN CONNECTION WITH THE ASSOCIATION FOR WHICH ALL CLUBS BELONGING TO THE ASSOCIATION SHOULD BE INVITED TO COMPETE."
>
> - CHARLES ALCOCK -

Above: A vintage illustration of Sheffield Football Club, the world's oldest existing club, pictured in the year in which they first took part in The FA Cup, 1874. They were beaten in the Third Round by Clapham Rovers.

Opposite: A group portrait of the Harrow School football team in 1867. Harrow would produce many notable players in the early years of The FA Cup.

Association for which all clubs belonging to the Association should be invited to compete."

The minute book from that meeting records that this proposal was approved unanimously by a seven-man committee. Fittingly enough, and predictably enough given the period, a core of that group became key players on the pitch as well as important administrators off it. Captain Francis Marindin was Alcock's opposing captain for the Royal Engineers in the first Final, and within two years became president of The FA. Morton Peto Betts, one of many former Harrow schoolboys to play for Wanderers, was the scorer of that fixture's first goal. Alfred Stair, of Upton Park Club and honorary treasurer to The FA Committee, refereed the first three Finals. The other three present are recorded as Charles William Stephenson, of Westminster School; J.H. Gifford, of the Civil Service, and D. Allport, also of Harrow School.

A further meeting, on 16 October 1871, saw the rules of the competition formalised and the first entries received. Fifteen clubs initially took the leap. They were Barnes; Civil Service; Clapham Rovers; Crystal Palace; Donington School; Great Marlow; Hampstead Heathens; Harrow Chequers; Hitchin;

Maidenhead; Queens Park; Reigate Priory; Royal Engineers; Upton Park; and Wanderers.

Among the original rules were a couple of proposals that have persisted throughout the history of The FA Cup: the idea of a player being cup-tied ("no individual shall be allowed to play for more than one competing club") and the notion that games ending in a draw would be settled by replays.

These former public schoolboys departed the office, content in the formation of their new competition. The reception wasn't unanimous when the plans were made public, however. There was opposition to what detractors called the cup's "incidental evils", namely fears that it would give rise to excessive rivalry, selfish interests, undesirable elements flocking to the game and a general lowering of the standard of morality among competitors

that would in turn undermine the true spirit of football. That last criticism was, of course, proved spectacularly wrong. On the contrary, this was really the spirit of football being forged. That's what truly happened that autumn day in 1871.

A first trophy was commissioned. Made by Martin, Hall and Company at a cost of £20, it was 18in (46cm) high and had a capacity of one quart (1.1 litres), reflecting the relatively modest nature of the cup in its infancy.

Alcock had other aims, though, and his big idea was about to take hold.

Above: A team portrait of the Royal Engineers side who competed in the inaugural FA Cup Final, losing 1–0 to Wanderers at the Kennington Oval in March 1872.

Opposite: The FA Cup trophy awarded to winners between 1896 and 1910. It was made from a mould of the original, which had been stolen when held by Aston Villa in 1895, and was known as "the little tin idol".

Following pages: Sketches of events and key figures from Blackburn Olympic's 2–1 victory over Old Etonians in the 1883 Final, the first won by a northern team. Etonians were captained by Lord Kinnaird, Blackburn Olympic by Albert Warburton.

THE HON: A: F: KINNAIRD:

CAPTAIN OF THE
"OLD ETONIANS"

THE ENCLOSURE

CROSSLEY KICKING THE DECISIVE GOAL;

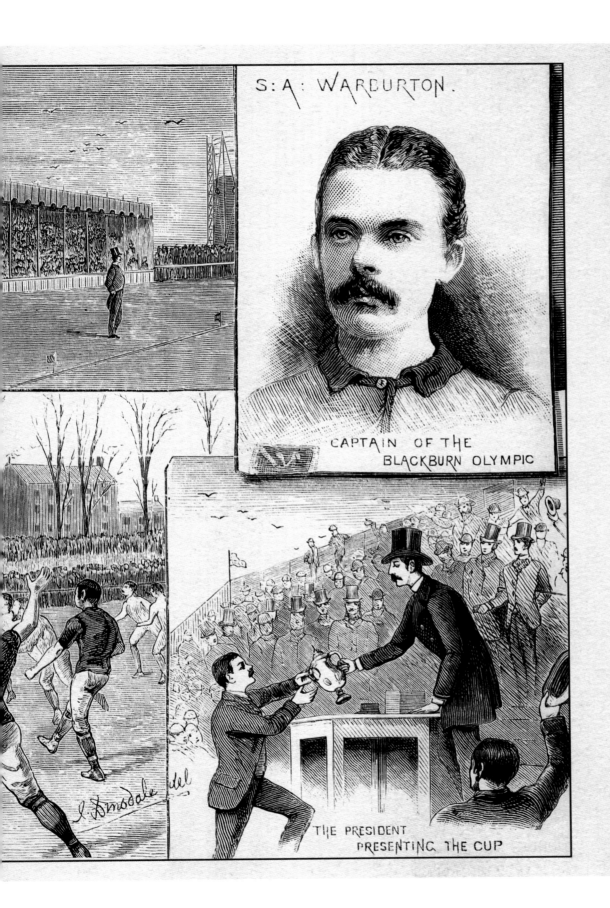

S: A: WARBURTON.

CAPTAIN OF THE
BLACKBURN OLYMPIC

THE PRESIDENT
PRESENTING THE CUP

CHAPTER THREE

THE FIRST FINALS

1871–1879

AS THE EIGHT TEAMS LINED UP FOR THE FIRST EVER FA CUP MATCHES ON A WINDY 11 NOVEMBER 1871, THERE WAS SOME CONSTERNATION IN BARNES. THE CIVIL SERVICE HAD ARRIVED WITH ONLY EIGHT PLAYERS. UNWILLING TO BE GIVEN ANY FAVOURS, THEIR CAPTAIN WENT ABOUT "CAREFULLY LOSING THE TOSS, THUS ENABLING BARNES TO OBTAIN THE AID OF A STIFF BREEZE".

The newspaper *The Sportsman*, central to the foundation of the cup, said it was typical of "the urbanity which distinguishes the 'CS' in general". Many would have said it was typical of the "gentleman amateur" spirit that governed the game at the time. It went way beyond spirit.

All the players in that first season were from the public school network and were made up of army officers, barristers and solicitors. It was the same among the crowds watching, since the shilling needed for entry was high for sporting events of the time. This was the football of the 1870s and was also why the first decade of The FA Cup was almost removed from the rest of its history, a time capsule that was only the inspiration for everything to follow.

Much of the sport was unrecognisable. The first FA Cup tie may have kicked off at 3pm on a Saturday but that was one of only a few customs that would become commonplace. Shirts didn't have numbers or consistent colours and opposing teams were differentiated by caps or stockings. The notional goalkeeper wore the same as everyone else, since this position had only been invented two years earlier. Players would freely interchange in the role, which allowed handling anywhere on the pitch so long as it conformed to the vague idea of protecting their own goal. That goal was a pair of upright posts with a rope or tape across the top and no net, at the end of pitches that were to be a maximum of 200yd (183m) by 100yd (91m). There were no markings inside those lines. Referees were not allowed on the pitch, didn't have whistles and only intervened when team-appointed umpires appealed.

The actual play was chaotic, with most of it revolving around a primitive form of dribbling. The other 10 players would adopt a pyramid formation "backing up" their teammate on the ball, so as to force it forward if it became free. Throw-ins were two-handed (like today) but had to touch the ground first. Players switched ends after every goal, and there were no penalties because it was inconceivable that gentlemen would seek to gain any unfair advantage.

Despite that, the Barnes–Civil Service match was one of many that saw a dispute over rules, in this case the difference between "fisting" – striking the ball with a closed fist – and just handling. This showed how unformed the newly codified game was, as the thousands of football players outside the 50 FA member clubs still wavered between rules that were closer to rugby. This competition was an attempt to remedy these inconsistencies, pushed ahead by a distinct, privileged few.

The first 12 years of The FA Cup were dominated by the era's own "big four". Wanderers won it five times in the first seven seasons. Old Etonians got to six Finals and won two. Royal Engineers and Oxford University both got to four Finals and won one each.

A key figure in many of those matches, and the game's first star, was Arthur Kinnaird. He was almost as important to the early game as Charles Alcock, and became synonymous with the early FA Cup – the Kensington native was the first cup specialist. The view at the time was that there could barely be a Final without Alcock and his famous auburn beard, and there rarely was as Kinnaird played in nine of the first 12 Finals and won five.

Opposite top left: Newspaper article describing the laws of the Football Association.

Opposite bottom left: Newspaper article describing proposed changes to the laws of the Football Association for its 1872 meeting.

Opposite right: Newspaper article listing the first laws of the Rugby Football Union, which represented the split on which the sports were founded.

Previous pages: Arthur Kinnaird (1847–1923), later known as Lord Kinnaird, a five-time winner of The FA Cup who was one of the early game's great figures and perhaps its first star.

"I HAVE BEEN CONNECTED WITH THE ASSOCIATION GAME EVER SINCE ITS COMMENCEMENT."

- ARTHUR KINNAIRD -

THE FOOTBALL ASSOCIATION.

The annual general meeting of the Football Association, to discuss the amendments proposed in the rules, as well as for the transaction of general business, took place at the Freemasons' Tavern on Monday evening last. The attendance was in excess of any witnessed in former years, including representatives of the Royal Engineers, Harrow Pilgrims, Wanderers, Barnes, Crystal Palace, Civil Service, Nottingham, Clapham Rovers, Queen's Park Club, Glasgow, C.C.C., Lausanne, Hampstead Heathens, Westminster School, Brixton, Forest, Upton Park, and other clubs that support the same laws. After the minutes of the last meeting had been confirmed, the following officers were elected for the coming season, only three of the committee of the previous year, it is worthy of remark, being re-elected:—President, E. C. Morley (Barnes Club); treasurer, A. Stair (Upton Park Club); hon. sec., C. W. Alcock (Wanderers); committee—A. F. Kinnaird (Old Etonians), Capt. Marindin (Royal Engineers), D. Allport (Crystal Palace Club), A. J. Baker (Wanderers), M. P. Betts (West Kent), J. Kirkpatrick (Civil Service), R. W. Willis (Barnes Club), C. W. Stephenson (Westminster School), J. Cockerell (Brixton Club), and J. H. Giffard (Civil Service). Mr Stair was appointed to the office of treasurer, it should be remarked, in order to relieve the hon. sec. of some of the onerous duties incidental to the post, and generally for the purpose of taking on his shoulders the active management of the affairs of the Association in concert with the secretary.

Some animated discussion then followed on the various alterations and additions to the rules proposed by the several clubs, those especially relating to "off-side" and handling evoking much difference of opinion as well as warmth of debate. Eventually the following propositions were carried:

RULES OF THE ASSOCIATION.

RULE II.—Proposed by the Wanderers:
In place of words "one year's standing," to insert playing Association Rules.

RULE VII.—Proposed by the Wanderers:
To add the words "the privilege being granted to provincial clubs of sending deputies, no two clubs to be represented by the same deputy."

LAWS OF THE GAME.

RULE V.—Proposed by the Wanderers:
To insert after the words "at right angles with the boundary lines" "to a distance of at least six yards."

RULE VIII.—Proposed by Upton Park Club:
To add the words "except in the case of the goal-keeper, who shall be allowed to use his hands for the protection of his goal."

The proposition by the Oxford Association to introduce the strict offside rule met with little favour, being supported chiefly by Capt. Marindin, of the Royal Engineers, C. W. Alcock, of the Wanderers, and R. H. Birkett, of the Clapham Rovers, and was negatived by a large majority. The various proposals relative to handling were subjected to a lengthy discussion, that emanating from Upton Park being ultimately easily victorious, although there were many adherents to the views promulgated by the C.C.C. and Barnes Clubs. Again, after some further ventilation of the points at issue it was, on the suggestion of Mr C. L. Rothera, of the Notts Club, agreed to add a memorandum to the rules to the effect that "handling is understood to be playing the ball with the hand or arm." The remaining proposals from the Chesterfield Club relative to the establishment of umpires, and by the Wanderers, advocating a penalty in case of an infringement of the rules, having been lost, the meeting was brought to a close with the usual vote of thanks to the president (Mr E. C. Morley) for his services in the chair. We had almost omitted to add that the financial position of the Association was of a most healthy character, the statement of the hon. sec. showing a goodly balance in hand.

FOOTBALL ASSOCIATION.

The following are the alterations proposed in the Rules of the Football Association for the ensuing year, for discussion at the general annual meeting, to be held on Tuesday, February 27:

RULES OF THE ASSOCIATION.

Rule IV.—Proposed by Wanderers:
Insert "seventeen" instead of "ten;" and add "That it be in the power of the committee to appoint one of their body to act as assistant secretary if required."

Rule X.—Proposed by Harrow Chequers:
"That a fixed size be appointed for the Association football."

LAWS OF THE GAME.

Rule III.—Proposed by Wanderers:
To add the words, "After the call of half-time ends shall not again be changed."

Rule IV.—Proposed by Wanderers:
To add the words, "The ball hitting one or other of the goal-posts and rebounding into play is considered in play, and not as having passed behind the goal line."

Rule VI.—Proposed by Nottingham Club:
To erase the present rule and substitute following:—"Any player nearer to his opponent's goal than the player of his own side who last played the ball without having followed him, shall be off-side and out of play until the ball has been played by an opponent."

Proposed by Sheffield Association:
To erase rule, and substitute following:—"Any player between an opponents' goal and goal-keeper (unless he has followed the ball there) if off-side, and out of play. The goal-keeper is that player on the defending side who for the time being is nearest to his own goal."

Rule VII.—Proposed by Harrow Chequers:
To add the words, "In the event of one of the defending side kicking the ball behind his own goal line, a free kick shall be forfeited to the opposite party from the point where the ball passed behind the goal-line."

Proposed by Sheffield Association:
To erase rule and substitute following:—"When the ball is kicked over the bar of the goal, it must be kicked off by the side behind whose goal it went, within six yards from the limit of their goal. The side who thus kick the ball are entitled to a fair kick-off in whatever way they please; the opposite side not being allowed to approach within six yards of the ball. When the ball is kicked behind the goal-line, a player of the opposite side to that which kicked it out shall kick it in from the nearest corner flag. No player to be allowed within six yards of the ball until kicked."

Rule VIII.—Proposed by Great Marlow Club:
To omit rule, and insert following:—"The goal-keeper shall be allowed to handle the ball in any way he pleases for the protection of his goal, but no other player shall be allowed to handle the ball further than merely stopping it with the hand or arm, all carrying or knocking on being strictly prohibited, and provided always that no goal shall be allowed when the ball has gone in off the hand or arm."

Proposed by Harrow Chequers:
To add "in the event of any infringement of this rule, a free kick shall be forfeited to the opposite side from the spot where the infringement took place, but in no case shall a goal be scored from such free kick."

Proposed by Maidenhead Club:
To revise rule Rule XII.

Proposed by Great Marlow Club:
Between wear and "iron" omit "projecting nails" with a view to insert "any nails excepting such as have their heads driven in flush with the leather."

THE LAWS OF THE GAME OF FOOTBALL

AS PLAYED BY

THE RUGBY FOOTBALL UNION.

1. A *drop kick*, or *drop*, is made by letting the ball fall from the hands and kicking it the *very instant* it rises.

2. A *place kick*, or *place*, is made by kicking the ball after it has been placed in a nick made in the ground for the purpose of keeping it at rest.

3. A *punt* is made by letting the ball fall from the hands and kicking it *before* it touches the ground.

4. *Each goal* shall be composed of two upright posts, exceeding 11ft in height from the ground, and placed 18ft 6in apart, with a cross bar 10ft from the ground.

5. *A goal* can only be obtained by kicking the ball from the field of play direct (*i.e.*, without touching the dress or person of any player of either side), over the cross bar of the opponent's goal, whether it touch such cross bar or the posts or not; but if the ball goes directly over either of the *goal posts* it is called a *poster*, and is not a goal.

6. A goal may be obtained by any kind of kick except a *punt*.

7. A match shall be decided by a majority of goals only.

8. The ball is dead when it rests absolutely motionless on the ground.

9. A *touch-down* is when a player putting his hand upon the ball on the ground in touch or in goal stops it so that it remains dead or fairly so.

10. A *tackle* is when the holder of the ball is held by one or more players of the opposite side.

11. A *scrummage* takes place when the holder of the ball being in the field of play puts it down on the ground in front of him, and all who have closed round on their respective sides endeavour to push their opponents back, and by kicking the ball to drive it in the direction of the opposite goal-line.

12. A player may take up the ball whenever it is rolling or bounding, except in a scrummage.

13. It is not lawful to take up the ball when dead (except in order to bring it out after it has been touched down in touch or in goal) for any purpose whatever; whenever the ball shall have been so unlawfully taken up it shall at once be brought back to where it was so taken up, and there put down.

14. In a scrummage it is not lawful to touch the ball with the hand under any circumstance whatever.

15. It is lawful for any player who has the ball to run with it, and if he does so it is called *a run*. If a player runs with the ball until he gets behind his opponents' goal-line and there touches it down, it is called *a run in*.

16. It is lawful to *run in* anywhere across the goal-line.

17. The goal-line is in goal, and the touch-line is in touch.

18. In the event of *any* player holding or running with the ball being tackled and the ball fairly held, he must at once cry *down*, and there put it down.

19. A *maul in goal* is when the holder of the ball is tackled inside goal-line, or being tackled immediately outside is carried or pushed across it, and he or the opposite side, or both, endeavour to touch the ball down. In all cases the ball when so touched down shall belong to the players of the side who first had possession of it before the maul commenced, unless the opposite side have gained entire possession of it.

20. In case of a maul in goal those players only who are touching the ball with their hands when it crosses the goal-line may continue in the maul in goal, and when a player has once released his hold of the ball after it is inside the goal-line he may not again join in the maul, and if he attempts to do so may be dragged out by the opposite side.

But if a player when *running in* is tackled inside the goal-line, then only the player who first tackled him, or if two or more tackle him *simultaneously* they only may join in the maul.

21. *Touch in goal* (see plan).—Immediately the ball, whether in the hands of a player (except for the purpose of a punt-out, see Rule 29) or not, goes into touch in goal it is at once dead and out of the game, and is brought out as provided by Rules 41 and 42.

PLAN OF THE FIELD.

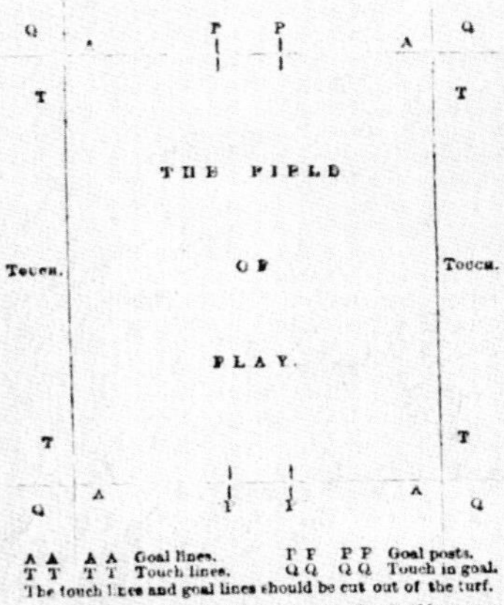

A A A A Goal lines. P P P P Goal posts.
T T T T Touch lines. Q Q Q Q Touch in goal.

The touch lines and goal lines should be cut out of the turf.

22. Every player is *on side* but is put *off side* if he enters a scrummage from his opponents' side, or being in a scrummage gets in front of the ball, or when the ball has been kicked, touched, or is being run with by any of his own side behind him (that is, between himself and his own goal-line).

23. Every player when *off side* is out of the game and shall not touch the ball in any case whatever, either in or out of touch or goal, or in any way interrupt or obstruct any player, until he is again *on side*.

24. A player being *off side* is put *on side* when the ball has been run five yards with or kicked by or has touched the dress or person of any player of the opposite side, or when one of his own side has run in front of him either with the ball or having kicked it when behind him.

25. When a player has the ball none of his opponents who at the time are off side may commence or attempt to run, tackle, or otherwise interrupt such player until he has run five yards.

26. *Throwing back*.—It is lawful for any player who has the ball to throw it back towards his own goal, or to pass it back to any player of his own side, who is at the time behind him in accordance with the rules of *on side*.

27. *Knocking on*—*i.e.*, deliberately hitting the ball with the hand—and *throwing forward*—*i.e.*, throwing the ball in the direction of the opponents' goal-line—are not lawful. If the ball be either knocked on or thrown forward, the captain of the opposite side may, unless a fair catch has been made, as provided by the next rule, require to have it brought back to the spot where it was so knocked or thrown on, and there *put down*.

28. A *fair catch* is a catch made direct from a kick or a throw forward or a knock on by one of the opposite side, or from a punt out or a punt on (see Rules 29 and 30), provided the catcher makes a mark with his heel at the spot where he has made the catch, and no other of his own side touch the ball. (See Rules 43 and 44.)

29. A *punt out* is a *punt* made after a touch-down by a player from behind his opponents' goal-line, and from touch-in-goal, if necessary, towards his own side, who must stand outside the goal-line and endeavour to make a fair catch, or to get the ball and *run in* or *drop* a goal. (See Rules 49 and 51.)

30. *A punt on* is a punt made in a manner similar to a punt out, and from touch if necessary, by a player who has made a fair catch from a *punt out* or another *punt on*.

31. *Touch* (see plan).—If the ball goes into touch the first player on his side who touches it down must bring it to the spot where it crossed the touch-line, or if a player when running with the ball cross or put any part of either foot across the touch-line he must return with the ball to the spot where the line was so crossed, and thence return it into the field of play in one of the modes provided by the following rule.

32. He must then himself, or by one of his own side, either bound it out in the field of play, and then run with it, kick it, or throw it back to his own side, or (2) throw it out at right angles to the touch-line, or (3) walk out with it at right angles to the touch-line any distance not less than five or more than fifteen yards, and there put it down, first declaring how far he intends to walk out.

33. If two or more players holding the ball are pushed into touch the ball shall belong in touch to the player who first had hold of it when in the field of play and has not released his hold of it.

34. If the ball when thrown out of touch be not thrown out at right angles to the touch-line, the captain of either side may at once claim to have it thrown out again.

35. A catch made when the ball is thrown out of touch is not a *fair catch*.

36. *Kick off* is a place-kick from the centre of the field of play and cannot count as a goal. The opposite side must stand at least ten yards in front of the ball until it has been kicked.

37. The ball shall be *kicked off* at the commencement of the game, after a goal has been obtained.

38. The sides shall change goals as often as and whenever a goal is obtained, unless it has been otherwise agreed by the captains before the commencement of the match.

39. The captains of the respective sides shall toss up before the commencement of the match; the winner of the toss shall have the option of choice of goals or the kick-off.

40. Whenever a goal shall have been obtained the side which has lost the goal shall then kick-off.

41. *Kick-out* is a drop-kick by one of the players of the side which has had to touch the ball down in their own goal, or into whose touch in goal the ball has gone (Rule 21), and is the mode of bringing the ball again into play, and cannot count as a goal.

42. *Kick-out* must be a *drop-kick*, and from not more than twenty-five yards outside the kicker's goal-line; if the ball when kicked out pitch in touch it must be taken back and kicked out again. The kicker's side must be behind the ball when kicked out.

43. A player who has made and claimed a *fair catch* shall thereupon either take a *drop-kick* or a *punt*, or *place* the ball for a place-kick.

44. After a fair catch has been made the opposite side may come up to the catcher's mark, and (except in cases under Rule 50) the catcher's side retiring, the ball shall be kicked from such mark or from a spot any distance behind it.

45. A player may touch the ball down in his own goal at any time.

46. A side having touched the ball down in their opponents' goal, shall *try at goal* either by a place-kick or a punt out.

47. If a *try at goal* be made by a *place-kick* a player of the side who has touched the ball down shall bring it up to the goal-line (subject to Rule 48) in a straight line from and opposite to the spot where the ball was touched down, and there make a mark on the goal-line, and thence walk straight out with it at right angles to the goal-line such distance as he thinks proper, and there place it for another of his side to kick. The kicker's side must be behind the ball when it is kicked, and the opposite side must remain behind their goal-line until the ball has been placed on the ground. (See Rules 54 and 55.)

48. If the ball has been touched down between the goal-posts, it may be brought out in a straight line from either of such posts, but if brought out from between them the opposite side may charge at once. (See Rule 54.)

49. If the *try at goal* be by a *punt out* (see Rule 29), a player of the side which has touched the ball down shall bring it straight up to the goal-line opposite to the spot where it was touched down, and there make a mark on the goal-line, and then *punt out* from touch in goal, if necessary, or from any part behind the goal-line not nearer to the goal-post than such mark, beyond which mark it is not lawful for the opposite side, who must keep behind their goal-line, to pass until the ball has been kicked. (See Rules 54 and 55.)

50. If a fair catch be made from a *punt out* or a *punt on*, the catcher may either proceed as provided by Rules 43 and 44, or himself take a *punt on*, in which case the mark made on making the fair catch shall be regarded (for the purpose of determining as well the position of the player who makes the *punt on* as of the other players of both sides) as the mark made on the goal-line in the case of a *punt out*.

51. A catch made in touch from a *punt out* or a *punt on* is not a fair catch. The ball must then be taken or thrown out of touch as provided by Rule 32; but if the catch be made in touch in goal the ball is at once dead, and must be *kicked out* as provided by Rule 21.

52. When the ball has been touched down in the opponents' goal, none of the side in whose goal it has been so touched down shall touch it or in any way displace it or interfere with the player on the other side who may be taking it up or out.

53. The ball is dead whenever a goal has been obtained, but if a *try at goal* be not successful, the kick shall be considered as only only an ordinary kick in the course of the game.

54. *Charging*—*i.e.*, rushing forward to kick the ball or tackle a player—is lawful for the opposite side in all cases of a place-kick after a fair catch or upon a *try at goal*, immediately the ball touches or is placed in the ground; and in cases of a drop-kick or punt after a fair catch, as soon as the player having the ball commences to run or offers to kick, or the ball has touched the ground; but he may always draw back, and unless he has dropped the ball or actually touched it with his foot, they must again retire to his mark (see Rule 56). The opposite side in the case of a punt out or a punt on, and the kicker's side in *all* cases, may not charge until the ball has been kicked.

55. If a player having the ball when about to *punt it out* goes outside the goal-line, or when about to *punt on* advances nearer to his own goal line than his mark made on making the fair catch, or if after the ball has been touched down in the opponents' goal or a fair catch has been made, more than one player of the side which has so touched it down or made the fair catch touch the ball before it is again kicked, the opposite side may charge at once.

56. In cases of a fair catch the opposite side may come up to and stand anywhere on or behind a line drawn through the mark made by the player who has made the catch, and parallel to their own goal-line; but in the case of a fair catch from a *punt out* or a *punt on* they may not advance further in the direction of the touch-line nearest to such mark than a line drawn through such mark to their goal-line, and parallel to such touch-line. In all cases (except a punt out and a punt on) the kicker's side must be behind the ball when it is kicked, but may not charge until it has been kicked.

57. No *hacking* or *hacking over* or tripping up shall be allowed under any circumstances.

58. No one wearing projecting nails, iron plates, or gutta percha on any part of his boots or shoes shall be allowed to play in a match.

59. The captains of the respective sides shall be the sole arbiters of all disputes.

That number of appearances remains a record, while the number of medals won was only bettered in 2010, when Ashley Cole made it six, with Chelsea, and then seven in 2012.

The first decade of The FA Cup is as much the story of Kinnaird and his social group as it is his social class. In 1865, the young Kinnaird went on a trade mission to America with his father. It was led by Morton Peto, who brought his nephew, Morton Peto Betts – a future Wanderers teammate of Kinnaird. Betts had just left Alcock's Harrow and would be on The FA committee that approved the cup, before scoring the first ever Final goal.

Kinnaird actually missed the first 1871–72 edition because he was on a tour of Christian missions in India. He consequently missed a lot of chaos, in the logistics as much as the rules. The FA Cup still had much to figure out.

An initial draw for that First Round had been made on 23 October 1871 – again at *The Sportsman's* offices – although it was not final as The FA wanted to encourage more London clubs to play. Only Donington Grammar School from Lincolnshire and Glasgow's Queen's Park had entered from outside the capital. As promised by The FA for those outside London, both were

Above: Representation of a football match in 1894, from the book *Athletics and Football*.

Above left: Ludgate Circus in London, the area where *The Sportsman's* offices were based. That was where The FA Cup was first proposed on 20 July 1871.

Left: Ebenezer Cobb Morley (1831–1924), left, and Charles Alcock (1842–1907), right.

paired together in a draw that also featured Wanderers v Harrow Chequers; Barnes v Civil Service; Crystal Palace v Hitchin; Royal Engineers v Reigate Priory; Upton Park v Clapham Rovers. Hampstead Heathens were awarded a bye but that was far from the only compromise.

In fact, only four of the seven fixtures took place, and that first season only featured 13 games in all. Wanderers and Royal Engineers – who would become the first finalists – got through after both Reigate Priory and Harrow Chequers withdrew, while the Queen's Park–Donington match was rearranged for the Second Round because they couldn't decide on a venue. When that match was finally arranged to be played in Glasgow, Donington withdrew because of the cost, and never played in The FA Cup again.

The very first FA Cup goal came at West Ham Park, where Clapham Rovers' Jarvis Kenrick scored just two minutes into their away match against Upton Park. *The Sportsman* described it as a "first-rate piece of play" that came "after a good rush". It was far from Kenrick's only historic contribution to the cup. In this match, Clapham went on to win 3–0, to go with Barnes' 2–0 victory over the Civil Service, and Maidenhead's 2–0 win over Marlow. Hitchin

Above: The Oxford University team that won their first FA Cup in 1874, beating Royal Engineers 2–0 in the Final.

Following pages: Famous representation of the international match between England and Scotland, at the Oval, in 1879.

"I KNOW OF NO SPORT WHICH HAS SO QUICKLY ASSUMED NATIONAL IMPORTANCE AS FOOTBALL."

- ARTHUR KINNAIRD -

and Crystal Palace drew 0–0, but were both permitted to advance, which also happened with Wanderers and Crystal Palace in the Third Round. The first-ever replay took place in the Second Round, Hampstead Heathens beating Barnes 1–0.

Queen's Park's logistical issues meant they were eventually exempted until the Semi-finals, which were both due to take place at the Kennington Oval, along with the Final. Their very first match was against Wanderers, and the cross-border nature of the tie led it to become the first FA Cup fixture to really capture public interest, as well as to inspire a community spirit. Queen's Park's supporters rallied to raise funds for the trip, which brought a creditable 0–0 draw. Observers were struck by the effectiveness of the Scots' passing game, but the club couldn't play a replay as they ran out of money and had to return to Glasgow. The other Semi-final did go to a replay after another 0–0 draw, Royal Engineers eventually beating Crystal Palace 3–0.

Top: The Royal Engineers team that won The FA Cup in 1875, beating Old Etonians in a replay.

Above left: The only known surviving medal from the first FA Cup Final in 1872, awarded to a Wanderers player after the defeat of Royal Engineers.

Above right: Major Francis Marindin (1838–1900).

Opposite: Arthur Kinnaird (1847–1923), attends a match.

History beckoned on 16 March 1872. After four months, The FA Cup had just about worked its way to a first showpiece. The occasion at Kennington Oval didn't yet have any of the pageantry to come, but did have plenty of fans. An estimated 2,000 supporters attended, although *The Sportsman* reported that this was less than expected due to the price of entry. The venue, which had also hosted the first "representative" international between England and Scotland in 1870, reflected football's deep crossover with cricket at the time. Most of these gentlemen amateurs observed the sports calendar of the day, which was football in the winter and cricket in the summer. The *Bell's Life* newspaper reported the day as being "too hot for the winter game".

There was a deeper crossover between players and administration. Captaining Wanderers was Alcock, who had founded the club as a team for the best players from former public schools. They were so-called because they didn't have their own pitch. Captaining Royal Engineers was their own founder, Major Francis Marindin, who would become president of The FA in

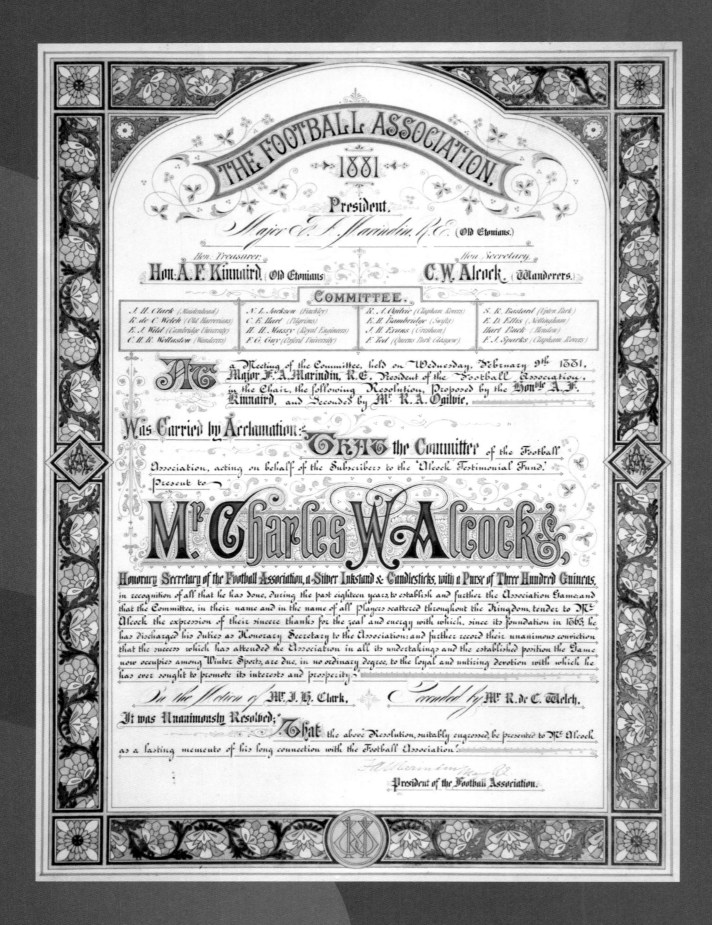

"THE FASTEST AND HARDEST MATCH THAT HAS EVER BEEN SEEN AT THE OVAL."

- THE FIELD -

1874. He had served in the Crimean War and formed the club as a team for officers from Chatham.

Such influence would prove useful. The first ever FA Cup Final scorer was initially recorded as "A.H. Chequer". This stood for "A Harrovian Chequer", and was taken by Betts as a reference to his status as a Harrow player. Once they withdrew without playing, he switched to Wanderers, despite rules on cup ties. Serving as a member of The FA committee, and playing with its most prominent figures, ensured that wasn't a problem.

It might have been argued that Wanderers needed the help, since Royal Engineers were favourites having won three games on the way to the Final. Wanderers had only beaten Clapham Rovers, otherwise progressing via a withdrawal and a draw.

That expectation swung the other way after 10 minutes of the 3.05pm kick-off, however, in a development that would become another of the Final's traits over the years. You might call it the Oval hoodoo – Royal Engineers' Lieutenant Edmund Cresswell was the first of many players to get injured in the showpiece, breaking his collarbone.

Five minutes after that, Betts – or, if you like, Chequer – scored the only goal. The fateful moment was forced by Walpole Vidal, known as "the prince of dribblers". His run eventually saw the ball fall to Betts who scored with what *The Sportsman* described as a "well-directed kick".

Wanderers won 1–0 and were the first name on the cup. It was to be presented by FA President E.C. Morley at the club's annual dinner, at Pall Mall Restaurant four weeks later. Alcock, the man who had the original idea, now had the trophy in his hands.

The name given the competition before the first season was The FA Challenge Cup, because that was precisely what it was intended to be: a challenge. As winners, Wanderers were given immediate passage to the 1873 Final, with everyone else playing off for the right to try and beat them. It meant the returning Kinnaird's

Above: Representation of a wrestling match at Lillie Bridge Ground, the site of the second FA Cup Final, in 1873.

Opposite: The Charles Alcock Scroll, outlining the Football Association in 1881.

FOOTBALL MATCH,

WANDERERS, London, v. QUEEN'S PARK,

Played on Hampden Park, Mount Florida, Glasgow, on Saturday, 9th October, 1875.

H. W. CHAMBERS,
Goal Keeper.

A. H. STRATFORD.
X
Back.

A. F. KINNAIRD.
Right X *Half-back*
Blue and white cap

W. S. RAWSON
Left X *Half-back*
Blue cap

J. TURNER,
Left X *Wing.*

W. D. GREIG,
Right X *Wing*
Blue stockings

R. L. GEAVES,
Centre X
Red and white cap

C. W. ALCOCK,
Captain X *and Centre.*
Cap— blue and white chequers.

H. S. OTTER,
X *Centre*
Pink cap

HUBERT HERON,
Left X *Wing*
Grey stockings and orange,
violet and black cap

J. KENRICK,
Right X *Wing*
Cerise and French grey
cap

UMPIRE—ROBERT GARDINER, Clydesdale Club
REFEREE—THOMAS HASWELL 3RD L.R.V. Club
UMPIRE—W. C. MITCHELL, Queen's Park Club

HENRY M'NEILL,
Left X *Front*
Orange and black stockings

W. MACKINNON,
Centre X *Front*
Red stockings

JAMES B. WEIR,
Right X *Front*
Red and white stockings

M. M'NEIL,
Left X *Back-up*
Blue and white stockings

C. HERRIOT,
Centre X *Back-up*
Black and white cap—no
stocking.

THOMAS LAWRIE,
Right X *Back-up*
White stockings

JAS. PHILIPS
Left X *Half-back*
Red and black stockings.

CHAS. CAMPBELL,
Right X *Half-back*
Red, white, and black stockings

R. W. NEIL,
Left X *Back*
Heather mixture stockings

JOSEPH TAYLOR,
Captain and X *Right Back*
Black and white stockings

JOHN DICKSON,
Goal Keeper.

Colours : Wanderers, White Jersey — Queen's Park, Black and White Stripe.
Play will begin at 3.30 p.m. and end at 5 p.m.

PLEASE DO NOT STRAIN THE ROPES.

first ever FA Cup match was the second Final, against Oxford University, when he was captain and also scored.

It was an introduction that would set the tone for his influence on the cup, and the game. As well as playing in nine Finals, Kinnaird organised the first official international, earned a cap for Scotland and was an administrator and leader in The FA for 55 years. As many as 33 of those were as president. He would also become Lord High Commissioner to the Church of Scotland and Baron Kinnaird of Inchture. On his death in 1923 at the age of 75, by which time he had been presented with the second FA Cup trophy, fellow administrator Frederick Wall described him as having done more "to popularise soccer than any man who ever lived".

Kinnaird's prowess as a player for Wanderers, and then Old Etonians, was a huge part of that. Alcock described him as the best player of the time, and he could play anywhere, although preferred half-back. Kinnaird was fast, physical and fired by a huge hunger for the game. One story has it that his wife, Lady Alma Kinnaird, once complained to teammate William Kenyon-Slaney – scorer of the first ever international goal – that his vigour for the game would "end in a broken leg". She was told she was right but that it wouldn't be his own.

Nevertheless, Andy Mitchell's *Arthur Kinnaird: First Lord of Football* casts him as a fair player, and the respect for him at the time was clear. Another story describes an adoring crowd removing the horses from Kinnaird's carriage en route to the 1882 Final and pulling it themselves.

But back in that 1873 showpiece, *Sporting Life* said Wanderers' victory was "in great measure due to the extremely brilliant play of their captain". That Final was the only one to take place at Lillie Bridge, the home of London Athletic Club. Wanderers selected it since they didn't have a stadium of their own. Another season filled with byes and withdrawals again saw Queen's Park withdraw in the Semi-final due to travel costs. The Scots' planned opponents, Oxford University, at least won a total of four games throughout the competition to earn the right to "challenge" Wanderers. It wasn't much of a test. Kinnaird and Charles Wollaston both scored in a 2–0 win. Wollaston was actually the first player to win five FA Cups, doing so before Kinnaird, because he played in all of Wanderers' victories.

1872–73
WANDERERS **2–0** OXFORD UNIVERSITY
VENUE: **LILLIE BRIDGE**
ATTENDANCE: **3,000**

1873–74
OXFORD UNIVERSITY **2–0** ROYAL ENGINEERS
VENUE: **KENNINGTON OVAL**
ATTENDANCE: **2,000**

This second win actually kicked off at 11am so that the two teams could watch the Oxford v Cambridge university Boat Race, reflecting the nascent game's secondary status. But form and fervour were developing. That 1872–73 season was the first in which free-kicks were introduced for handling the ball, while author and FA Cup historian Geoffrey Green wrote that 1873–74 was when "the first germs of the epidemic of cup fever had begun to spread". And the game itself had spread – that campaign was the first in which Sheffield took part. Their first two matches were 0–0 draws with Shropshire Wanderers. A coin toss was used to decide the tie – which Sheffield won – for the only time in history. The cup was otherwise a much smoother process. The "challenge" concept was dropped after just one season, with the Final returned to the Kennington Oval, but out with it went the champions themselves in the Third Round. Oxford University gained revenge on Wanderers with a 1–0 victory after a replay, before beating Royal Engineers 2–0 in the showpiece. That 1874 match marked the only time that two brothers – William and Herbert Rawson – played on opposite sides in the Final.

Royal Engineers must have felt they were cursed, but made it third time lucky the following year against Old Etonians. Their most famous player had no such fortune. Marindin recused himself for the Final on the basis that he was a member of both teams.

Inspired by the spirit of the competition in the same way that Alcock was, Kinnaird felt the experience would be a good fit for a team of his old school friends from Eton. He actually got one together for 1873–74, but illness put him out and they withdrew without playing.

"[WANDERERS' VICTORY WAS] IN GREAT MEASURE DUE TO THE EXTREMELY BRILLIANT PLAY OF THEIR CAPTAIN."

- SPORTING LIFE -

Top: Arthur Kinnaird (1847–1923), left, and William Kenyon Slaney (1847–1908), right.

Opposite: A match card, which was the day's version of the programme, for a match between Queen's Park and Wanderers at Hampden Park on 9 October 1875. Alcock captained Wanderers, who had by then won two FA Cups.

Old Etonians were in full strength the following season, however, as they pushed Royal Engineers all the way. This was the first Final to go to a replay, after a 1–1 draw. It was also the last to see teams change ends after a goal was scored – not that Old Etonians actually did that in the second game. Having arrived an hour late, they were overwhelmed by Royal Engineers. Henry Renny-Tailyour scored the first FA Cup Final brace, in a 2–0 win.

It was now Old Etonians who would feel cursed. They got to the Final again the following season, but Wanderers reasserted their authority. They also won it in a more arduous fashion than their previous triumphs. Unlike the open paths of their first two victories, Wanderers this time played six games, the Final again going to a replay. It was a strange occasion for Kinnaird, since he was associated with both clubs, and also ultimately a disappointing one, partly because he was still suffering from an injury in the first game that forced him to go in goal. Wanderers' 3–0 win – secured by Wollaston and two goals from Thomas Hughes – was their third victory, and the first of a three-in-a-row.

Wanderers, this time with Kinnaird back in the team, returned for another Final against Oxford University in 1877. Kinnaird was initially still in goal after the previous season's injury and suffered a rare moment of ignominy as he was responsible for the first own goal in a Final, having carried a ball over the line. Eager to rectify that, and with Wanderers 1–0 down in the Final minutes, Kinnaird went up front and inspired the comeback. Kenrick, the scorer of the first-ever goal in The FA Cup, equalised for Wanderers four minutes from time before William Lindsay won it.

1874–75
ROYAL ENGINEERS **1–1** OLD ETONIANS
AET
VENUE: **KENNINGTON OVAL**
ATTENDANCE: **2,000**

1874–75 (REPLAY)
ROYAL ENGINEERS **2–0** OLD ETONIANS
VENUE: **KENNINGTON OVAL**
ATTENDANCE: **3,000**

1875–76
WANDERERS **1–1** OLD ETONIANS
AET
VENUE: **KENNINGTON OVAL**
ATTENDANCE: **3,500**

1875–76 (REPLAY)
WANDERERS **3–0** OLD ETONIANS
VENUE: **KENNINGTON OVAL**
ATTENDANCE: **1,500**

1876–77
WANDERERS **2–1** OXFORD UNIVERSITY
AET
VENUE: **KENNINGTON OVAL**
ATTENDANCE: **3,000**

1877–78
WANDERERS **3–1** ROYAL ENGINEERS
VENUE: **KENNINGTON OVAL**
ATTENDANCE: **4,500**

"FANCY! A LOT OF WORKING CHAPS BEATING A LOT OF GENTLEMEN!"

- UNNAMED OBSERVER -

Wanderers by now had so much momentum that they overcame goalkeeper James Kirkpatrick's broken arm in the 1878 Final, although he stayed on to make one fine save. Kenrick ultimately scored twice in a 3–1 win, becoming the first player to score in successive Finals, as well as the showpiece's highest-ever scorer.

In lifting the trophy for a third successive year, Wanderers had earned the right to keep it. They declined, on the condition it would never be awarded to any club in perpetuity. It was a symbolic moment, not least for the fact Wanderers would never again play in a Final, and would actually disappear within just three years.

The trophy might have stayed in one place between 1876 and 1878, but those same three years saw the spread of the competition, and the game. By 1876, agreement was finally reached between The FA and the Sheffield Association on the offside law, and the two sets of rules were combined. Alcock's calculation had paid off. That 1876–77 season meanwhile saw a record 32 clubs enter, requiring the introduction of another round. Teams were now applying from all over the country, and 1877–78 saw the first from Lancashire.

One of them, Darwen, would change the course of football history. It was why this period was such a watershed for The FA Cup. It would not just herald the end of Wanderers, but also the end of the era they represented. Now came the rise of provincial football and professionalism.

A key moment in Wanderers' decline was the official formation of Old Etonians in October 1878. The former schoolboys had initially been a "scratch team", which generally involved Kinnaird and Marindin rounding up players when they were needed. This was why they withdrew in 1873–74 and didn't even enter in 1877–88, sparking Marindin into action. The new team quickly absorbed players from Wanderers, including Kinnaird. There was a sense of providence when Old Etonians immediately drew the holders in the First Round in November 1878. It was seen as the biggest cup tie of the age and produced one of the biggest defeats. Old Etonians thrashed Wanderers 7–2, but this still wasn't the most significant game of the season.

That accolade went to Darwen's Fourth Round tie with Old Etonians. It was a game rich in narrative, contrasts and consequence. It was also anything but the procession to the trophy many had expected when Old Etonians destroyed Wanderers in the opening round.

Darwen FC were a team of millworkers, of very different backgrounds to the men they were taking on. They also had two fine players in Fergie Suter and Jimmy Love, who attracted interest for more than their ability. The duo had come from Scotland's Partick Thistle, and many suspected they were being paid. There was no mention of payment in The FA rules of the time because it was a possibility that nobody had envisaged, but it was generally considered unethical. Suter and Love are now seen as pioneers, and the game's first professionals.

Darwen were planting a flag. Their earlier match against Remnant might have gone down in history itself had it not been overshadowed by the sensations to follow. It was probably the very first Third Round upset, even if the idea was unknown at the time. Suter had been influential in introducing some Scottish tactics to Darwen. The positioning of attackers in different places to facilitate passing confused the congested amateur

Above: The Darwen team that stunned Old Etonians and changed football in the 1878–79 FA Cup. Lying on the ground is Fergus Suter, who was almost certainly one of the first two professional footballers with teammate James Love.

teams, and brought Darwen a 3–2 victory in extra-time. The astonishing nature of the victory was revealed by one observer's quote, as reported by author Keith Dewhurst: "Fancy! A lot of working chaps beating a lot of gentlemen!"

Much as the victory was praised, it was still seen as a fluke. Darwen's next opponents, the mighty Old Etonians, would surely make that clear. In the build-up to the match, another new reality for the game also announced itself. Darwen had initially considered withdrawing due to the £31 cost of travelling to London by train for the Remnant game. But "cup fever" had overtaken the town and its people set up a "London Fund" to send their heroes off.

It was the first sign of the future to come, which was the game – and The FA Cup – binding communities. When the players finally made it to London, they were stepping into a different world, that of the football establishment. The match took place at the Kennington Oval – The FA's rules stated that all three final rounds should take place there – with Alcock the referee. Old Etonians won the toss and decided to play with the wind first half. They were 5–1 up by half-time. Kinnaird was in the form of his career, his throws causing havoc.

Then, as far as Old Etonians were concerned, everything went downhill rapidly. Darwen clearly had one of the great half-time team talks as they produced an amazing comeback. In seeking to avoid humiliation, they embarrassed Old Etonians. Darwen began to properly apply their passing game, pulling the opposition everywhere. It was 5–2 with 15 minutes to go but Old Etonians were exhausted. Two further Darwen goals followed, before Love claimed a late equaliser, to excited astonishment in the stands. Custom suggested extra time should be played, but that had not been agreed beforehand. No doubt knowing his side were exhausted, Marindin – Old Etonian's captain and The FA president – refused. A replay was required, along with another trip to London for Darwen.

The northerners again challenged Old Etonians, drawing 2–2. Extra-time had been agreed this time, but there were no further goals. In the face of an expensive third trip south, Darwen tried everything to get the game switched to their home ground, Barley Bank – including offering £40 to cover their opponents' travel expenses. But Old Etonians again refused. For the third game, with the players already sapped from two previous trips, work demands meant Darwen had to travel overnight. That proved the difference on the day (not to mention highlighting the social difference between the players). A fatigued Darwen were defeated 6–2.

Old Etonians would go on to win their first FA Cup, and Kinnaird's fourth, by beating Clapham Rovers 1–0 in the Final. Charles Clerke scored the only goal of a poor game. Clapham had been the first club from outside the original "big four" to reach the Final and would, in 1880, become the first outside that group to win it, but their inexperience that day was personified by James Prinsep. At the age of 17 years and 245 days, he would remain the youngest player to appear in the showpiece until 2004, when Curtis Weston of Millwall took that accolade.

Old Etonians won the cup, but had lost some good will. The press were shocked by the lack of sportsmanship shown towards Darwen: "Whatever satisfaction it may be to the Old Etonians' that they have compelled the Darwen club to spend this large sum of money they are heartily welcome to it," the *Athletic News* said.

It was all a long way from the attitude that opened the cup. Under huge public pressure, The FA changed the rule that all three final rounds had to be played at the Oval. But that wasn't all that was changing. Darwen had opened the game to a new world.

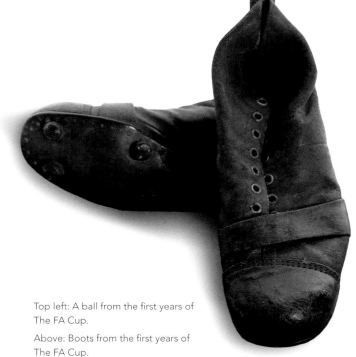

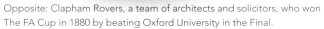

Opposite: Clapham Rovers, a team of architects and solicitors, who won The FA Cup in 1880 by beating Oxford University in the Final.

Below: Engraving of a match between Old Etonians and Blackburn Rovers, who would meet in the 1882 FA Cup Final.

Top left: A ball from the first years of The FA Cup.

Above: Boots from the first years of The FA Cup.

1879 OLD ETONIANS.
1880 CLAPHAM ROVERS.
1881 OLD CARTHUSIANS.
1882 OLD ETONIANS.
1883 BLACKBURN OLYMPIC
1884 BLACKBURN ROVERS.
1885 BLACKBURN ROVERS.
1886 BLACKBURN ROVERS.
1887 ASTON VILLA.
1888 WEST BROMWICH ALBION
1889 PRESTON NORTH END.
1890 BLACKBURN ROVERS.
1891 BLACKBURN ROVERS.
1892 WEST BROMWICH ALBION
1893 WOLVERHAMPTON WANDERERS
1894 NOTTS COUNTY.
1895 ASTON VILLA.
1896 SHEFFIELD WEDNESDAY.
1897 ASTON VILLA.

CHAPTER FOUR

ENTER THE PROFESSIONALS

1880–1892

1880 🏆 1892

THE LAST DECADE OF FA CUP FINALS AT THE KENNINGTON
OVAL FEATURED THE FIRST-EVER DOUBLE AND SO MANY SUPERB
PERFORMANCES, BUT THERE WAS NO MATCH AS SIGNIFICANT AS
A FOURTH ROUND DRAW ON 19 JANUARY 1884.

U pton Park had drawn 1–1 away to a burgeoning Preston North End, but were left unsettled by the nature of the game. The London club accused Preston of paying Nick Ross and George Drummond, two hugely talented Scottish players. Upton Park were one of The FA Cup's original sides and were staunch amateurs, but they inadvertently sparked the introduction of professionalism.

When Preston secretary Major William Sudell appeared before The FA, he had a choice. He could continue the custom of the time and deny the accusations, so Preston could continue to pursue the trophy, or he could admit it.

He astonished everyone in the room by going much further. Sudell didn't just admit the charge but confirmed that payment was widespread in northern football. The brazenness stunned The FA, and saw Preston immediately expelled from The FA Cup. If many wondered what Sudell's thinking was, that was the point. Sudell instantly changed the thinking of The FA. They were now forced to confront an issue that had been rumbling on ever since the competition spread outside the public school network. It could have potentially led to a split in the game. Instead, it shaped the future of football, although only after considerable upheaval. This, then, was a decade of deep change. It would bring professionalism, the Football League and many revolutionary rules and consequences, as well as the last Final at the Kennington Oval.

The true centre of the game was moving north, specifically to an area around Darwen and Blackburn, which was where professionalism was born. This was why Suter and Love were such pioneers and why Darwen were so important to the history of the game. They would influence Blackburn Olympic and Rovers to take a similar approach, the latter even poaching Suter, who was a key player in their three successive FA Cup wins between 1884 and 1886. Rovers' ambition would in turn inspire Sudell to create a team of stars at Preston, bringing the issue to a head.

All of this stemmed from the growing popularity of the game, which brought increasing amounts of money through the gates and created economic momentum. Blackburn were charging

sixpence for entry, which was double what Darwen were. Money was naturally diverted to better players as "bonuses", which then developed into regular rumours of pay.

It might be said that Charles Alcock could barely have imagined all this when he came up with the idea for The FA Cup, but he was already ahead of most of the game. Like Arthur Kinnaird, he recognised the way football was going, and argued that "the spread of the game depends upon professionalism". Its spread had been one of his motivations, after all.

Not everyone was so enlightened. There was a lot of tension, particularly within the competition itself. The "professors" – as paid players came to be called – didn't immediately take over. There were gradual steps.

Clapham Rovers learned the lessons of the 1879 defeat to win in 1880, beating Oxford University in the Final. Clapton Lloyd-Jones got the only goal in a 1–0 win. But this was very much the beginning of the end of the era of the gentlemen amateurs.

The 1879–80 season was the last time the universities of Oxford and Cambridge entered The FA Cup, with 1880–81 the

---

1879–80
CLAPHAM ROVERS **1–0** OXFORD UNIVERSITY
VENUE: **KENNINGTON OVAL**
ATTENDANCE: **6,000**

Opposite top: A colour lithograph of many of the leading players in the first decade of the FA Cup competition, from 1881. Back row, left to right: Charles Campbell, Charles Caborn, Tom Marshall, Harry Swepstone, John Hunter, Sam Weller Widdowson, Edwin Luntley, James Frederick McLeod Prinsep, Harry McNeil, William Lindsay, John Sands, Tom Brindle, William Mosforth; seated on right: Francis Sparks; front row, left to right: Herbert Whitfield, Norman Bailey, Edward Bambridge and F W Earp.

Opposite bottom: The Blackburn Rovers team that became the first northern club to reach The FA Cup Final, losing to Old Etonians 1–0 in the 1882 Final.

Previous pages: The original FA Cup, "the little tin idol", stolen in 1895.

1880–81
OLD CARTHUSIANS 3–0 OLD ETONIANS
VENUE: **KENNINGTON OVAL**
ATTENDANCE: **4,000**

1881–82
OLD ETONIANS 1–0 BLACKBURN ROVERS
VENUE: **KENNINGTON OVAL**
ATTENDANCE: **6,500**

1882–83
BLACKBURN OLYMPIC 2–1 OLD ETONIANS
AET
VENUE: **KENNINGTON OVAL**
ATTENDANCE: **8,000**

Old Carthusians had, meanwhile, adopted the "scientific" Scottish passing approach that was beginning to take over the game. They ended up convincingly beating Old Etonians 3–0, the victory also creating a rare record as Carthusians remain one of just three clubs – along with Royal Engineers and, over a century later, Wimbledon – to have won The FA Cup and The FA Amateur Cup. Canada's Edward Hagarty Parry, meanwhile, became the first foreign-born winning captain and first foreign scorer in a Final.

That 1881 Final was also played according to new laws, which saw the referee mentioned for the first time. This was the pace of change – every season offered evolutionary leaps.

Blackburn Rovers' 1882 appearance in the Final was the first by a provincial club. Their Semi-final against Sheffield Wednesday was actually played in Huddersfield, with the aim of showcasing football to a rugby stronghold. The good word was spreading and generated high emotion. Blackburn were greeted like heroes after confirming their place in the Final – fog signals were exploded and the players were carried through the streets. Hundreds of Rovers fans made their first-ever trip to London for the Final against Old Etonians, many on special trains.

Above: The Blackburn Rovers football team that won the 1884 FA Cup, pictured with the trophy, the East Lancashire Charity Cup and the Lancashire Senior Cup. Standing (left –right): Joe Lofthouse, Hugh MacIntyre, Joe Beverley, Herby Arthur, Fergus Suter, Jimmy Forrest and R Birtwistle. Seated: Jimmy Douglas, Joe Sowerbutts, James Brown (holding the FA Cup), G Avery and John Hargreaves.

last edition that would see two southern amateur teams contest the Final, as well as the last season that involved Wanderers. By 1887, the then-most successful team in FA Cup history would be dissolved altogether.

Tellingly, that 1881 showpiece was between two public school teams who had been most responsible for Wanderers' decline. Many of their prospective players instead appeared for Old Etonians and Old Carthusians, the latter another team of former pupils from Charterhouse. It got to the point that Wanderers could no longer field a side. It is still testament to the club's legacy that, in the more than 140 years since Wanderers' fifth FA Cup win, only nine clubs have exceeded that total – although Blackburn Rovers would match that haul within the next decade.

> ## "[THE CUP IS] VERY WELCOME TO LANCASHIRE. IT'LL HAVE A GOOD HOME AND IT'LL NEVER GO BACK TO LONDON."
>
> - ALBERT WARBURTON -

It was an occasion weighted with meaning, and the increasing popularity saw the showpiece moved from the side areas of the Oval to the very centre for the first time. That proved symbolic. This was really a match taking place across eras, the first-ever Final between two different worlds. The 6,000-strong crowd watched a tense game where Rovers looked nervous, but the amateur southerners just about held on to the trophy. William Anderson scored the only goal from a breakaway, between posts connected by a crossbar for the first time. Old Etonians had won their second FA Cup and Kinnaird did a handstand in celebration, but the tide was turning as an increasing number of southern clubs were getting eliminated earlier.

The Final was also played amid increasing protests about payment. A month before the game, The FA Cup formally banned the "disease" of professionalism. A sub-committee was later set up to investigate the many protests that payment was persisting.

In 1883, the cup at last went north, and to Blackburn, but not yet to Rovers. Blackburn Olympic had been founded just five years earlier and were built on the best modern practices. Their influential half-back Jack Hunter even took the players to a training camp in Blackpool before the Final. This didn't fit with the amateurs' idea of a game played as pastime. These new professional attitudes brought planning and calculation. It's no coincidence this period saw two forwards withdrawn to create the new position of centre-half, as well as the 2-3-5 formation that would dominate until the 1930s. Given the Scottish influence on their shape and tactics, it was ironic that Olympic would also become the first team to win the cup with an all-English line-up, listed as a team of plumbers, metal workers and spinners.

Old Etonians – in their last ever Final – just couldn't cope with Olympic's sweeping passes. It was from one of those that Tommy Dewhurst set up Jimmy Costley for the winner in extra time.

Below: The Blackburn Olympic team who became the first northern club to win The FA Cup, beating Old Etonians 2–1 in the 1883 Final.

Below right: The changing styles of early English FA Cup winners' medals. Top: 1876, the winners were Wanderers; middle left:1877, again the winners were Wanderers; middle right: 1886, the winners were Blackburn Rovers, and this medal belonged to Fergus Suter; Bottom: 1907, the winners were Sheffield Wednesday, and this medal belonged to Andrew Wilson.

1883–84
BLACKBURN ROVERS 2–1 SCOTLAND QUEEN'S PARK
VENUE: KENNINGTON OVAL
ATTENDANCE: 4,000

Major Marindin, the former Old Etonian and one of the figures in The FA against professionalism, handed over the trophy. The silverware that symbolised the game's elite, and had been the exclusive preserve of society's elite, was now among the working people. So was the competition as a whole. That 1882–83 season marked the first time more northern clubs entered than southern clubs.

One famous story has it that, during the jubilant celebrations back in Blackburn, one local complained the trophy looked "more like a tea kettle". Olympic captain Albert Warburton responded: "Aye, it might do. But it's very welcome to Lancashire. It'll have a good home and it'll never go back to London."

That was prophetic. The trophy was eventually stolen in 1895, having barely left Blackburn. Rovers, for their part, were about to fulfil their potential, initially with three FA Cups wins in a row.

The first two involved successive Final victories over Queen's Park, the only time in history the final pairing has been repeated the following year. The "mother club of Scottish football" surprised The FA by finally overcoming travel costs to compete, and at last play their second-ever match in the cup at the start of the 1883–84 season. They then astonished the football world with how they played, scoring 44 goals in seven games on the way to the Final, including a 4–0 Semi-final win over Blackburn Olympic.

Queen's Park featured the finest Scottish players that hadn't yet been lured to England, and it meant the 1884 Final was almost seen as an international match. That attracted the biggest crowd yet – 12,000. Open questions about professionalism were not the only tension. A rivalry between the nations arose during the match following a dispute about the offside law. Queen's Park argued it should only feature two defenders rather than three. Marindin went with the English definition, and disallowed two goals apiece.

Above: Illustration of events and faces from the 1884 FA Cup Final between Blackburn Rovers and Queens Park, at Kennington Oval.

Opposite: Charles W Alcock (right) with Dr William Gilbert Grace at the Kennington Oval in London, the venue for 22 of the first 23 Finals.

No. 189. New Series.—(Vol. VIII.)   APRIL 8th, 1886   Price Sixpence. Post Free, 6½d.

REGISTERED AT THE GENERAL POST OFFICE FOR TRANSMISSION ABROAD.

THE FINAL TIE: BLACKBURN ROVERS v. WEST BROMWICH ALBION.

FOOTBALL ASSOCIATION CHALLENGE CUP.

There was also tension that was exclusively English. This fixture prompted a more distasteful trend, where the southern press would openly mock travelling fans from the north. "London witnessed an incursion of northern barbarians, hot-blooded Lancastrians, sharp of tongue, rough and ready, of uncouth garb and speech," the *Pall Mall Gazette* wrote.

This caused bad feeling in Blackburn, but even greater joy when they took the trophy north. In the end, Queen's Park were beaten 2–1 in the first Final and 3–2 in the second, James Forrest scoring in both. By the time of Rovers' third victory, however, the world of football would be very different.

Rovers had eliminated Upton Park en route to their first FA Cup win in 1883–84, after Preston had been disqualified for professionalism. But Rovers were themselves paying players, illustrating the depth of the challenge The FA faced in trying to stamp it out. Accrington were another side expelled, but there was too much for The FA to actively police.

Alcock, Kinnaird and more progressive minds felt nothing could be done to stop the trend so it was more logical to try and regulate it. At an FA general meeting at the Freemasons' Tavern in 1884, it was proposed that "professionalism be legalised". That fitted with Alcock's idea of what football was supposed to be, although he did initially suggest The FA Cup be kept for amateurs as a sop.

But the opposition to professionalism, driven by the intransigent Birmingham and Sheffield associations, was vociferous. Some of the reasoning was purely traditionalist, as these gentlemen didn't want to give up their idea of the game they'd grown up with. Some of it was more self-serving, as they didn't want to give up their place at the top of it. Some of it went much deeper, undoubtedly coming from class divides of the day. W.H. Jope, of the Birmingham association, said it was demeaning for gentlemen to play with professionals. There were mutterings about how working men couldn't be trusted, and that this whole episode was fundamentally immoral.

Many Birmingham and Sheffield clubs feared for their futures if professionalism was introduced. Others just couldn't get their heads around it. They needed more time to register it all, and that meant Alcock's proposal only received three votes. The problem was the opposition was too entrenched. Having rejected Alcock's proposal, those against professionalism sought to shut down pay altogether. A new FA law was passed in June 1884 that clubs had to list players from outside their area. The thinking was that these players were likely to have been paid to move.

This was a step too far and the northern clubs revolted. Marshalled by Sudell, a rebellion of 70 clubs threatened to break away and form a "British Football Association". The FA was

1884–85
BLACKBURN ROVERS 2–0 SCOTLAND QUEEN'S PARK
VENUE: **KENNINGTON OVAL**
ATTENDANCE: **12,500**

1885–86
BLACKBURN ROVERS 0–0 WEST BROMWICH ALBION
VENUE: **KENNINGTON OVAL**
ATTENDANCE: **15,000**

1885–86 (REPLAY)
BLACKBURN ROVERS 2–0 WEST BROMWICH ALBION
VENUE: **RACECOURSE GROUND**
ATTENDANCE: **12,000**

rocked. Many members were already wavering and there was now real danger there could be a split, as was to happen with rugby. The new law about non-local players was suspended, and Alcock seized the opportunity to draft another recommendation in January 1885. Most were now in favour of professionalism, although some politicking and newspaper pressure was still required to secure the two-thirds majority needed to pass the law.

Finally, at a Special General Meeting of The FA on 20 July 1885, professionalism was legalised. The future of football was set. There were still some lingering issues, but it was like a cloud had lifted.

That first season of professionalism saw 130 clubs enter The FA Cup, although all players now had to be registered. Clubs could no longer just turn up with a team on the day. That did bring more disqualifications for teams who fielded unregistered players, with Preston among them.

It also ensured the further spread of FA Cup success. Birmingham was soon to have its time and that season the city had its first finalist. West Bromwich Albion forced Blackburn Rovers to a replay after a 0–0 at Kennington Oval, but couldn't prevent them making it three wins in a row. The holders ultimately won 2–0 in a replay at the Racecourse Ground in Derby, the first time the fixture had been held outside London. It also produced a classic Final goal, the Ricky Villa strike of its age, with Jimmy Brown scoring after dribbling past a series of West Brom players.

Right: A vintage match card, featuring the teams and line-ups for the 1886 FA Cup Final.

Opposite: Cover illustration from the *Pictorial World*, published in April 1886, featuring action from the first game of that year's FA Cup Final, between Blackburn Rovers and Bromwich Albion at the Kennington Oval. Blackburn won the replay 2–0 at the Racecourse Ground.

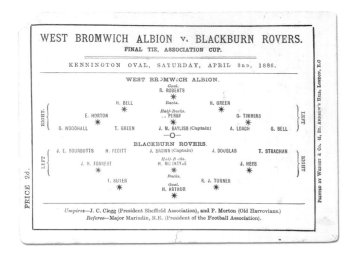

The moment enthralled the crowd of 15,000, a remarkable number given the snow on that April day. Unable to keep the cup due to the precedent set by Wanderers, Blackburn were instead presented with a silver shield.

Rovers were now the most popular team in England, having scored 87 goals in their 22 games on their way to those three FA Cup victories, but their eventual conquerors came from Scotland. Rovers were finally eliminated by Renton, as the 1886–87 season saw The FA allow entries from all over Britain and Ireland for the only time in history. That all-inclusive rule fostered some quirks, such as Nottingham Forest becoming the only club to play a cup tie in all four countries of the United Kingdom. Glasgow Rangers also reached the Semi-final, ultimately going out to the growing force that was Aston Villa.

It also fostered other tensions. The Scottish FA had been furious about professionalism, only accepting it as late as 1893. Already aggravated by so many players going south, they prohibited Scottish clubs from appearing in The FA Cup from 1887–88. The Irish FA followed, although the Welsh did not, recognising the unique glory of the competition.

On the other side, Marindin had always been unsettled by the signing of Scottish players, which the ambitious Preston did more than any other club. This brought a telling incident when West Brom beat Sudell's great side in the other 1887 Semi-final. Marindin walked into West Brom's dressing room and asked whether they were all English. When that was confirmed, he replied: "Then I have much pleasure in presenting you with the ball. You have played a very good game and I hope you will win the cup."

That Semi-final had other notable figures in the line-ups. Preston's goalkeeper was Arthur Wharton, English football's first black professional player. Earlier in the club's run, a Carthusians player named C.A. Smith had missed a fine chance. He would get over it. The player was Aubrey Smith, Hollywood legend.

Opposite: Arthur Wharton, the first black professional footballer, who played for Preston North End in the 1886–87 Semi-final against West Brom.

Below: Nottingham Forest team photograph, after they won the 1884–85 Notts senior cup.

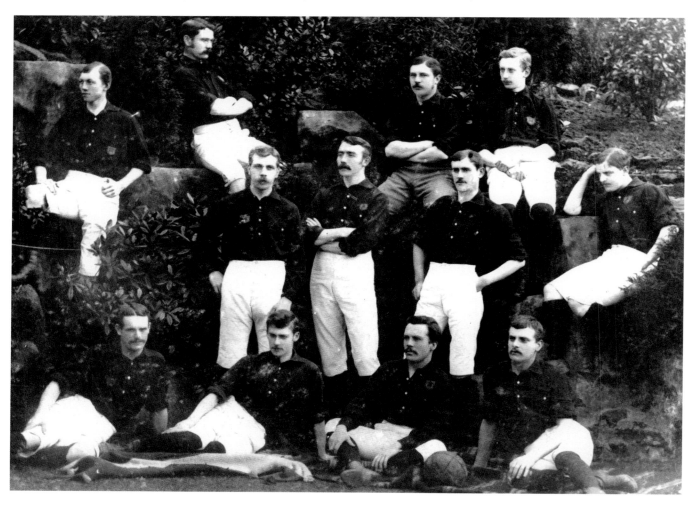

"THEN I HAVE MUCH PLEASURE IN PRESENTING YOU WITH THE BALL. YOU HAVE PLAYED A VERY GOOD GAME AND I HOPE YOU WILL WIN THE CUP."

- FRANCIS MARINDIN -

West Brom had meanwhile ended the run of Notts County, and consequently the cup career of Harry Cursham. He remains the competition's top goalscorer, with 49 goals in 44 games, although he always felt the number should have been higher. Cursham had been credited with six in an 11–1 win over Wednesbury Strollers, but he insisted it was nine.

The results ensured that the 1887 Final was the first-ever provincial derby, as Birmingham was electrified by West Brom's meeting with Villa. West Brom were expected to win on account of their experience, but it was instead to be the first trophy for another FA Cup legend – Villa manager George Ramsey. His first signing, Archie Hunter, meanwhile became the first player to score in every round of the cup, including the first in a 2–0 Final win.

West Brom finally did lift the trophy the following year, beating Preston 2–1. The club that had prompted professionalism still hadn't shown their true value, although their quality was

Above left: Sir C Aubrey Smith: 1881 FA Cup winner, England cricket XI captain 1888–9 and Hollywood actor who between 1911–1948 appeared in 76 films including *The Prisoner of Zenda* and *Tarzan of the Apes*.

Above right: Aston Villa director William McGregor, who is credited with founding the English Football League in 1888.

Top: Aston Villa club photo, featuring players and officials, after their first ever FA Cup win, in 1887. They beat local rivals West Brom 2–0 in the Final.

Opposite: Henry Cursham, Notts County 1880–1887, the scorer of a record 49 FA Cup goals.

undeniable. Star man James Ross was free-scoring, and the whole team was free-flowing, having scored 49 goals in six games en route to the Final. This should have been their year, as it was probably when they were at their best. The only flaw was that "Proud Preston" were too confident. In the build-up to the 1888 Final, it occurred to the squad that their pristine white kit might be sullied by dirt for the celebratory photos. So they asked Marindin – of all people – if they could have their picture taken with the trophy before kick-off. His response was predictable: "Hadn't you better win it first?"

A fall immediately followed such arrogance. West Brom won 2–1 with the brilliant Billy Bassett inspirational in another big-game performance. No matter how good you were, sudden death made any one-off match perilous. That was a beauty of The FA Cup, made even clearer by the next historic development.

Growing crowds had created professionalism, but now professionalism required more crowds. Clubs needed regular income, and meaningful fixtures. There was also huge appetite for more. A record 27,000 people had watched Preston beat Villa 3–1 in the 1887–88 edition of the cup.

Inspiration this time came from America. Journalist W.H. Mounsey felt The FA could benefit from a league system like in baseball, and Aston Villa director William McGregor ran with it. A group of clubs met on the eve of the 1888 FA Cup Final, where Sudell proposed "Football League" as a title. The new competition was to begin in September 1888, without a single southern club among its 12 founding members.

The Football League inevitably influenced the cup to a profound degree, but it didn't just bring fixtures or regular income. It brought structure and meaning, as well as a ranking to assess pairings and performance. Gaps in quality had become a problem, as Preston's record 26–0 win over Hyde in the 1887–88 cup First Round illustrated. So, The FA decided to split the cup into qualifying and the competition proper, with bigger clubs exempted until the First Round.

Some tensions again lingered. The FA didn't automatically consider all professional clubs the best in England, so some Football League members had to qualify, but Old Carthusians were exempted on account of their historic success.

Preston would nevertheless make good on Sudell's long-stated ambition to create "the finest team in the country", by immediately staking their claim to be the best side of all time.

The first year of the league brought the first-ever double, as they won the Football League and FA Cup. In fact, Preston didn't lose a game in either competition, and didn't concede a single goal in the cup.

It was remarkable. It was also, pointedly, a little more restrained than the previous season. Lessons had been learned. Wolverhampton Wanderers, in their first Final (and lying third in the league), couldn't get close to Preston. A record crowd of 22,000 saw history being made, and were able to buy the first-ever match programme to commemorate the occasion, for no more than a penny.

Sudell's more lavish spending could be witnessed in the goals from Fred Dewhurst, James Ross and Sammy Thomson, though Preston arguably never really showed their true worth in the cup.

Following pages: A composite illustration of the main events from the 1889 Final, that saw Preston North End complete the first ever double by beating Wolverhampton Wanderers at the Kennington Oval.

Opposite: West Bromwich Albion club photo, featuring players and officials, following their victory over Preston North End in the 1888 FA Cup Final at Kennington Oval.

Right: The official match card for the 1889 FA Cup Final, where Preston North End's famous "invincibles" completed the first ever double by beating Wolverhampton Wanderers 3–0.

Below: A vintage postcard featuring a reunion of the 1888–89 Preston North End team.

ENGLISH ✳ CUP ✳ COMPETITION.

FINAL TIE MARCH 30th, 1889,

BETWEEN

PRESTON NORTH END v. WOLVERHAMPTON WANDERERS.

PRESTON NORTH END.

Dr. Mills-Roberts

Hawarth   Holmes

Drummond   Russell   Graham

Gordon   Ross   Goodall   Dewhurst   Thomson

WOLVERHAMPTON WANDERERS.

Baynton

Baugh   Mason

Fletcher   Allen   Lowder

Hunter   Wykes   Brodie   Wood   Knight

Umpires : Lord Kinnaird (Old Etonians) and Mr. J. C. Clegg, (Sheffield). Referee : Major Marindin, R.E., C.M.G., (president Football Association).

Foul.

"Two heads are better than one"

View of the play from the Press Seats:

He backe
Wolv

"The man who does the chucking"

The Goal-keeper beaten.

Putting his soul into it.

He backed Preston.

The Guardians of the Cup.

record of five FA Cups, with James Forrest equalling Kinnaird and Wollaston in winning five medals.

The 1890 Final had meanwhile been Marindin's last as a referee, and his last as FA president. He had been opposed to professionalism, but in a less vociferous manner than many peers, and gracefully stepped down when the argument was lost.

There were still echoes of those fundamental disagreements in seasons to come. The end of the 1891–92 season saw a flashpoint after two key changes to the rules. The referee was given complete authority on the pitch (as linesmen replaced umpires), while the penalty kick was introduced.

The latter stemmed from an incident in the previous season's Quarter-final, when Notts County's John Hendry prevented a Stoke City goal by hitting the ball with his fist. There had been no law in place to cover this.

The 1888–89 victory was the only time the Sudell team won it, as they were eliminated by Bolton Wanderers the following season. Meanwhile, neighbours Blackburn Rovers remained the ultimate cup team. They defeated Sheffield Wednesday in the 1890 Final with a record 6–1 win, the second-highest winning margin in the showpiece. William Townley scored the first hat-trick in a Final, and would score again in the 3–1 Final defeat of Notts County the following season. Blackburn had now matched Wanderers'

Opposite: West Brom's Jem Bayliss heads towards goal during the 1887 FA Cup Final. It was an unsuccessful effort, as Aston Villa won 2–0.

Below: The Blackburn Rovers team that won the club's fifth FA Cup in 1891, beating Notts County 3–1 in the Final at Kennington Oval.

Many amateurs felt the very idea of a penalty was an affront to their integrity and refused to implement it. The feeling was they were being pushed out of the game. The truth was that it was leaving them behind. You couldn't have a more fitting representation of that than the fact the Final was leaving the Kennington Oval.

With a crowd of 32,810 for another Birmingham derby between Villa and West Brom in 1892, it was clear the genteel surroundings of a cricket club no longer suited the huge popularity of the fixture. For their part, the Surrey County Cricket Club were concerned that the pitch was getting ruined. This was to be the last FA Cup Final there.

The ground had been crucial to the popularisation of the game, having served as the stage for a fixture that went from hosting 2,000 people to 32,000; for a competition that had gone from including 15 clubs to 163; and for a sport that had evolved from a pastime to a profession. The Oval's last FA Cup Final featured appropriately glorious sunshine, and one last glimpse of the world that had outgrown it. Villa were favourites, as the wealthier club, having finished eight places ahead of West Brom in the league. They had

> ## "I AM OFTEN ASKED: 'DO I NOT REGRET THE PART I HAVE TAKEN IN PROMOTING THE DEVELOPMENT AND POPULARITY OF FOOTBALL?' I UNHESITATINGLY SAY 'NO!'"
>
> - ARTHUR KINNAIRD -

even thrashed that season's title-winners, Sunderland, 4–1 in the Semi-finals.

West Brom would render all that irrelevant, however, by gaining revenge for 1887, with Bassett again brilliant. Their three unanswered goals hit the back of a new innovation – the net – with the last of them scored by Jack Reynolds. Reynolds had attracted the interest of Villa, and was especially good on the day. Albion's furious directors later accused Reynolds of playing for a transfer, in a bad-tempered episode. The Kennington Oval hadn't witnessed anything like it. It had, however, seen so much.

MATCH OFFICIALS

So many different elements make The FA Cup what it is, but an old truth is always worth remembering in the most heated ties: none of it could take place without the figures at the centre of it all – the referee and their assistants. The officials naturally see the Final in the same way the players do. It is a career peak, and the greatest honour in the domestic game. Refereeing The FA Cup Final is seen as such a privilege that officials are usually only allowed to do so once, a rule that has been in place since 1902. Referees are permitted to have previously worked on the fixture as an assistant or fourth official, however.

It was a rule only loosened during the restrictions of the COVID-19 pandemic, the idea being that an official should have the opportunity to enjoy a full Final experience, rather than an occasion without a capacity crowd. That meant that Anthony Taylor and Michael Oliver got to rule on second Finals, in 2020 and 2021 respectively, becoming the first referees to whistle on more than one showpiece since Arthur Kingscott in 1901. Francis Marindin, one of The FA's founding figures, is the official to have refereed more Finals than anyone else, with nine.

The significant period in the late nineteenth century gave The FA Cup a much stronger relationship with referees than arguably any other football competition. That was because its fixtures were often the first to see crucial early rule changes, as well as the rise of referees as a position within the game. The 1880–81 FA Cup season saw the title of "referee" referenced in the laws of the game for the first time. In the gentleman amateur era, the belief was that debate about any play against the rules could be settled between two "umpires" designated by either team, who would then "refer" any disagreement to the timekeeper. By the turn of the century, the referee was the sole authority on the pitch.

That position has, of course, put referees at the centre of the action at times. One of the most famous refereeing moments in FA Cup history was the first-ever red card given in a Final, shown by Peter Willis to Manchester United's Kevin Moran in 1985. A further four referees have had to send players off since, with Anthony Taylor becoming the first to do so twice. He issued red cards to Victor Moses and Mateo Kovacic, following on from Rob Styles to José Reyes, Andre Marriner to Pablo Zabaleta, and Mark Clattenburg to Chris Smalling.

If issuing red cards has become more of a tradition in recent years than referees would like, they do have much more pleasant rituals of their own that only add to the occasion. Among them are banquets and, of course, their own medals.

Officials are assessed on performances before they are awarded a Final, making it a huge achievement and honour for those ultimately selected, something to be celebrated by the refereeing community.

In 2021, Sian Massey-Ellis became the first female official to be involved in The FA Cup Final, as assistant video assistant referee (VAR). She followed a line begun by Liz Fordwick, who was the first woman to officiate an FA Cup tie at all, working as an assistant in the 1981–82 Third Qualifying Round game between Burgess Hill Town and Carshalton Athletic. In 1988–89, Kim George became the first female referee in The FA Cup, taking charge of a Preliminary Round tie.

The first VAR in a Final was Neil Swarbrick in 2018, just the latest development in a role that continues to evolve along with the competition that helped birth it.

Opposite top: Peter Willis enters history as the first referee to issue a red card in an FA Cup Final, Kevin Moran the recipient of the dubious honour in 1985. The Manchester United defender is to Willis' immediate right, in between his protesting teammates – from left to right - Gordon Strachan, Bryan Robson, Mark Hughes, Frank Stapleton and John Gidman.

Opposite middle: Graham Poll and his officials lead out Aston Villa and eventual winners Chelsea, ahead of the last Final at the old Wembley Stadium, in 2000.

Opposite bottom left: Anthony Taylor collects the referee's medal after the 2017 Final between Arsenal and Chelsea. In the 2020 Final, between the same clubs, Taylor became the first official to take charge of two Finals since 1901 due to a loosening of the rules during the Covid pandemic.

Opposite bottom right: The LED screen shows the crucial VAR decision to rule a Ben Chilwell goal offside in the 2021 Final between Chelsea and Leicester City. It was just the latest in a long series of football innovations that The FA Cup has showcased.

CHAPTER FIVE

THE CUP TAKES FORM

1893–1922

WHEN WINNING PLAYERS GET TO LIFT THE FA CUP TODAY, A HUGE PART
OF THE MOMENT IS TOUCHING HISTORY. IT IS 150 YEARS OF GLORY IN
THEIR HANDS. IT IS SOMETHING UNIQUE THAT ONLY THAT PIECE OF
SILVERWARE CAN DELIVER, AND THAT FEELING GOES RIGHT BACK.

By the early 1900s, it was fair to say that The FA Cup was already the most prestigious knock-out competition on the planet. The world-record crowds were testament to this. It was the one everyone wanted to win. The FA soon realised, however, that the trophy itself wasn't as distinctive as it should have been. It certainly wasn't unique. The first "little tin idol" was never recovered after it was stolen, following Aston Villa's victory in 1895. The FA had a new version made, but didn't copyright the design. This allowed several pirate versions to surface.

So, in July 1910, The FA decided to commission a trophy worthy of the cup's gravitas. A budget of 50 guineas (about £6,000 in today's money) was set, with The FA intent that the look of the cup should match its prestige. Britain's finest silversmiths were invited to submit designs, with the work of Bradford's Fattorini & Sons getting the nod out of a huge range of proposals.

The new trophy was described as an "antique votive urn" and weighed 175oz (5kg), standing 19in (48cm) high. The body was decorated with grapes and vine leaves, surrounding one simple inscription: "The Football Association Challenge Cup". This is the trophy we know today, imbued with so much magic. The FA Cup had found its form.

The same was true of the competition as a whole throughout this period. If the 1880s had provoked upheaval, the years straddling the start of the twentieth century would see the game settle into something much closer to what we know today, including some classic cup characteristics.

Professionalism raised standards to new levels, which in turn raised crowds to astonishing numbers. This was the era of six-figure attendances before the world was ready for them, as The FA Cup Final became a mega-event way ahead of its time. The game even received establishment approval, as the Prince of Wales agreed to become the patron of The FA in 1892. All of this made the game increasingly commercial. Industries around football became big business and Sunderland's Alf Common became the first £1,000 player in 1905.

This era also saw the first steps of some of the country's most successful clubs, such as Manchester United, Liverpool and Arsenal, as well as English football's first dynasties. Aston Villa, Sunderland and Newcastle United set the example that managers such as Bill Shankly, Alex Ferguson and Arsène Wenger then followed. The duels between Villa and Sunderland, who repeatedly met in huge FA Cup ties, represented England's first great footballing rivalry.

Just as importantly, the period saw the settling of many of the little traditions and observations that make The FA Cup so beloved. Among them were the tying of the winning club's ribbons to the trophy, and the idea that the Final had a propensity for anti-climax – a huge number from this era were single-goal wins.

The very first Final outside the Kennington Oval featured something never to be repeated as the game took place at Fallowfield Stadium in Manchester in 1893. Holding the showpiece in the city made sense due to the new supremacy of the northern clubs, but Fallowfield was an athletics venue and wasn't suitable or secure enough. The official crowd of 45,000 probably became 65,000 after a stampede to get in. The press complained they couldn't see, and Everton actually protested their 1–0 defeat to Wolverhampton Wanderers due to fans

1892–93
WOLVERHAMPTON WANDERERS   1–0   EVERTON
VENUE: FALLOWFIELD STADIUM
ATTENDANCE: 45,000

Opposite: Fans look on during the 1893 Final between Wolverhampton Wanderers and Everton, at Fallowfield Ground in Manchester. It was the only showpiece held at the venue, due to concerns about crowd management.

Previous pages: The Football Association Challenge Cup trophy, and the image known all around the world today. This model was first introduced in 1911.

spilling onto the pitch, though the real reason was probably fatigue. This was an indication of the new difficulty clubs had of adapting to different competitions. Everton had beaten Preston in the Semi-final after a taxing chase in the league between the two clubs behind champions Sunderland. Everton couldn't cope with Wolves' energy, as Harry Allen won their first FA Cup with an ambitious lob. That it was a team of mostly local players only added to Wolves' celebrations.

Notts County followed with their first and only FA Cup win the next season, also becoming the first lower-league club to claim the trophy. The Second Division had only been set up the previous year, as the growing game required an expanded structure. First Division Bolton Wanderers were beaten 4–1, with Jimmy Logan scoring a hat-trick – only the second time that had happened

in a Final. The game had taken place at Everton's recently constructed Goodison Park after the problems in Manchester the previous year, but The FA were mindful that the showpiece should really take place in the capital.

A medium-term solution was offered by a day out of a different kind. By 1894, the Crystal Palace in south London was one of England's most popular tourist attractions. The dazzling glasshouse had been built for the Great Exhibition of 1851, and was later transported piece by piece from Hyde Park in central London. Its surrounding gardens offered a playing area with a natural bowl, perfect for what The FA required.

The gardens also influenced the nature of the fixture, making it a great day out as well as a great occasion. Thousands of supporters congregated for picnics. The splendour of the glasshouse seemed an appropriate backdrop to the great feats on the pitch. This was particularly true of Villa, who had constructed a great house of their own and were influential in the establishment of twentieth-century footballing standards.

Top left: A mock funeral card made for Everton after the 1893 Final defeat. These were hugely popular at the time and a sign of football's growing culture.

Below: A crowd of more than 48,000 spectators looks on as the 1896 Final between The Wednesday and Wolverhampton Wanderers kicks off. The Crystal Palace is clearly visible in the background.

1893–94
NOTTS COUNTY **4–1** BOLTON WANDERERS
VENUE: **GOODISON PARK**
ATTENDANCE: **37,000**

1894–95
ASTON VILLA **1–0** WEST BROMWICH ALBION
VENUE: **CRYSTAL PALACE**
ATTENDANCE: **42,560**

1895–96
THE WEDNESDAY **2–1** WOLVERHAMPTON WANDERERS
VENUE: **CRYSTAL PALACE**
ATTENDANCE: **48,836**

Villa's 1895 FA Cup Final was their second after 1887, and came in a spell where they won five league titles (1894, 1896, 1897, 1899 and 1900), plus another cup in 1897 to secure England's second-ever double.

Their dominance was sparked by the drive of Frederick Rinder, later known as the "Grand Old Man of Aston Villa". A member of the club since 1881, Rinder had grown frustrated with poor management at the club, who were one of the Football League's founding members and who he felt should have been much more successful. He instigated the famous "Barwick Street meeting" in February of that year, where he lambasted the standards at the club – right down to the players' drinking – and forced the resignation of the board. They were replaced by a five-man committee led by Rinder himself.

He quickly built the best and most admired team in the country, primarily on a formidable half-back line of Jack Reynolds, James Cowan and Jimmy Crabtree. Villa immediately took the league title from Sunderland, who themselves were hailed as "the team of all the talents". This created the first of one of those vintage rivalries that pushed both sides – and the game – to higher standards. Villa were perhaps the first team to show the extent of the benefits that professionalism could bring, as their grandiose stadium was gradually installed with gyms, steam rooms and even an X-ray machine. Sunderland couldn't keep up with them and lost three FA Cup ties to Villa in four years. One of those was the 1895 Semi-final at Ewood Park, which set up another grand rematch, Villa v West Brom, at the first Crystal Palace Final.

This was the third meeting between these two sides in the showpiece, a record not matched until Newcastle United and Arsenal reached the same number in the 1950s. The Crystal Palace crowd didn't have to wait long for the first goal. In fact, it was so quick that many latecomers missed it, as Villa scored within 30 seconds. The goal was credited to Bob Chatt, although there was dispute over whether his shot had deflected off John Dewey. There was no dispute over the result, though, and Villa should have won by more than their single goal. Reynolds had some revenge for 1887.

Villa, by then England's most admired team, did subsequently earn some rancour, though, having been held responsible for "a national disaster". On 11 September 1895, the original FA Cup was stolen. The club had been granted permission to exhibit it in the shop window of shoemaker William Shillock, a friend of Villa's William

Above: An early example of an FA Cup Final programme, for the 1897 showpiece between Aston Villa and Everton played at the Crystal Palace. It features details of the players, officials, venue and a number of contemporary advertisements.

Top: A reward notice posted by Birmingham Police after The FA Cup had been stolen from a shop display following Aston Villa's victory in 1895. It was never recovered, and was seen as a "national disaster".

THE ASSOCIATION CHALLENGE CUP MATCH AT THE CRYSTAL PALACE.

WATCHING THE GAME.

FROM A PHOTOGRAPH BY NEGRETTI AND ZAMBRA, HOLBORN

| G. B. Ramsey (Sec.). | H. Spencer. | T. Wilkes. | T. Welford. | J. T. Lees (Com.). | J. Grierson (Trainer). |
| W. Athersmith. | R. Chat. | J. Devey. | D. Hodgetts. | S. Smith. | |

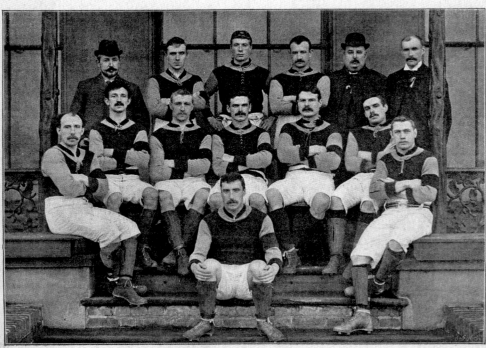

J. Reynolds.   G. Russell.   J. Cowan.

ASTON VILLA, THE WINNING TEAM.

FROM A PHOTOGRAPH BY SYMMONS AND THIELE, CHANCERY LANE, W.C.

McGregor. The next morning, a small hole was discovered in the roof of the shop, which allowed the thieves to lift the trophy out. A £10 reward was offered, but later investigations indicated it was likely melted down by a gang of four in the yards near the shop. Poor Shillcock fretted he would be ruined and despised, which indicated the strength of feeling around the incident.

A company founded by Villa's 1887 FA Cup winner, Howard Vaughton, was commissioned to create a replacement trophy, using replicas that Wolves had given their 1893 winners. It cost £25 – precisely the sum that Villa were fined for losing it. When the club won the cup again, two years later, they stored the trophy in a vault.

Aston Villa's double of 1897 was naturally the zenith of this era, amplified by the fact that Villa won the league by a mammoth 11 points. That was by far the biggest winning margin of the era, all the more remarkable given it was only a 30-game season, and wins were then only worth two points.

It was no coincidence the 1896–97 FA Cup season was similarly seen as one of the greatest of the age, and its Final maybe the finest ever. After symbolically eliminating Preston in a three-game series, Villa faced a burgeoning Everton team in the Final at Crystal Palace. Another record crowd of 62,891 watched a blistering match that ended 3–2 to Villa, and which contained maybe the best 25 minutes in The FA Cup's pre-war history. All of the goals came between the 18th and 44th minutes, with Villa's John Campbell opening the scoring and Crabtree finishing it. The drama was by no means over, though, as Everton's Edgar Chadwick missed a fine chance with just two minutes left that would have brought the scores level.

The FA Cup's silver anniversary season had brought a gold-standard achievement, as Villa also became the only team to win

> ## "THE PREMISES WERE BROKEN INTO BETWEEN THE HOURS NAMED, AND THE CUP, TOGETHER WITH CASH IN DRAWER, STOLEN."
>
> – BIRMINGHAM POLICE POSTER –

Above: The Aston Villa team that won the double of FA Cup and league title in 1897, only the second time the feat had been achieved after Preston North End in 1889. The achievement wouldn't be secured again until Tottenham Hotspur in 1961.

Opposite: An image of the 1895 FA Cup Final between Aston Villa and West Bromwich Albion, and a photo of the victorious Villa team. They won 1–0 thanks to a goal scored by Robert 'Bob' Chatt.

S.T.DADD.

THE ILLUSTRATED LONDON NEWS, APRIL 27, 1901.— 619

THE FOOTBALL ASSOCIATION CUP FINAL TIE AT THE CRYSTAL PALACE, APRIL 20.

PHOTOGRAPHS BY RUSSELL.

TOTTENHAM HOTSPUR v. SHEFFIELD UNITED: THE KICK OFF.

1897–98
NOTTINGHAM FOREST **3–1** DERBY COUNTY
VENUE: **CRYSTAL PALACE**
ATTENDANCE: **62,017**

1898–99
SHEFFIELD UNITED **4–1** DERBY COUNTY
VENUE: **CRYSTAL PALACE**
ATTENDANCE: **73,833**

1899–1900
BURY **4–0** SOUTHAMPTON
VENUE: **CRYSTAL PALACE**
ATTENDANCE: **68,945**

1900–01
TOTTENHAM HOTSPUR **2–2** SHEFFIELD UNITED
VENUE: **CRYSTAL PALACE**
ATTENDANCE: **110,820**

1900–01 (REPLAY)
TOTTENHAM HOTSPUR **3–1** SHEFFIELD UNITED
VENUE: **BURDEN PARK**
ATTENDANCE: **20,470**

the league and FA Cup on the same day – Derby County lost 1–0 at Bury that afternoon, gifting Villa the title.

The previous season, Sheffield Wednesday – then just known as 'The Wednesday' – had become the first club to lift the replica FA Cup, beating Wolves 2–1 in 1896. It was near the start of a period, sparked by Wolves themselves at Fallowfield in 1892, when there were a series of maiden winners. Their geographical spread exemplified the game's explosion. Nottingham Forest won their first cup in 1898, Sheffield United in 1899, Bury in 1900, Tottenham Hotspur in 1901, Manchester City in 1904 and Everton in 1906.

All of these wins of course have their own special stories and moments. When Wednesday won in 1896, Wolves' keeper Billy Tennant didn't even realise his team lost – Fred Spiksley's second goal in Wednesday's 2–1 win was so fierce that the ball rebounded out of the net. At the final whistle, Tennant asked Wednesday captain Jack Earp when the replay was. Earp replied: "There's no replay, old man! We won by two goals to one, as you'll see when we take the medals!"

"You can't have," Tennant replied, "for only one shot passed me!"

When Forest had their winning photo taken in 1898, they had to use Derby County's shirts, as their red apparently looked too dark on camera. Derby went on to lose in successive Finals, as not even their free-scoring Steve Bloomer could beat the 22-stone (140kg), 6ft 2in (188cm) figure of William "Fatty" Foulkes in goal for Sheffield United. All manner of stories existed about Foulkes, from snapping crossbars to dangling opposition players by their ankles. He pulled a thigh muscle in the 1898–99 Third Round win over Forest and had to be carried off by six men, although only after his heroics in goal kept United in the game. Foulkes was probably the best goalkeeper of the time, instrumental in the club's 1897–98 title and the two cups of 1899 and 1902.

Derby must have felt they were cursed. The much-loved Bloomer would never win The FA Cup and was injured for their 1903 Final. That was possibly for the best since Bury beat them 6–0, a score that remains a joint-record loss. And it made it 10 goals scored, none conceded, in two Finals for Bury, who had also beaten Southampton 4–0 in 1900.

Southampton had been the first southern club to reach the showpiece since Old Etonians in 1883, signifying a shift away from the north and pointing to one of many reasons why Tottenham's 1901 victory was arguably the most momentous of all these firsts.

That 1901 Final featured the first ever six-figure crowd for a football match anywhere, with a reported 110,820 people turning up, 40,000 of them from Sheffield. That world record stood until the 1913 Final, although the true number was again higher – many supporters had scaled trees to watch. It's remarkable to think that the last time a southern club – Old Etonians – had won the cup, 19 years earlier in 1882, a crowd just a fraction of that size showed up.

The FA Cup was by now attracting entries from more than 200 clubs per season and the 1901 Final was the first attended by a former prime minister, Lord Rosebury. He was joined by the future prime minister, Arthur Balfour, as well as Cecil Rhodes.

The old arguments against professionalism in London had evaporated. The Southern League had been formed in 1894, with Spurs winning it in 1900. Since that league hadn't yet been incorporated into the Football League, it meant Spurs were not just the first southern club

Above: The FA Cup, at that point the second version of the original "little tin idol" model, is presented to Bury after their 4–0 win over Southampton in 1900.

Opposite top: An illustration of John Mcpherson scoring Nottingham Forest's third goal in the 3–1 win over Derby County in the 1898 Final.

Opposite bottom: The moment of kick-off for the 1901 Final at Crystal Palace between Tottenham Hotspur and Sheffield United, for which a world-record crowd of a reported 110,820 turned up.

"THERE'S NO REPLAY, OLD MAN! WE WON BY TWO GOALS TO ONE, AS YOU'LL SEE WHEN WE TAKE THE MEDALS!"

- JACK EARP -

1901–02
SHEFFIELD UNITED **1–1** SOUTHAMPTON
VENUE: **CRYSTAL PALACE**
ATTENDANCE: 76,914

1901–02 (REPLAY)
SHEFFIELD UNITED **2–1** SOUTHAMPTON
VENUE: **CRYSTAL PALACE**
ATTENDANCE: 33,068

1902–1903
BURY **6–0** DERBY COUNTY
VENUE: **CRYSTAL PALACE**
ATTENDANCE: 63,102

1903–04
MANCHESTER CITY **1–0** BOLTON WANDERERS
VENUE: **CRYSTAL PALACE**
ATTENDANCE: 61,374

to win the cup since 1882 but the only non-league side to win it. They would do so again 20 years later, beating Wolves.

The 1901 victory came after a replay, and was perhaps the first-ever example of the media proving a refereeing error. It was the first true twentieth-century Final in that sense, since it was also the first to be filmed.

Amid raucous scenes before kick-off, many of the supporters in the trees around Crystal Palace almost fell out as Tottenham's Sandy Brown beat Foulkes to equalise after Alfred Priest's opener. It meant Brown joined Archie Hunter as the only player to score in every round of the cup, before adding another on 51 minutes, as well as the clinching goal in the replay.

The replay would not have been necessary were it not for football's first high-profile refereeing controversy. Just a minute after Brown's second goal, Spurs goalkeeper George Clawley fumbled a drive from Bert Lipsham. Walter Bennett attempted to force the ball over the line, but Clawley scrambled it wide. The linesman signalled a corner but the referee, Arthur Kingscott, overruled him. When Clawley went to take a goal kick, it became apparent a goal had been given. What followed was maybe the first instance of mass supporter irony. Every shot thereafter was met with shouts of "goal!".

The film of the games shown at Spurs' celebratory banquet showed their suspicions were right. The goal shouldn't have stood. It was just as well it didn't matter, as Spurs won the replay 3–1. That match inexplicably took place at Bolton's Burnden Park, with railway work reducing the crowd to just 20,470.

But in London, far bigger numbers celebrated Spurs' win for days. At the same banquet, the wife of one of the directors tied ribbons to the trophy in club colours, creating a distinguished tradition.

The ribbons were in sky blue in 1904, as the maverick Billy

Opposite top: The legendary goalkeeper William 'Fatty' Foulkes watches the ball go just wide of the Sheffield United goal in the 1901 FA Cup Final against Tottenham Hotspur.

Opposite bottom: The Sheffield United team that beat Southampton in the 1902 Final, with the famous Foulkes third from the left in the back row.

Below: The atmosphere of the cup could be felt all around London, as football fans gather around St Paul's Cathedral before making their way to the 1904 Final, between Manchester City and Bolton Wanderers.

1904–05
ASTON VILLA 2–0 NEWCASTLE UNITED
VENUE: **CRYSTAL PALACE**
ATTENDANCE: **101,117**

Meredith led Manchester City to victory over Bolton in the first all-Lancashire Final. Sandy Turnbull scored the only goal.

The third great dynasty of the age also began, as Newcastle United succeeded Aston Villa as England's dominant team. Their legacy can be seen in Herbert Chapman's comments when he was first intrigued by the Arsenal job in London – he felt he could "build a Newcastle United there". With stars like Bill Appleyard and Colin Veitch, in a classic blend of British and Irish players, Newcastle filled stadiums whenever they played, winning three league titles in five years (1905, 1907 and 1909) and reaching five FA Cup Finals. The problem was, the little tin idol just kept eluding them.

All sorts of explanations were offered for this, from whether their style of football suited the cup, to whether the thick Crystal Palace turf suited their football, to whether they had a stadium "hoodoo" – all familiar football chat today.

Villa were the first club to stop Newcastle in a Final, in 1905, which also denied the Magpies the double. Villa's lightning football was just too much on the day, going ahead after just three minutes through Harry Hampton, who later clinched the 2–0 win. Newcastle were criticised for being "too fancy". They received

Above left: Sandy Turnbull, who scored the only goal of the 1904 Final, to give Manchester City the cup against Bolton Wanderers.

Above right: Harry Hampton, the Aston Villa forward who scored both goals in Aston Villa's 2–0 win over Newcastle United in the 1905 Final.

Top: Crystal Palace is once again packed, with the penalty area much the same, in Aston Villa's 2–0 win over Newcastle United in the 1905 Final.

Opposite: A spread of the events at the 1905 Final, between Aston Villa and Newcastle United, in *The Illustrated Sporting and Dramatic News* edition of 22 April 1905.

THE F.A. CUP FINAL.—ASTON VILLA WIN FOR THE FOURTH TIME.

Drawn by Ralph Cleaver.

THE NEWCASTLE UNITED GOALKEEPER IS KEPT BUSY

THE VILLAN'S HALVES CONSTANTLY SLIP IN AND TAKE THE BALL

PARTISANS OF NEWCASTLE UNITED

ASTON VILLA'S SECOND GOAL

PARTISANS OF ASTON VILLA

PLAY UP VILLANS

"VAULTING AMBITION"

BRAWN ENJOYING HIMSELF

This game, which was played before 100,000 people at the Crystal Palace, on Saturday last, resulted in Aston Villa beating Newcastle United by 2 goals to nil, the first goal coming within three minutes of the start.

2–1 by The Wednesday in another surprise result, but the main talking point was how Newcastle had been cleared from their path.

The notion of a cup upset was another of The FA Cup's developing mythologies, and the shock of the 1906–07 First Round further shaped mindsets. Crystal Palace, at that point only recently reformed and near the foot of the Southern League, went to Newcastle and won 1–0. It was seen as a miracle, but was to mark the start of a trend.

The cup was becoming that bit harder to win; now more of a marathon than a sprint, since the proliferation of entrants saw the competition expanded by another round. It all just seemed out of reach for Newcastle. In 1908, they were the vanquished in another historic defeat, as Wolves followed Notts County in winning the cup from the Second Division. This was one of those vintage upsets, as Wolves picked off a frustrated Newcastle on the break. It was a 3–1 win that could have been 2–7. One report described

some physical treatment, as Newcastle goalkeeper Jimmy Lawrence complained of double vision after a charge from Hampton, who was a battering ram of a forward. The match was seen as one for the ages, as Villa's great champions refused to cede ground.

The following year's Final was the opposite in a few senses, bar Newcastle again losing. It was a poor Final, though Everton won their first major trophy through Alex Young's goal. Everton were back the next year, having beaten league winners Liverpool in the first Merseyside derby Semi-final. They were ultimately defeated

Opposite top: Charlie Roberts leads out the Manchester United team for the 1909 FA Cup Final against Bristol City.

Opposite bottom: Sandy Turnbull scores the only goal of Manchester United's first FA Cup Final, in 1909, having scored the only goal of City's in 1904. Billy Meredith is the player in white on the furthest left.

Below: The Wolverhampton Wanderers team that beat Newcastle United 3–1 in the 1908 FA Cup Final. It was the third of five Finals Newcastle reached in seven years, losing four.

it as: "Hare and Tortoise: a new version of an old proverb – how pretty football failed to win the cup."

The arguments about Newcastle and the cup were never fiercer. It was said the elaborate nature of their passing wasn't decisive enough for sudden-death football. That, of course, overlooks how many knock-out games they'd won in reaching three Finals, although their football was more direct the following season. It was mostly just one of those things, and Newcastle's Alex Gardner was philosophical after this latest defeat: "Never mind. We shall come again, and our turn will surely arrive some day."

It arrived as soon as 1910, although not at Crystal Palace. Newcastle just about survived another scare there in coming from behind to draw 1–1 with Second Division Barnsley. At the Goodison Park replay, though, The FA Cup Final at last saw the true Newcastle. They expressed themselves with beautifully expansive football, Albert Shepherd scoring both goals in a commanding 2–0 win. Ironically, they'd actually been criticised that season for uncompromising play, even getting labelled "Dirty Newcastle".

Their "hoodoo" had nevertheless been overcome. It was almost fitting that Newcastle were the last recipients of the "little tin idol", since they were at that point the club to have been to the most Finals without lifting it. The trophy was presented to Lord Kinnaird to celebrate 21 years as FA president in 1911. Newcastle even lost the very next showpiece for good measure, as a resilient

"NEVER MIND. WE SHALL COME AGAIN, AND OUR TURN WILL SURELY ARRIVE SOME DAY."

- ALEX GARDNER -

Bradford City became the first winners of the trophy that had been crafted in their town. The very shape of the silverware seemed to better fit the moment of glory.

That 1911 climax also went to a replay, this time at Old Trafford after Newcastle had again failed to win at Crystal Palace. This grand new stadium had been completed the year before, a literal monument to the rapid rise of Manchester United. One of The FA Cup's most successful ever clubs had an inauspicious start in the competition, reaching the last 16 in their first appearance in 1896–97, as Newton Heath. It was the investment of businessman John Henry Davies that really transformed the club – and their name – as they began to sign a series of stars, including Meredith

Above: Crystal Palace as it stood for the 1911 FA Cup Final, when Bradford City beat Newcastle United. The famous glass edifice can be partially seen on the right.

1909–10
NEWCASTLE UNITED 1–1 BARNSLEY
VENUE: **CRYSTAL PALACE**
ATTENDANCE: **77,747**

1909–10 (REPLAY)
NEWCASTLE UNITED 2–0 BARNSLEY
VENUE: **GOODISON PARK**
ATTENDANCE: **69,000**

1910–11
BRADFORD CITY 0–0 NEWCASTLE UNITED
VENUE: **CRYSTAL PALACE**
ATTENDANCE: **69,068**

1910–11 (REPLAY)
BRADFORD CITY 1–0 NEWCASTLE UNITED
VENUE: **OLD TRAFFORD**
ATTENDANCE: **58,000**

1911–12
BARNSLEY 0–0 WEST BROMWICH ALBION
VENUE: **CRYSTAL PALACE**
ATTENDANCE: **54,556**

1911–12 (REPLAY)
BARNSLEY 1–0 WEST BROMWICH ALBION
AET
VENUE: **BRAMALL LANE**
ATTENDANCE: **38,555**

and Turnbull from City. That brought a league win in 1908 and a first FA Cup against Bristol City in 1909. With both sides in neutral kits due to the clash of reds, Turnbull scored the only goal. It was one of many turgid one-nils during this era.

"Battling Barnsley" fought their way back from the 1910 defeat to beat West Brom by that scoreline in 1912, although only after another Final replay. This was the third replay in a row, leading to complaints that the grand climax didn't finish on the day despite the extra expense for supporters. Rule 20, which covered replays, was consequently altered so that Finals would go to extra time in the event of a draw.

The 1914 Final was another drab 1–0, as Burnley beat Liverpool, but this was one where the action was very much secondary to the sense of occasion. Tommy Boyle became the first winning captain to receive the trophy from a reigning monarch, as King George V had decided to attend. It was quite a send-off for the last-ever Final at

Top right: Newcastle United finally bring home The FA Cup in 1910, after their fourth Final, having beaten Barnsley.

Below: The victorious Bradford City line up in 1911 to become the first team to lift the new FA Cup model, the first of the current version, which had been created in the city by a local silversmith.

1912–13
ASTON VILLA 1–0 SUNDERLAND
VENUE: CRYSTAL PALACE
ATTENDANCE: 121,919

1913–14
BURNLEY 1–0 LIVERPOOL
VENUE: CRYSTAL PALACE
ATTENDANCE: 72,778

1914–15
SHEFFIELD UNITED 3–0 CHELSEA
VENUE: OLD TRAFFORD
ATTENDANCE: 49,557

Crystal Palace as real-world events were about to intervene. On that happier day, the king's entry had been marked by a rendition of the national anthem by the Irish Guards and Liverpool regiment. It was the start of another tradition and another triumph for football.

The Times' match report summed up the change: "The fact that the king himself has attended a cup-tie… will, let us hope, put an end to the old, snobbish notion that true-blue sportsmen ought to ignore games played by those who cannot afford to play without being paid for their services." The king's presence was a step up from mere prime ministers, and there was also a significant step up in entries to The FA Cup. A record 476 clubs entered in 1914. Everyone was watching.

This never felt truer than for one of those landmark Finals, in 1913. Aston Villa met Sunderland in another game for the ages. This was not just a meeting of two great clubs, one aiming for a record fifth FA Cup victory and the other making their Final debut, it was the first ever meeting in the Final between the top two teams in the league. Both clubs were going for the double. Both had so many stars, from Clem Stephenson with Villa to Charlie Buchan with Sunderland. It was a greatly anticipated Final, and attracted another world-record crowd, this time 120,081.

They weren't disappointed. This was another 1–0 game but a very different 1–0 to the others, the low score belying the high intensity. The game ebbed and flowed, Sunderland missing a series of chances while Villa's Charlie Wallace missed the first-ever penalty in a Final.

Just as the game was ticking towards extra time, there was some extrasensory inspiration. Stephenson claimed that he had dreamed Tommy Barber would score the winning goal with a header, and that he had informed Buchan of this. On 78 minutes, Wallace sought to make up for his penalty miss with a fine cross… and a dream came true. There was Barber to head home.

Above: The official programme for the 1913 FA Cup Final between Aston Villa and Sunderland.

Opposite top: The "Khaki Cup Final" of 1915, so called because of the number of serviceman who attended as World War I continued. It was held at Old Trafford due to Crystal Palace being used as a war depot.

Opposite botttom: Chelsea captain Jack Harrow, left, shakes hands with his Sheffield United counterpart, George Utley, ahead of the 1915 Final. The Blades won 3–0 for their second cup.

Below: King George V becomes the first reigning monarch to attend an FA Cup Final, in 1914 for Burnley's 1–0 win over Liverpool.

"THE FACT THAT THE KING HIMSELF HAS ATTENDED A CUP-TIE… WILL, LET US HOPE, PUT AN END TO THE OLD, SNOBBISH NOTION THAT TRUE-BLUE SPORTSMEN OUGHT TO IGNORE GAMES PLAYED BY THOSE WHO CANNOT AFFORD TO PLAY WITHOUT BEING PAID FOR THEIR SERVICES."

- THE TIMES -

"YOU HAVE PLAYED WITH ONE ANOTHER AND AGAINST ONE ANOTHER FOR
THE CUP. IT IS NOW THE DUTY OF EVERYONE TO JOIN WITH EACH OTHER
AND PLAY A STERNER GAME FOR ENGLAND."

- EARL OF DERBY -

Villa had won a record-equalling fifth FA Cup. Sunderland would at least win the league title the following Wednesday – by drawing with Villa. Rinder's influence had raised standards so much that Villa were competitive even when they were not at their best. They went on to win The FA Cup again in 1920, beating Huddersfield Town to make it a record sixth win. Such an immense feat was secured in an innocuous manner, the ball bouncing off Billy Kirton's neck and in.

Huddersfield's own presence in the Final was something of a miracle. They'd been threatened with dissolution for lack of funds just months earlier, only for the townspeople to rally to the club's aid. That was to spark a remarkable rise, with Herbert Chapman leading them to victory – another 1–0 against Preston in 1922.

All of that was to come, though. Before it, all was to be disrupted. Concerns about football were put in their place as World War I began. Amid a lot of ugly debate about sport

continuing, the War Office initially advised The FA that matches were good for morale and recruitment. That led to the 1914–15 competition going ahead, albeit with altered rules about dates so war production was not affected. There was still some magic, as Swansea City knocked out Blackburn Rovers in the First Round, the last time a non-league club eliminated the reigning league champions. The overarching feel of the year was better reflected at the Final at Old Trafford, though. With Crystal Palace being used as a war depot, the sunny days of picnics seemed far away. This Final was played in front of just 49,557, most of the crowd staying silent on a wet afternoon. Known as the Khaki Cup Final due to the large number of servicemen in the crowd, it saw Sheffield United beat Chelsea 3–0, but the game didn't linger as long in the memory as the Earl of Derby's speech: "You have played with one another and against one another for the cup. It is now the duty of everyone to join with each other and play a sterner game for England."

1919–20
ASTON VILLA   1–0   HUDDERSFIELD TOWN
AET
VENUE: **STAMFORD BRIDGE**
ATTENDANCE: 50,018

1920–21
TOTTENHAM HOTSPUR   1–0   WOLVERHAMPTON WANDERERS
VENUE: **STAMFORD BRIDGE**
ATTENDANCE: 72,805

1921–22
HUDDERSFIELD TOWN   1–0   PRESTON NORTH END
VENUE: **STAMFORD BRIDGE**
ATTENDANCE: 53,000

Many footballers ended up losing their lives in the war, including cup heroes such as Hampton, Turnbull and most of the 1911 Bradford City team. Football was inevitably postponed, and the 1915 Final was the last for five years.

The yearning for the cup was never greater, though, not least after the horrors of war. There was even an attempt to get the FA Cup rebooted sooner, featuring only the top two divisions, the Southern League and four clubs selected by the council. The governing body instead rightly claimed the competition was about more than the elite. It was about openness. That was the essence of The FA Cup. That was what had become so apparent during this period.

By the time the cup restarted on January 10, 1920, crowds were huge again. Ticket prices even had to be raised for the Final to keep numbers down, because Stamford Bridge couldn't host enough spectators. The cup had form. It now just needed a true home.

Opposite: Prince Henry meets the Aston Villa team before the 1920 Final at Stamford Bridge, the cup specialists eventually beating Huddersfield Town 1–0.

Left: Bert Bliss attempts a shot on goal for Tottenham Hotspur during a memorably muddy 1921 FA Cup Final at Stamford Bridge.

Below: King George V presents the cup to Tottenham Hotspur captain Arthur Grimsdell after his team beat Wolverhampton Wanderers 1–0 to win The FA Cup Final at Stamford Bridge.

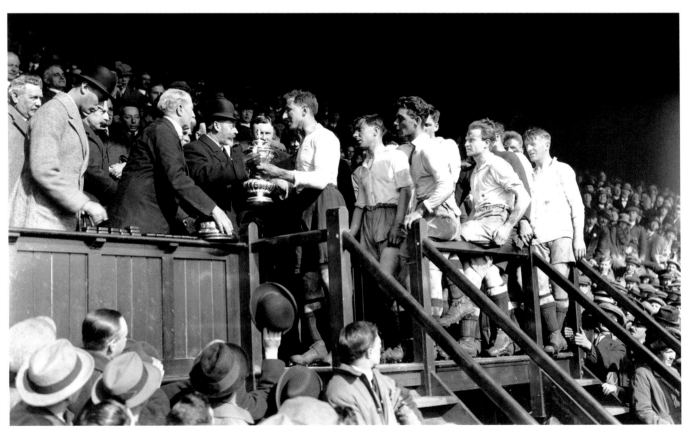

THE EARLY ROUNDS

As the 2021 FA Cup Final kicked off, Leicester City's Jamie Vardy could already celebrate a personal milestone. The striker became the first player to feature in 13 of The FA Cup's 14 stages, having only ever missed out on the very earliest round, the extra-preliminary. That breadth of FA Cup experience has afforded him a unique appreciation of the flow and feel of the whole competition.

If the Final is all about prestige and immortality, and the Third Round about the whole pyramid coming together, the early rounds embody the lifeblood of football at the grassroots level. Over 700 clubs from Level 10 upwards now enter The FA Cup, with the vast majority going through those early stages. Many of the fixtures are regionalised to save costs, reflecting the modest resources of the clubs involved. You might even say those parts of the competition are the non-league teams' equivalent of the Final. All are dreaming of the same thing as their Football League counterparts further up the pyramid, just on a different scale: a cup run that transforms the mood around a club – and potentially their finances.

More than anything, The FA Cup offers a chance at glory, the excitement around the luck of the draw only adding to that sense of opportunity. The very prospect of being in the same competition as the biggest names in the game, with just a few rounds separating them, electrifies clubs. The sheer number of teams involved in the early rounds also creates a glorious chaos, which has led to some of The FA Cup's most outlandish records.

In 1973–74, Bideford AFC went on the longest run in the competition's history, playing a total of 13 games. They entered in the First Qualifying Round (beating Penzance) before requiring two games to eliminate Newquay, five games to defeat Falmouth, four to knock out Trowbridge and then ultimately losing to Bristol Rovers in the First Round proper – just two rounds away from meeting the champions and eventual winners, Liverpool.

The 2005–06 Preliminary Round then saw a remarkable 40 penalty kicks in a shoot-out between Tunbridge Wells and Littlehampton Town, the former ultimately winning 16–15.

The earlier rounds also allow for stories that are only really possible at that stage. Amateur side Corinthian Casuals reached the First Round in 1983–84, with Team Bath following in 2002–03, capping a campaign where they became the first university side to compete in The FA Cup since Oxford University in 1880. The 1980–81 campaign saw semi-pro club Wembley FC reach that stage for the only time in their history, the closest they've yet come to the famous stadium nearby. Wembley ultimately lost 3–0 to Enfield, who had been responsible for another notable elimination in 1977–78, beating a Wimbledon side that three years earlier had knocked out Burnley as part of their incredible rise.

Clubs like Bedford Town, Telford United, Emley and a series of others have enjoyed similar runs over the years, but the early rounds have also seen big clubs get brought down to earth. Blackpool, Bolton Wanderers, Burnley, Cardiff City, Coventry City, Notts County, Preston North End, Sunderland and Wolves are all among former FA Cup winners who have been eliminated in the First Round proper. A reminder that status really can mean little in this most open of competitions.

"FA CUP...COMPLETED IT MATE!"

- JAMIE VARDY -

Opposite top: Team Bath, in orange and blue, become the first student team to contest The FA Cup First Round since Oxford University in 1880. They were beaten 4–2 by Mansfield Town in 2002, after a hugely creditable display.

Opposite bottom: Jamie Vardy, on the right of Fleetwood Town teammate Jamie McGuire, has played in more rounds of The FA Cup than any other player in history. This picture was taken after a 2–0 win over Yeovil Town in a 2011–12 Second Round replay at Huish Park.

CHAPTER SIX

THE CUP FINDS ITS HOME

1923–1939

IT WAS THE IMAGE THAT STOPPED PEOPLE IN THEIR TRACKS AND INSPIRED SO
MANY CUP RUNS. WHEN SUPPORTERS GOT OFF THE TRAIN AT WEMBLEY PARK
FOR THAT FIRST GLIMPSE BACK ON 28 APRIL 1923, THEY WERE AWE-STRUCK.
SOME PLAYERS COULDN'T HELP LOOKING UP DURING FA CUP FINAL MATCHES.

What was that image? The resplendent twin towers, now replaced by the arch, all monuments to Wembley's distinguished place in the game. The walk up Wembley Way from station to stadium is one of many traditions that have become unique to time and place, making the allure of The FA Cup inseparable from the ground that has become its home.

The dream of lifting the trophy is also the dream of Wembley. That is made clear by one of those other traditions that has grown with the ground – the songs that accompany so many cup runs: "Whatever will be will be, we're going to Wembley."

The stadium makes the day and the day has made the stadium. The world's oldest football competition is bound to the world's most famous football ground. This was Arsène Wenger's idea of football "perfection". That feeling has inspired the same ambitions in so many young footballers across so many generations.

Wembley's first few years didn't just see The FA Cup settle into a home, but also set a path there. It was in this period that the Third Round proper became the Third Round as we know it now, the competition by that point becoming so large that in 1925–26 this became the stage at which the top clubs entered. These seasons would similarly conjure perhaps the greatest Third Round upset of all, ingraining the concept in the public consciousness. Walsall, then languishing in the lower reaches of the regional Division Three, knocked out the dominant team of the era, the mighty Arsenal, in 1932–33.

It's in keeping with the cup's inherent unpredictability that the move to Wembley was itself almost happenstance. Stamford Bridge was only ever a temporary option and in 1921 The FA started discussions about building a new stadium at Crystal Palace. This was at the same time that plans were made to host the British Empire Exhibition in Wembley, then an expanse of green space in the London suburbs. The idea behind the exhibition was to forge better relationships with the dominions and colonies Britain then presided over and it was this that inspired the famous twin towers. They were designed by Sir Robert McAlpine to take in styles from around the empire and were supposed to be the centrepiece of a

new stadium, which was then to be torn down. It was put to The FA that this site might make "a great national sports ground" and, on 8 May 1921, the association's ground committee paid a visit. It so impressed them that Charles Clegg, the president of The FA, signed a 21-year agreement to stage fixtures here. This really got things moving. Although the response to the exhibition had been indifferent due to how remote Wembley seemed, the idea of a national football stadium was exciting. Money poured in.

On 10 January 1922, the Duke of York – George VI from 1936 – cut the first piece of turf. A mere 300 working days later, at a total cost of £750,000 (approximately £46 million today), the stadium was completed. The main ground stood 890ft (271m) long, 650ft (198m) wide and 76ft (23m) high, with towers rising a further 50ft (15m) to elevate the stadium as the most elegant of visions.

The final touches were made a mere four days before the first FA Cup Final held at Wembley, on 28 April 1923, between Bolton Wanderers and West Ham United. The only sadness was that Lord Kinnaird had passed away in January of that year – this stadium was part of his legacy.

It's impossible not to wonder what he would have made of a day that became known as the "White Horse Final". It's remarkable to

1922-23
BOLTON WANDERERS **2-0** WEST HAM UNITED
VENUE: **WEMBLEY STADIUM**
ATTENDANCE: **126,047**

Opposite: An aerial view of Wembley Stadium, London, during the 1923 FA Cup Final. An estimated 200,000 people attended, resulting in the crowd overflowing onto the pitch.

Previous pages: King George V overlooks the first FA Cup Final to be held at Wembley, in 1923. Bolton Wanderers beat West Ham United 2–0 in front of an enormous crowd in what came to be known as the "White Horse Final".

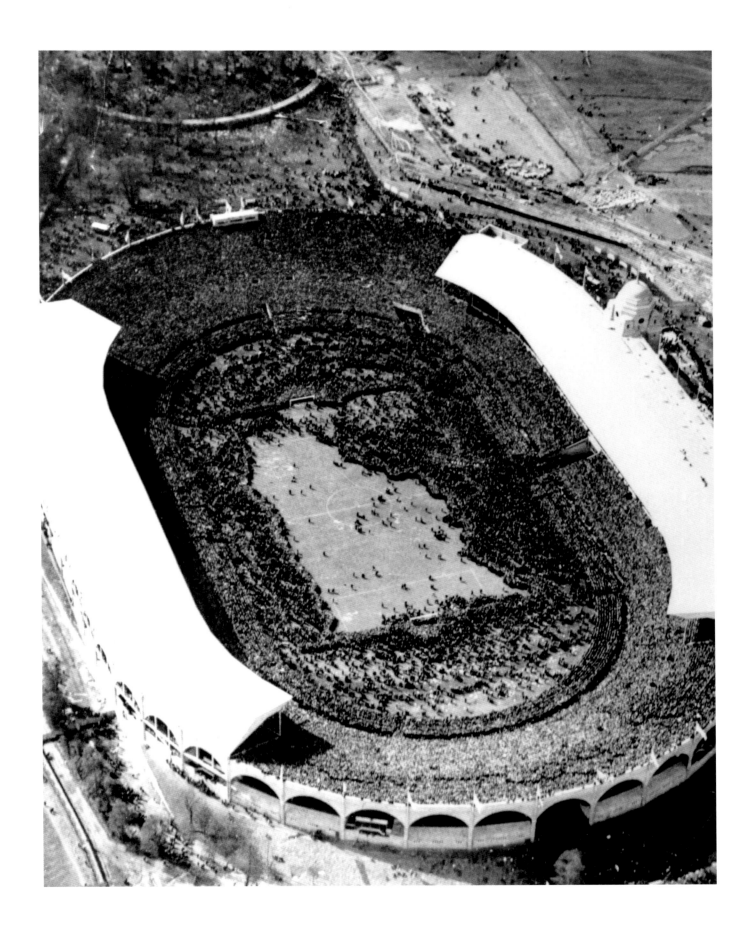

think the first of the old Wembley's 72 Finals went down in history for something other than its opening and the awe that was felt at first seeing those towers. Other images of the day became far more striking. The photo of PC George Scorey and his horse Billy – who was actually a grey – amid an ocean of spectators is one of the most famous in English football. The sheer mass of people remains astonishing. Those images have all become part of FA Cup folklore – there was the popularity, there was the spirit. There was also the possibility that it could have been very different. It was only the good mood of the crowd that prevented disaster, and that was in no small part down to the assured control of Scorey.

The main problem was that the Wembley authorities had been ill-prepared. The stadium could hold 127,000 and there was a complacency that would be more than enough, even though a London club, West Ham, were making their debut in the Final. Ticketed admission had not even been considered. That was a key mistake, as it just encouraged somewhere between 250,000 and 300,000 spectators to turn up on the day, although the true figure will never be known.

Whatever the truth, it's generally accepted that Wembley's first-ever game saw what was probably the largest-ever crowd at any football match, anywhere. The official attendance is recorded as 126,047. It's likely that figure was only accurate at around 1pm, two hours before kick-off, when the seats and stands were filled. The gates were closed at 1.45pm but they were soon broken down as the multitudes tried to get in. That inevitably drove people inside towards the pristine green pitch. A memorable account came from John Squires in *The Observer*, as he described the scene at 2.30pm: "There is no field now: nothing but people in the bowl and the far people above them."

One of those was soon to be King George V, who arrived at 2.45pm and was given a panicked warning by Frederick Wall, The FA secretary: "I fear, sir, that the match may not be played."

It is illustrative of the mood that, even amid such chaos, the people stood to sing the national anthem when the king entered. That perhaps made Scorey's task more manageable. Assured of himself atop the 13-year-old Billy, he began to ask people, "Don't you want to see the game?" Scorey started to request that supporters "join hands and heave" back. Billy meanwhile nudged people with his nose, so the green pitch began to present itself again. It was expertly judged crowd management, aided by the appearance of the players, who helped. Scorey later gave credit to Billy, who came up as white in the news images that enraptured the world. "I felt like giving it up as hopeless. Billy knew what to do."

Opposite top left: Programme for the first Final to be held at Wembley Stadium in 1923.

Opposite top right: Crowds pack the turnstiles before the 1923 FA Cup Final at the newly opened Wembley Stadium.

Opposite bottom: The famous Billy, with PC George Scorey atop, starts to succeed in clearing the Wembley pitch.

Right: The front page of the *Sunday Pictorial* displays images of the chaotic and eventful game at Wembley the previous day.

"I FELT LIKE GIVING IT UP AS HOPELESS. BILLY KNEW WHAT TO DO."

- PC GEORGE SCOREY -

By 3.45pm, only 45 minutes late, enough of the pitch was visible for English football's biggest match to begin. It remained quite a scene. "It was an unforgettable sight, with a solid wall of spectators around the touchlines," Bolton's Ted Vizard later said about the teams' entrance. "It felt as though we were going to play in a human box."

It also influenced the occasion, often directly. As Bolton's prolific David Jack scored Wembley's first-ever goal after just two minutes, West Ham's Jack Tresadern was trying to extricate himself from the crowd after the momentum of his defensive run took him into it.

The crowd otherwise frequently broke onto the pitch, causing constant stoppages. The congestion even caused the players to stay on the pitch at half-time, with West Ham captain George Kay suggesting to referee David Asson that the game should be abandoned. Bolton's Joe Smith was having none of it, saying, "We'll play until dark to finish if necessary."

The truth was that Bolton were always likely to win their first

FA Cup. West Ham were at that point a Second Division side, although they enjoyed some consolation by gaining promotion that same season. Bolton ensured they would become Wembley's first FA Cup winners by the 52nd minute, with another illustration of what the game would be remembered for. Jack Smith's goal rebounded out of the net, as it had hit one of the supporters wedged up behind.

Such quirks have made the game a happy memory but a serious inquest and a government committee on crowd management followed. This saw the introduction of proper match policing, crush barriers, channelled approaches and licences for stadiums. Every cup Final since has been fully ticketed. The 1922–23 season was as influential as it was momentous.

It also saw the competition return to its roots, just as it had found a new home. This was the season when the amateurs of Corinthians finally graced the competition, playing their home games at the storied locale of Crystal Palace. The ground witnessed their replay with Brighton and Hove Albion and a second successive 1–1 draw, before the Third Division South side narrowly knocked them out.

Corinthians didn't just go one better the following season, they offered a cup run for the ages. The amateurs became one of just ten non-league clubs since 1900 to knock out top-tier opposition, as Blackburn Rovers were beaten 1–0. This was no backs-against-the-wall display either. Corinthians took Blackburn aback with their famously adventurous play, which saw Graham Doggart score the only goal.

The amateurs were eventually beaten 5–0 by West Brom in the next round, but they'd made their mark and almost forced Newcastle to a replay three years later, in 1926–27. There were two other records that season. Billy Meredith, now back at Manchester City, became the oldest player to appear in a Semi-final at the age of 49 years and eight months. His side's defeat to Newcastle then meant that the Magpies' Billy Hampson would become the oldest player to appear in a Final, at 41 years and eight months.

Newcastle again faced Aston Villa in the showpiece, Wembley seeing its first meeting of the cup's great names in what turned out to be a superb Final. After a back-and-forth that surprisingly produced no goals for 83 minutes, Villa were undone by two strikes in quick succession. Neil Harris scored in the 83rd minute before Stan Seymour sealed it in the 85th. Villa had actually thrashed Newcastle 6–1 in the league only a few days earlier,

Above: Corinthians meet West Bromwich Albion in the Second Round, after the amateur side shocked Blackburn Rovers in 1923–24.

Far left: Billy Meredith, who in 1926–27 became the oldest player to appear in an FA Cup Semi-final.

Left: Billy Hampson, who in the same season became the oldest player to appear in The FA Cup Final.

Opposite top: The *Bernicia* and many of the Newcastle United fans that the ship carried to London for the 1924 FA Cup Final against Aston Villa.

Opposite bottom: Bolton Wanderers beat Manchester City in the 1926 Final, their second of three FA Cup wins in seven years.

possibly because Newcastle had been fielding weakened teams in the run up to the Final, a tactic for which they were fined £750.

While those two clubs had been giants of the early game, the move to Wembley would itself herald a wider geographical shift. The big city clubs began to rise, eventually outgrowing those then dominating from Lancashire and South Yorkshire. As ever, the shift wasn't sudden and Blackburn matched Villa's all-time record with their sixth FA Cup in 1928, beating Huddersfield Town 3–1 in an epic Final. It was also the first time in 18 years both finalists scored. Sheffield United had already won their fourth cup in 1925, beating Wales' first finalists, Cardiff City. West Brom would then claim their third in 1931, in another derby Final, although this time defeating Birmingham City rather than Villa. Billy Bassett, the hero of the Baggies' early victories, watched proudly as chairman.

It was Bolton who were the defining cup team of the decade, though, as they managed a perfect hat-trick. Victories in 1926 and 1929 followed that historic 1923 win. Manchester City were defeated in the second of the three matches, a reverse of the 1904 Final. Jack, of course, scored the only goal, but as impressive was Dick Pym's clean sheet. City had scored 31 goals on the way to Wembley, including an 11–4 victory over Crystal Palace, but they were too porous. They suffered their own ignominious double that season, as they were also relegated.

Portsmouth were then defeated 2–0 in their first Final in 1929,

> "I CAN SAY HERE AND NOW THAT ONE DAY SOON OUR FOLLOWERS CAN BE SURE THAT CARDIFF CITY WILL BRING THAT CUP TO WALES."
>
> – FRED KEENOR –

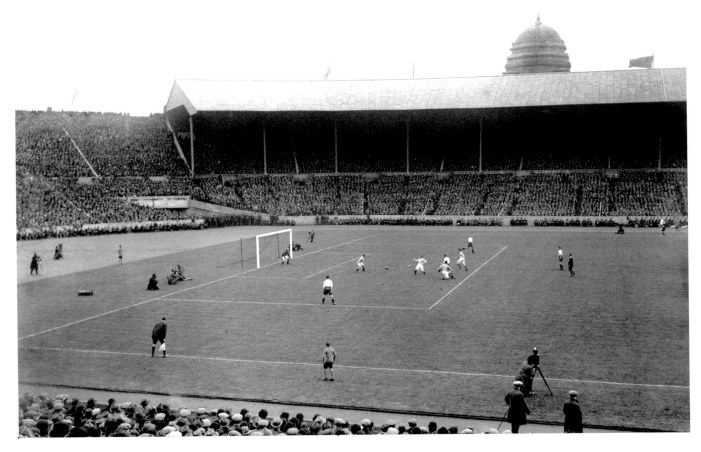

1926–27
WALES CARDIFF CITY 1–0 ARSENAL
VENUE: **WEMBLEY STADIUM**
ATTENDANCE: **91,206**

1927–28
BLACKBURN ROVERS 3–1 HUDDERSFIELD TOWN
VENUE: **WEMBLEY STADIUM**
ATTENDANCE: **92,041**

with William Butler and Harold Blackmore striking for Bolton. Jack, the first scorer at Wembley and the Trotters' main force, had by then moved to Arsenal in the world's first five-figure deal. It was an indication of the new power in the game, as was the nature of the negotiation.

Whether Jack's fee was £10,000 or up to £11,500 was open to debate, due to hazy memories. During talks with Bolton, Arsenal manager Herbert Chapman reputedly ordered rounds of gin and tonics but asked the waiter to keep gin out of his while doubling those of the Burnden Park representatives.

Chapman was generally a step or four ahead, which made him one of the greatest managers in history and one of the first to define the role. Prior to his arrival at Huddersfield, the manager – in fact, the "secretary manager" – had been little more than an administrative role, with directors making most decisions. This, to Chapman, was ridiculous. "Team picking is a complicated and scientific matter requiring expert knowledge," he wrote in a *Sunday Express* article. "In my experience, comparatively few directors are qualified to undertake it."

Chapman wasn't just qualified but way ahead of his time. His approach would lead Huddersfield to that 1922 FA Cup and two consecutive league titles in 1923–24 and 1924–25, before being tempted to Highbury. Chapman knew there was huge potential in Arsenal, who at that point were an idiosyncratic club. They refused to sign players under 5ft 8in (172cm) tall, or those

from outside their immediate area, and reversing this culture was probably why progress was initially slow. Arsenal didn't win anything in Chapman's first four seasons and lost the 1927 cup Final to Cardiff. That was considered a sensation, but the Welsh side – the only non-English club to win The FA Cup – had been a growing force. They'd lost the league on goal average to Chapman's Huddersfield in 1923–24 by a mere 0.2 goals. Had goal difference been used as a tie-breaker, Cardiff would have become the only non-English league winners, too.

Both Finals were national events for Wales. A quarter of a million supporters greeted the team on their return from the victory in 1927, after a 1–0 win. Arsenal, despite bringing in players such as the esteemed Charles Buchan and rapid Joe Hulme, had still never won a major trophy. The winning goal was that kind of vintage mishap that goes against you when victory remains so tantalisingly elusive. A tame Hughie Ferguson shot was caught by Arsenal's goalkeeper Dan Lewis – himself Welsh – only to squirm under his elbow and just over the line. He blamed his new woollen jersey. The cup was leaving England for the only time.

That Final had nevertheless given the occasion something new: a conductor. This became a tradition that would last until the 1970s, and the Welsh fans were only too happy to sing. It was in this spirit that King George V was asked whether he'd like a hymn played. He requested a favourite of his wife, Queen Mary. 'Abide With Me' was played for the first time at an FA Cup Final. It was a spine-tingling moment for the crowd, that seemed to fit the emotional depth of the occasion. The FA Cup was almost acquiring new traditions by the year, with Wembley's distinctiveness lending itself to little touches that made the day more than just a game.

Many of those traditions, as with 'Abide With Me', came about from circumstances specific to one Final that happened to fit the occasion. Another classic illustration came in 1930. Huddersfield and Arsenal made it to Wembley in another of those Finals that marked a historical watershed. One had dominated the 1920s, the other

Above: Cardiff City captain Fred Keenor shakes hands with his Arsenal counterpart, the famous Charlie Buchan, before the 1927 Final.

Opposite top: A child mascot, dressed as a cat, hands a lucky horse shoe to Southampton captain Michael Keeping before an FA Cup tie.

Opposite bottom: The ball squirming out of Arsenal goalkeeper Dan Lewis' grasp to give Cardiff City a goal and the cup in the 1927 Final. He later blamed the new jersey.

> "IN MY PLAYING DAYS NO ATTEMPT WAS MADE TO ORGANISE VICTORY. THE DAY OF HAPHAZARD FOOTBALL HAS GONE."
>
> - HERBERT CHAPMAN -

1928–29
BOLTON WANDERERS 2–0 PORTSMOUTH
VENUE: WEMBLEY STADIUM
ATTENDANCE: 92,576

1929–30
ARSENAL 2–0 HUDDERSFIELD TOWN
VENUE: WEMBLEY STADIUM
ATTENDANCE: 92,488

was to dominate the 1930s. Both wished to recognise Chapman's considerable influence, so the two sets of players walked out side by side for the first time, a gesture that was to continue. Something else that was to persist was Chapman's effect on Arsenal, as he started to repeat the alchemy he'd displayed at Huddersfield.

Chapman's first great feat at Huddersfield was the 1922 FA Cup Final win over Preston, which was the first to be settled by a penalty. It was a controversial one at that, as the foul seemed to happen outside the penalty area. Bill Smith scored, giving Huddersfield the win as well as the confidence to become the first club to win three successive league titles, between 1923 and 1926. The first two were under Chapman, and they were enough to convince Arsenal to go for him. It was all the more remarkable since Huddersfield had almost been out of business as recently as 1920. Their subsequent transformation was almost exclusively down to Chapman's drive, judgement and innovation. He is credited with one of football's most influential tactical adaptations, after another key change in the game. In 1925–26, the offside law was amended to its modern form, so an attacker only required

two defending players – rather than three – to be between him and the goal to remain onside. This was done to address an increasing suppression of attacking play, and had immediate effect. The number of goals shot up, going from 4,700 in the Football League in 1924–25 to 6,373 the next season. Both Swindon Town and Oldham Athletic claimed 10–1 victories, over Farnham and Lytham respectively.

It was the perceptive Buchan who realised the problem this posed defences and that more protection was required. Chapman was always shrewd enough to listen and experiment. A centre-half was pulled back to become a third defender, known as "the stopper". This developed into the famous "WM" formation, so called because of the shapes made by the 3-2-2-3 arrangement of players on the pitch. It suited Arsenal's mercurial attackers, as their first great team took shape.

There was Hulme on the right, Cliff Bastin on the left, Alex James and Jack inside, with Jack Lambert up front. The only pity in 1930 was that the injured Lewis missed the chance

Opposite top left: Bolton Wanderers' James Seddon drinks from the cup with teammates Dick Pym and Harold Blackmore after their 2–0 win over Portsmouth in 1929, the third time in seven years the club had won the competition.

Opposite top right: The brilliant Herbert Chapman, who was perhaps the first modern football manager. He won The FA Cup twice, with Huddersfield Town in 1922 and Arsenal in 1930.

Opposite bottom: The German Graf Zeppelin flying over Wembley during the 1930 FA Cup Final between Huddersfield Town and Arsenal.

Below: Thousands of Arsenal fans pack the streets outside Islington Town Hall to greet The FA Cup winners in 1930.

1930–31
WEST BROMWICH ALBION 2–1 BIRMINGHAM
VENUE: **WEMBLEY STADIUM**
ATTENDANCE: 92,406

1931–32
NEWCASTLE UNITED 2–1 ARSENAL
VENUE: **WEMBLEY STADIUM**
ATTENDANCE: 92,298

at redemption for 1927. He wouldn't have been that tested. Huddersfield were good but Arsenal were on another level. James ran the game and won it, scoring after a clever exchange with Bastin, before Lambert made it 2–0.

All of this was described to radio listeners by Arsenal director George Allison, who doubled up as a radio commentator. This was another reason Wembley became so revered, as its first years coincided with the early period of sports broadcasting, and the manner in which it was so vividly described painted the most alluring image for listeners. There was also the fact that the Football League had blocked radio coverage of its games, fearing it would harm attendances, leaving The FA Cup as the sole competition people grew up with in their homes.

Something almost other-worldly happened that day in 1930, as Allison had to find the words for the sight of a German Graf Zeppelin airship casting a shadow over Wembley and going so low

as to become part of the day. Some players briefly stopped to look up, as the airship dipped its nose in salute of King George V before moving on. Another aspect of the day that wasn't repeated was the two squads joining together for a post-game banquet. They were otherwise going in different directions. Huddersfield had won their last major trophy. Arsenal had just won their first, as Chapman had promised. The Gunners won the title the next season, before echoing Huddersfield's achievement in winning three successive leagues – between 1932 and 1935 – and then another in 1938.

Arsenal would consequently become the benchmark for FA Cup success, though that's not to say they didn't suffer setbacks. That was summed up by how, in 1932, they became the first team to score the opening goal at Wembley and lose. It was a controversial defeat to Newcastle, too, in what became known as the "over the line" Final. Bob John had given Arsenal the lead and that was considered enough against an unconvincing Newcastle. As

Above: Tommy Glidden, captain of West Bromwich Albion, victorious 1931 FA Cup finalists, poses with the trophy in front of a train at Paddington Station.

Opposite top: Crowd surround Newcastle United's car, as it arrives at King's Cross station before the 1932 Final against Arsenal.

Opposite bottom: Jack Allen heads Newcastle United's controversial equaliser in the so-called "over the line" 1932 Final against Arsenal. Photos later showed that the ball had crossed the line beforehand and Arsenal should have had a goal kick.

often happens on such occasions, however, the Magpies found something extra. Many pointed to a matter of inches being the difference. On 38 minutes, Arsenal thought they'd defended an attack as the ball rolled out of play. In chasing a lost cause, Newcastle's Jimmy Richardson won the game, hooking the ball over for Jack Allen to score. Photos later vindicated the Arsenal players' disbelief – the ball had gone out of play. The Gunners couldn't get back in the game, although they were later praised for the restraint of their reaction.

Restraint didn't suit what happened next, however. Arsenal weren't just the benchmark for success in the 1930s. They became the benchmark for all upsets. Their Third Round elimination to Walsall on 14 January 1933 has a claim to be the most sensational in history. It was one with all the ingredients to set the template for giant killing.

First, there was the contrast. Arsenal were on course for the

second of those five league titles, and were the wealthiest club in the country. They had a player, Jack, who cost five figures, and much was made before the game about how their boots cost £87. Walsall's entire team cost £69 as they sat in the Third Division North. There was then the context of the day. Arsenal had travelled from their palatial surroundings in London to the rickety Fellows Park, that had a laundry wall behind one goal and was often clouded in smoke from surrounding factories. Walsall had not won in four games and one of those included a 5–0 defeat to Stockport County. Arsenal, meanwhile, had hammered Sheffield United 9–2.

As tends to happen on such days, though, little developments started to grow into something more substatial. Arsenal hadn't actually won an away game in three, and were hit by flu. They took to the pitch on that afternoon with five first-team players missing, although some of that was possibly squad rotation, and

Opposite: The 1933 Final, between Everton and Manchester City, saw shirt numbers worn for the first time. They were numbered 1–22, though, as seen on City goalkeeper Len Langford.

Below: The Walsall team that beat Arsenal in one of the most sensational ever upsets, a 2–0 win in the 1932–33 Third Round.

they still fielded Jack, Bastin and James. All of them felt the force of Walsall's challenges in the first few minutes. Bastin said they were "more like steamrollers than footballers". The gameplan was clear, as was the effect. Arsenal were cowed. Reserve striker Charles Walsh missed chance after chance. The crowd at Fellow Parks responded, with locals swelling the attendance to 24,000 as news of Walsall's performance spread. On the hour, there was an eruption. Gilbert Alsop managed to lose the inexperienced Tommy Black at a corner, and powered home. Black was rattled, as he followed that with a desperate hack to give away a penalty. Bill Shepherd got up to finish.

Arsenal should still have had enough to overturn a 2–0 deficit in the remaining 20 minutes, but it was one of those days – and the first of those upsets. The opening lines of the report in the *Walsall Times* summed up the mood: "Is it true? Is it not really a dream

that I shall awake and smile at?" Chapman was furious that the chance of the double had gone. On the train back, he told Black he would never even set foot at the training ground again. The defender was sold to Plymouth Argyle within days. Walsh was sold to Brentford within weeks.

Walsall went on to lose narrowly to Manchester City, who met Everton in the Final. The Toffees were, at that point, one of Arsenal's main rivals, having in 1931–32 become the first club to win the league immediately after promotion. They would follow that with The FA Cup, convincingly beating City 3–0. This was also the first Final to feature numbers on shirts, although City wore 12 to 22. It meant The FA Cup's first number nine was the archetypal number nine: the legendary William Randolph Dean. More widely known as 'Dixie', he had scored an incredible 60 league goals in 1927–28. Dean, of course, scored here.

City's right-half, a young Matt Busby, was already proving himself a shrewd football mind and felt the side had got their preparation wrong by arriving at Wembley too early, allowing some stage fright to set in. That could have been a problem when they returned to the Final in 1934 to face Portsmouth, because 19-year-old goalkeeper Frank Swift had to cover for the injured Les Langford. Swift was "desolate" when Septimus Rutherford's 38th-minute shot slipped through his fingers to give Portsmouth a 1–0 lead. He later wrote that he feared becoming "just another

"IS IT TRUE? IS IT NOT REALLY A DREAM THAT I SHALL AWAKE AND SMILE AT?"

– WALSALL TIMES –

1933–34
MANCHESTER CITY 2–1 PORTSMOUTH
VENUE: WEMBLEY STADIUM
ATTENDANCE: 93,258

1934–35
SHEFFIELD WEDNESDAY 4–2 WEST BROMWICH ALBION
VENUE: WEMBLEY STADIUM
ATTENDANCE: 93,204

1935–36
ARSENAL 1–0 SHEFFIELD UNITED
VENUE: WEMBLEY STADIUM
ATTENDANCE: 93,384

Opposite top left: Legendary Everton number-nine Dixie Dean holds up The FA Cup during their victory parade in Liverpool after the 1933 win over Manchester City.

Opposite bottom left: Manchester City goalkeeper Frank Swift makes a save in his side's 2–1 win over Portsmouth in the 1934 Final. He would later faint at the final whistle.

Opposite right: The referee for the 1934 Final, Stanley Rous, right, and Sir Frederick Wall, who he would succeed as FA secretary.

Below: Alex James holds up The FA Cup after Arsenal beat Sheffield United in the 1936 Final.

Wembley goalkeeper", overwhelmed by the size of the stage. Seeing Swift crestfallen at half-time, Fred Tilson casually told him not to worry. "I'll plonk two in the next half."

And so he did, although only after an injury to Portsmouth's £10,000 centre-half, Jimmy Allen. City finally had the space to play the fluid game that had enraptured the country. They had put six past Aston Villa in the Semi-finals and their Sixth Round game against Stoke City had attracted 84,569 – a record for a British crowd outside of London or Glasgow. Here, Tillson got the equaliser on 74 minutes and the winner on 88. He'd stayed true to his word. Swift couldn't stay on his feet. He fainted at the final whistle, blown by future FA secretary Stanley Rous.

As if to sum up the era, two of the next four winners knocked out Arsenal. Sheffield Wednesday beat them, before defeating West Brom in sensational fashion in the 1935 Final. Jimmy Rimmer made it 3–2 in the 85th minute and then 4–2 in the 88th, to join the exclusive club of players to score in every round.

Arsenal won the cup again in 1936, but sadly without Chapman, who died in tragic circumstances in 1934. He had gone to scout Wednesday on a cold January evening and picked up a heavy cold. He then insisted on attending an Arsenal third-team game despite being ill. His illness developed into pneumonia and he died within a few days. Arsenal's perseverance in 1936 was a testament to him.

It meant that Allison took charge for the 1934–35 title and the 1935–36 cup run, giving up his commentary duties. There was some irony to that since this was a year of media upheaval. The Third Round draw was broadcast on radio for the first time, despite opposition from newspapers. The broadcast was described as an experiment, but it lasted decades. Rous had been asked to shake the velvet bag so that it made "a distinctive and suitable sound" on air. Another dispute even saw cameras banned from the 1936 showpiece, which made for another Final where there was something in the air. Autogyros – small aircraft – were hired to circle Wembley from above with cameras to try and catch some of the action. The newsreels showed snatched footage.

Those in the air might have caught a glimpse of Ted Drake scoring the only goal. Sunderland actually prised the league title from Arsenal that season, but only after they had lost to Third Division Port Vale in the Third Round. It was a dismal low in the cup for the Black Cats, but the prelude to their sweetest moment. Sunderland finally won their first-ever FA Cup in 1937, with local boy Raich Carter driving them to a 3–1 win over Preston. The

1936–37
SUNDERLAND **3–1** PRESTON NORTH END
VENUE: **WEMBLEY STADIUM**
ATTENDANCE: **93,495**

Lilywhites would immediately rectify their own struggles in the cup the following year, winning their first since the double of 1889. That 1938 Final was the first to be televised live, even though there were only 10,000 TV sets in the country. It was a poor game that led to a notorious prediction from commentator Thomas Woodruffe with just a minute of extra time left: "If there is a goal now, I will eat my hat."

Within seconds, George Mutch was brought down at the edge of the area. A penalty was given, a silence descended. That transformed into a deafening roar when Mutch scored off the bar. Woodruffe duly ate a marzipan hat on TV the following week.

"I'LL PLONK TWO IN THE NEXT HALF."

- FRED TILSON -

Above: An autogyro flying in the foreground above Wembley during the 1936 Final. A dispute meant media were banned, leading to some enterprising broadcasters renting small aircraft to try and capture the action.

Opposite: The crowd at Wembley during Sunderland's 3–1 win over Preston North End in the 1937 Final.

1937–38
PRESTON NORTH END   1–0   HUDDERSFIELD TOWN
AET
VENUE: **WEMBLEY STADIUM**
ATTENDANCE: **93,497**

1938–39
PORTSMOUTH   4–1   WOLVERHAMPTON WANDERERS
VENUE: **WEMBLEY STADIUM**
ATTENDANCE: **99,370**

The media was again shocked by developments the following year. A brilliant Wolves team, built on the rock-solid foundation of centre-half Stan Cullis, froze in the Final. They were said to be so nervous that many of the players' signatures were illegible in the official autograph book. That was the effect of Wembley. That was how little superstitions took hold, to ward off hoodoos. Portsmouth manager Jack Tinn wore his "lucky white spats" right through every round, to the point his team destroyed Wolves 4–1 to lift the cup.

All of those stories were soon to be put away for some time, though. The brutal reality of war was about to intervene again. Wembley would become an image to be yearned for in a different way, as a reminder to people of normality.

"THE BALL HIT THE BAR, WHICH WAS SQUARE THEN, TOOK THE PAINT OFF IT […] THE PAINT IS ON THE BALL TO THIS DAY."

- BILL SHANKLY -

Above: Portsmouth Jimmy Guthrie receives the cup from King George V after the shock 4–1 win over Wolverhampton Wanderers in the 1939 Final. It was the last Final for seven years.

Top left: Portsmouth manager Jack Tinn has his lucky white spats fastened by winger Freddie Worrall at Fratton Park.

Opposite top: Scarborough footballers enjoy a seaweed bath to get ready for an FA Cup tie. This was the era when the Third Round became the Third Round as we know it today, when top clubs entered, strengthening the mythology of the competition as well as the mystique of upsets.

Opposite bottom left: Preston North End captain Tom Smith holds up The FA Cup after the 1938 Final win over Huddersfield. On the right, with his arm outstretched to touch the cup, is a young Bill Shankly.

Opposite bottom right: BBC commentator Thomas Woodruffe keeps his promise and eats his hat after saying there wouldn't be a goal in the 1938 Final – although it is made of marzipan.

THE THIRD
ROUND

It takes place in January, but it is almost English football's version of Christmas Day. The date involves sparkling winter weather, brings everyone together, has a magic air to it and often involves gifts. Year after year, so many people wake up giddy on the morning, excited by what the day has in store, after a month of build-up.

There is ultimately nothing in the football calendar that can compare to The FA Cup Third Round. It is the heart of the competition, but also its spirit. The Third Round is the stage that finally gathers everyone in the game together, as clubs from the top two divisions enter the draw. It is this entry that offers those in divisions below such a great opportunity: the chance for a big day out, to host a top-tier team or – maybe, just maybe – to conjure one of the upsets that really make the cup what it is.

The Third Round is where everyone meets, so anything can happen. It distils the famous democracy of The FA Cup, and remains the one date in football synonymous with unpredictability. It's for that reason that the Third Round weekend isn't completely self-contained. An enchanting prelude is the draw. This sets out the games to come, but also sets up the excitement. So many famous FA Cup heroes talk as fondly about their memories of the draw as of their favourite games or greatest moments. A classic cup tradition was squads gathering around the radio on a Monday afternoon in December, to find out what that weekend had in store. Any non-league teams are naturally hoping for that grand occasion, either to host a big club or get that rare chance to play in one of football's most renowned stadiums.

The drama of this anticipation offered compelling scenes of its own, which was why television companies eventually started to film clubs' reactions to the draw, too. It has become a broadcasting event in itself, though the quaint old velvet bags and wooden balls, that had lent such a gravitas, were eventually replaced by more modern equipment in another sign of the cup's evolution.

All of this is still just build-up, though. There is no feeling in football like the anticipation of entering a stadium in the Third Round. It's an occasion rich with possibility. Players themselves have always loved the change of scenery it offers, as the marathon of the league campaign momentarily gives way to a one-off where anyone can win. The way it matches the 64 remaining clubs together naturally means that the majority of the most famous FA Cup upsets have inevitably come in the Third Round, too. It is where Bournemouth beat Manchester United in 1984, Hereford United eliminated Newcastle United in 1972, and Walsall knocked out Arsenal in 1933.

The Third Round has also featured its share of mega-ties, which have set the pace for the cup season. The Merseyside derby has taken place at this stage three times, the Manchester and North London derbies twice each. The Third Round's timing in the middle of the season also means it can offer a shot at rebirth, and a chance to save a campaign. There are countless examples of an early January win recharging a team, but none so consequential as Mark Robins' goal for Manchester United against Nottingham Forest in 1990. That was the day when things finally began to come together for Alex Ferguson. It was fitting that it happened on the one day that brings the game together. That is why the Third Round is unique.

Opposite top left: The balls being prepared for an FA Cup draw at Soho Square, in 2006.

Opposite top right: An old cup tradition, as non-league Gravesend and Northfleet players gather around a radio to listen to what the luck of the draw had for them in the 1962–63 Third Round. That was a trip to Carlisle United, which they won 1–0, in one of the stage's great stories.

Opposite middle: Gianfranco Zola, a cup winner in 1997 and 2000, helps conduct the draw for the Third Round in 2011–12.

Opposite bottom: Liverpool's Virgil van Dijk rises highest to score a late winner in another of the cup's Merseyside derbies, this time knocking Everton out of the 2017–18 Third Round.

CHAPTER SEVEN

MATINEE IDOLS

1945–1958

1945 1958

IT WAS A SCENE THAT WAS ALMOST CINEMATIC. AS THE CLOCK TICKED CLOSER TO 3PM ON SATURDAY 2 MAY 1953, THE STREETS OF BLACKPOOL WERE DESERTED. THE CITY'S FAMOUS TOWER WAS EMPTY. ALMOST EVERYONE HAD GATHERED AROUND THEIR NEWLY PURCHASED TELEVISIONS, AND THE RECORD VIEWING FIGURES SHOWED THE REST OF THE COUNTRY WAS DOING THE SAME.

Tens of millions of people were captivated by a single event, and most of the focus was on one man. Stanley Matthews was playing in his third FA Cup Final with Blackpool and almost all of Britain was willing him to finally win it.

His was one of the great sporting quests; one which enriched The FA Cup and enchanted the public. Privately, it was something even more important to Matthews himself. His life's ambition to win The FA Cup was well known, but a deeply personal part of it was not. In the minutes before his father, Jack, died in 1945, he beckoned his son over and told him to fulfil that last great dream of his distinguished football career. Matthews told no one about this promise until he revealed it in his autobiography years later.

Back in the dark Wembley tunnel in 1953, all of this was playing on the 38-year-old's mind. The widespread belief was that this would be Matthews' last chance at FA Cup glory, and there was a real fear that football's most revered career would go unfulfilled. Matthews later admitted he had never felt worse before a match.

Then, the players went out into that brilliant light.

The emotional power of such moments lies in a lore that can't be bought or copied. It can only grow over years, through the emotional investment of so many people. A competition has to have a distinguished history. A career has to have a certain distinction. So much of this came together in The FA Cup of the 1950s, a footballing era akin to Hollywood's golden age.

There were the stories. There were the stars. There were moments of huge significance to the national psyche, propelled by the spread of television that at once made these narratives more accessible and more special. The 1953 Final was the era's centrepiece, deepening the mythology of the competition. So many future players would cite it as the memory that made The FA Cup their dream. Neville Cardus, the celebrated cricket writer, resignedly accepted that this was the day football became "the game of the people".

Matthews' pursuit of his holy grail was just one of many entrancing, epic stories during this period. Newcastle United dominated the cup like no one else this century, Bert Trautmann showed the physical lengths a player would go to in order to achieve

victory, and managers like Matt Busby and Stan Cullis enjoyed their first successes. The era was closed by an even more emotional quest – the resurgent cup run of Manchester United, after the tragedy of the Munich air disaster.

All of this was underscored by English football's battle with itself. Hungary's 6–3 win over England at Wembley – again in 1953, again with Matthews playing – offered a glimpse of the future of the sport. That "match of the century" heralded huge technological and tactical changes. Floodlights allowed evening games and European football. Kits became lightweight. Tactics were afforded new importance, which started to usher out the great wingers that defined this era, such as Tom Finney, Wilf Mannion and Matthews himself. For a time, stars like these, and Len Shackleton, put huge numbers on gates, in the same way matinee idols guaranteed a box office smash. Matthews was the most admired of all, and it was said his mere appearance could add 10,000 to a crowd.

This was amplified by the yearning for something as joyful as football after the war. The effects of conflict were still visible. Players such as Colchester United's giant-killing hero Bob Curry had been wounded at Dunkirk, while many others had been denied their best years. Clubs had been left in ruins. Old Trafford had been bombed. The FA Cup itself had narrowly escaped destruction. The trophy had been constantly showcased throughout the war in aid of charities and, at one point, was moved mere days before the house where it was kept was bombed. One story has it that Jack Tinn, of the white spats, spent a night during the Blitz protecting it under his stairs. Portsmouth had become the longest-ever holders of the cup, keeping it safe for seven years.

Opposite: The FA Cup returns to the Bird in Hand pub, where it spent some of WW2, for a 2009 recreation of the period. Portsmouth held the trophy for seven years after winning it in 1939.

Previous pages: At the age of 38, Stanley Matthews finally claims an FA Cup winners' medal, after Blackpool's epic 4–3 win over Bolton Wanderers in 1953. He is hoisted up here by Blackpool teammates Jackie Mudie, on the left, and Stan Mortensen, who hit a hat-trick.

There had been such a desire for football that The FA Cup's organising committee had sanctioned its return for the 1945–46 season as early as 1 June 1945 – the day the Allied Control Council formally took control of Germany.

Since the league's return had not yet been formalised and clubs were so desperate for money, this first year back would bring a unique change. Every tie until the Sixth Round would be two-legged, with unlimited replays until there was a decider. As supporters went to games, they passed government posters encouraging cheerfulness. Football did more for this than anything else. It was vivid colour at a time when rationing only added to the grey.

Post-war attendances were the highest in history and they were occasionally astounding. When 80,000 turned up at Maine Road for the Wednesday afternoon FA Cup replay between Derby

Above: Women and children being passed over the crowd to safety at Burnden Park on 9 March 1946, during the FA Cup tie between Bolton Wanderers and Stoke City. The crush was one of the worst disasters ever seen in English football, with 33 people dying.

Above left: Moelwyn Hughes is shown plans of Burnden Park, as part of an inquiry that would bring changes to how matchdays were organised. Sir Alexander Rouse is examining the crash barrier.

Left: A concrete wall is constructed at Burnden Park after the disaster.

Opposite: Charlton Athletic captain Don Welsh, left, shakes hands with Derby County counterpart Jack Nicholas ahead of the 1946 Final, the first after WW2. In the middle is referee Eddie Smith, who famously predicted the ball wouldn't burst, only for exactly that to happen.

1945–46
DERBY COUNTY **4–1** CHARLTON ATHLETIC
AET
VENUE: **WEMBLEY STADIUM**
ATTENDANCE: **98,000**

1946–47
CHARLTON ATHLETIC **1–0** BURNLEY
AET
VENUE: **WEMBLEY STADIUM**
ATTENDANCE: **99,000**

County and Birmingham City, there were so many absences from work that the government banned daytime, midweek fixtures.

That enthusiasm to watch games – not to mention a star like Matthews – would sadly create new tragedy so soon after the war, principally because the sport was unprepared. Bolton's Burnden Park on 9 March 1946 saw one of English football's worst disasters when 33 people died at a Sixth Round second-leg match between Bolton Wanderers and Matthews' Stoke City. A reported 85,000 turned up at a ground that could only accommodate around 50,000, with many areas still blocked off due to the stadium's use during the war. That created a bottleneck and then a crush when another gate was opened. Two barriers collapsed and a brick wall crumbled, which saw people pile on top of each other and onto the pitch. After a mere 12 minutes of play, the teams were sent back to the dressing room. Unconscious fans were by then being passed over shoulders.

Astonishingly, the players went back on. Matthews recalled tears in his eyes. Nat Lofthouse, who would of course be on the other side to Matthews in that fateful 1953 Final, was in a state of shock. The Home Office initiated the Moelwyn Hughes Report, which recommended proper crowd control as well as automated turnstiles.

It wasn't like the game was stunned into stopping, though. Bolton went through and were back playing their Semi-final against Charlton Athletic just two weeks later. The likelihood was that Britain was just desensitised after the war. The show had to go on. Charlton beat a subdued Bolton to meet Derby in the Final. It was a fixture that seemed a surprise at the time but was very much a product of it. Since clubs had greatly changed from 1939, and there was no league to judge performance, it was hard to say what was expected.

One famous prediction was undone on the day. Referee Eddie Smith had gone on radio before the Final and ended up talking about how the chances of the ball bursting were one in a million. It of course burst. The same thing then happened again the next year,

with the quality of leather due to war shortages blamed. Another consequence of that was that this was the only time in history that bronze medals were given to FA Cup winners due to the rarity of gold. They were eventually replaced when proper medals could be made, and it was Derby County who received them.

Derby finally won their first FA Cup after a fourth Final, and a match that encapsulated the joy of the game. It had initially looked like it was going to end disappointingly. With the score 0–0 on 85 minutes, Charlton's Bert Turner deflected the ball into his own net. That would have been the first time an own goal had settled the Final, only for Turner to intervene by scoring with a free-kick. This made him the first player to score at both ends in an FA Cup Final, as well as the oldest to score in the fixture at all, at 36 years and 312 days. His equalizer brought extra time, but also something more out of Derby. With former Sunderland hero Raich Carter influential and Peter Doherty excelling with a goal, they won 4–1 after extra time.

The defeated Charlton swiftly followed another fine cup tradition, in becoming the 10th club to lose a Final and then immediately come back to win it the following year. When Christopher Duffy finally scored against Burnley after 114 minutes of the 1947 Final, manager Jimmy Seed put his head in his hands, unable to watch. He was unable to cope with the glory of victory either, as after the match he accidentally dropped the cup getting out of a taxi and broke the lid. A mortified Seed immediately got a local garage to do some initial repairs for a presentation that night, before silversmiths restored it to normal the next day.

> **"IT WAS NOT UNTIL I WAS MOTORING HOME THAT EVENING THAT THE SHADOW OF GRIM DISASTER DESCENDED ON ME LIKE A STORM CLOUD."**
>
> - STANLEY MATTHEWS -

1947–48
MANCHESTER UNITED 4–2 BLACKPOOL
VENUE: **WEMBLEY STADIUM**
ATTENDANCE: 99,000

1948–49
WOLVERHAMPTON WANDERERS 3–1 LEICESTER CITY
VENUE: **WEMBLEY STADIUM**
ATTENDANCE: 99,500

If there was a sense at that point the competition was getting back to normal, the 1947–48 season would see it return to its best. It was the true start of one of The FA Cup's great quests, if only after a restart for Matthews. He was perhaps the first player to completely dominate the collective football consciousness. Hungary captain Ferenc Puskás described Matthews as the greatest of all time. Most of the appeal lay in the ingenuity and exhilaration of his play. Matthews had myriad ways of drawing a defender in, before just whizzing past. He was variously known as "Wizard of Dribble", "King of Soccer" and, soon, Sir Stanley. Matthews remains the only player to have been knighted while still playing.

The only place where there seemed to be any doubt about Matthews was at his club: Stoke City. His relationship with manager Bob McGrory and the Stoke board had been strained after a knee injury, following on from pre-war tensions created by his popularity. Matthews was finally allowed to move to Blackpool in May 1947 for a fee of £11,500. There might have seemed some logic in Stoke's decision given that this was a 32-year-old, notionally past his prime, but the war had skewed careers. Like many players, Matthews had been denied six years of top-level football between the ages of 24 and 30. This may have prevented these stars from reaching their true peak, but it also prolonged careers. There was meanwhile a reticence about signing young players due to national service. In 1951–52, Chelsea had to bring the 18-year-old Bobby Smith over from his barracks at Aldershot for their Sixth Round win over Leeds United. In borrowed boots, he scored the equaliser in the first game and a hat-trick in the 5–1 replay victory.

The overall effect was that the average player's age of the era was higher, with Arsenal's XI for their 1950 Final win over Liverpool the oldest ever, at 30 years and two months. Perceptions nevertheless remained the same. Much of the emotional swell around Matthews was that he was 32 and had not even played in a Final. The feeling was that there wasn't much time left. This was reflected by Blackpool manager Joe Smith's question when his side completed the signing: "You're 32 – do you think you can make it for another couple of years?"

Smith, for his part, had full faith. He told Matthews he would

win that FA Cup. There was still an awful lot of anguish to go through, however. Every Third Round of the 1940s and early 1950s brought the discussion of whether this would finally be Matthews' year.

The 1947–48 season at least brought his debut in a Final, and the first of many epic contests across the era. Blackpool met Busby's first great Manchester United team, who were captained by the commanding Johnny Carey. United had shown their quality by becoming the first finalists to beat top-tier opposition in every round. That generated a collective attendance of 300,000, which is still a record. United's home games were at Maine Road due to the bomb damage at Old Trafford, although the most remarkable game came on the road. Aston Villa were beaten 6–4 in one of the great Third Round matches. That stage also saw the Southern League's Colchester United knock out Huddersfield, and it would not be the last time the Essex club would make their mark.

Blackpool had eliminated the upstarts, as well as an improving Tottenham Hotspur, to set up a superb Final. Showing how it stirred the emotions, United became the first side to go behind twice and win the cup. It was Matthews, and the response to him, that typically conditioned the game. Busby had initially told Charlie Mitten to drop back and help Johnny Aston when Matthews was on the ball, but that just invited him on and sapped United's own threat. Eddie Shimwell gave Blackpool the lead from the spot after Allenby Chilton had fouled Stan Mortensen. Mortensen himself made it 2–1 following Jack Rowley's equaliser, ensuring the Blackpool striker had scored in every round.

At half-time, Busby accepted his mistake. Mitten was freed and United were instructed to play high and just cut Matthews off. United were transformed, winning 4–2. Rowley hit the equaliser on 70 minutes before Pearson and John Anderson scored in the space of three minutes in a brilliant climax.

Bobby Charlton described it as "the greatest cup Final of all time", and the game that inspired him to go to United. The wait was getting heavier for Matthews. He was named the inaugural Footballer of the Year, but it was not individual awards he craved. Insult was added to injured pride the following season, in 1948–49, as Matthews' former club Stoke eliminated Blackpool in the Fourth Round.

That result paled next to the biggest story of that round, however, as Yeovil Town knocked out Sunderland. Sunderland weren't quite the force they had been before the war, but they were still the biggest spenders in the country. Known as the "Bank of England", they had lavished £250,000 on assembling a team, the pick of it Shackleton, signed for a record £20,050.

"THE GREATEST CUP FINAL OF ALL TIME."

- BOBBY CHARLTON -

Opposite: Manchester United captain Johnny Carey is lifted up by teammates Charlie Mitten, left, and Jack Crompton after the 4–2 win over Blackpool in the 1948 Final.

The gap in quality was immense but Yeovil had one advantage that levelled things a little, so to speak. Much was made of their sloping pitch at Huish Athletic Ground, which dropped by 6ft (3.3m) at some points. More significant was the manner in which player-manager Alec Stock cut the grass himself, showing the spirit at the club, although Stock wouldn't allow Sunderland to train on it.

An injury to goalkeeper Stan Hull forced Yeovil to bring in Dickie Dyke for just his second game, but he was not as busy as expected. Yeovil just went for it. Before half-time, they were ahead. Stock, of all people, scored his first goal of the season. Yeovil's attitude was exemplified when they kept going even after Sunderland's Jackie Robinson forced extra-time from a rare Dyke slip. The biggest error was to come from the biggest name. On 104 minutes, Shackleton attempted a speculative overhead pass. It only served to put Eric Bryant through for a sensational winner.

Yeovil's reward was a match at Maine Road against the holders, Manchester United, in front of 81,565 people. United won 8–0, but Yeovil had had their moment, and Stock had shown his

1949–50
ARSENAL 2–0 LIVERPOOL
VENUE: **WEMBLEY STADIUM**
ATTENDANCE: **100,000**

1950–51
NEWCASTLE UNITED 2–0 BLACKPOOL
VENUE: **WEMBLEY STADIUM**
ATTENDANCE: **100,000**

potential. Stan Cullis then followed Busby by winning his first trophy with one of the best teams of the 1950s, as his disciplined Wolves beat Leicester City 3–1 in the 1949 Final. Arsenal reclaimed the cup in 1950 with a 2–0 win over Liverpool.

Meanwhile, Matthews' longing for the cup only became more acute. Blackpool returned to Wembley in 1951 but ended up feeling like they hadn't turned up. Newcastle easily won 2–0, as Stan Seymour became the first figure to win the cup as a player and manager with the same club. The Magpies' great number nine Jackie Milburn scored twice, his second one of the memorable Final goals – Ernie Taylor opened up the entire Blackpool defence with a back heel, before Milburn smashed it in from distance.

Above: The famous Compton brothers, Denis and Leslie, in the Wembley dressing room after Arsenal's 2–0 win over Liverpool in 1950.

Above right: King George VI shakes hands with Stanley Matthews, ahead of the Blackpool star's second Final, the defeat to Newcastle United in 1951.

Opposite top left: Yeovil players celebrate with local fans at Huish Park after their incredible elimination of Sunderland in 1948–49, two of their beaten opponents walking through disconsolately.

Opposite top right: Wolverhampton Wanderers supporters at the 1949 Final, to watch their team beat Leicester City.

Opposite bottom: Leicester City's Gordon Bradley makes a save in the 1949 Final, but he couldn't stop Wolves winning 3–1.

"I SIMPLY CREATED A YARDSTICK WHICH PEOPLE COULD CRITICISE ME AGAINST."

- STAN CULLIS -

That Newcastle team featured the Chilean-born George Robledo, who became the first South American to appear in the Final. He went on to score the only goal of the 1952 Final, a 1–0 win over Arsenal, made all the more special because he was joined by his brother Ted. That strike was the subject of a famous drawing by a young John Lennon.

Winston Churchill became the only prime minister to ever present the trophy, as Newcastle became the first club to retain it since Blackburn Rovers in 1891. While FA Cup success seemed to come so easily for some, it was only getting harder for Blackpool. There was deep dejection in their dressing room after the 1951 Final. Nobody said anything or even moved, most just stared at the floor.

When the Blackpool team were eventually able to talk about it, most would look to 'what-ifs'. Joe Smith pointed to the long gap between Semi-final and Final, describing it as a "miserable spell of anticipation". Matthews was more nervous than anyone had seen him, leading to a poor performance. The winger himself would lament a Mortensen header cleared off the line by Bobby Cowell at 0–0: "If we had got that goal…"

1951–52
NEWCASTLE UNITED   1–0   ARSENAL
VENUE: **WEMBLEY STADIUM**
ATTENDANCE: **100,000**

Above: Newcastle United celebrate in the dressing room following their FA Cup Final victory over Arsenal in 1952.

Opposite top left: Jackie Milburn scores the first of two goals in the 1951 Final against Blackpool, to seal the first of three FA Cup wins for Newcastle in the space of five years.

Opposite top right: Winston Churchill becomes the only prime minister to present the cup, handing it over to Newcastle captain Joe Harvey after the victory over Arsenal in 1952.

Opposite bottom: George Robledo, the first South American-born player to appear in the FA Cup Final, scores the decisive goal in the sixth minute of the 1952 Final, to beat Arsenal 1–0 and ensure Newcastle United become the first club to retain the trophy since 1891.

All of this hung over that day in 1953, as Blackpool returned to Wembley. There were other elements lifting the mood, too. The forthcoming coronation of Queen Elizabeth II created a spirit of optimism around Britain, as well as a rush for TV sets. Previous matches had been broadcast, including the 1950 Final, but none were close to the scale of this. It was a key moment for UK television as much as for football. The FA even rejected complaints about attendances dropping elsewhere by insisting the broadcast was of "national interest".

It was a truly national event, watched by more than 10 million people. Virtually all of them were willing a Matthews victory, in a manner never seen before. The anticipation had grown from the Sixth Round when Blackpool eliminated title-winners Arsenal. There was then the fact that Bolton were little more than a mid-table team, who hadn't even faced a top-tier side on the way to Wembley. Their own Sixth Round victory had come over Gateshead, who had offered one of the season's upsets by eliminating Liverpool.

That famous term, "The Matthews Final", was used in the press in the week before the game. Most of the headlines on the day highlighted the Queen's presence or Matthews' quest, despite Arsenal winning the league the night before.

It was far from a smooth build-up for Blackpool. Allan Brown had fractured his leg and missed out on the Final, as he did in 1951. Matthews himself had picked up a knock, but this was really about psychology. Before the Blackpool players went out, Smith told them he was proud no matter what – before delivering one last message: "Let's win this one."

Smith, for his part, always believed they would do it. He told Matthews as much when Stoke had tried to re-sign him before 1953. That faith was tested in just the first couple of minutes at Wembley, however, as Nat Lofthouse, the new Footballer of the Year, scored within 75 seconds. Adding to that sinking feeling, it looked like goalkeeper George Farm should have stopped it. Mortensen equalised on 35 minutes but that only made defeat feel more fated as Willie Moir instantly put Bolton back in front. When Eric Bell made it 3–1 even after getting injured, it really felt like Blackpool were destined to fall at the final hurdle for the third time. This was not just the same old story. It was the end.

But it was instead to prove the perfect plot line – the feeling that all was lost before everything changed. Matthews said later he couldn't believe the situation, but he'd already got the impression that this was not over by the way he was beginning to get at a tiring Bolton. By the 68th minute, Matthews crossed for Mortensen, the striker scoring a classically scruffy poacher's finish. "The tide had turned," Lofthouse would say. "We knew it. Blackpool knew it."

The only danger was running out of time. With the score still 3–2 on 88 minutes, Blackpool won a free-kick. Both Matthews and Mortensen stood over it, when the younger Stan said he could spot a gap. Matthews bet him sixpence he couldn't get through it. Mortensen accepted and duly drove the ball in, becoming the only player to score a hat-trick at a Wembley FA Cup Final. The force

Above: Stan Mortensen becomes the first player to score a hat-trick in an FA Cup Final, helping Blackpool to come back from 3–1 down against Bolton Wanderers in the famous 1953 Final.

Opposite: Blackpool captain Harry Johnston holds the FA Cup aloft after a long-awaited win, with the day's goalscoring heroes also lifting Stanley Matthews to celebrate his first winner's medal. Match-winner Bill Perry is on the left, with Stan Mortensen on the right.

1953–54
WEST BROMWICH ALBION   3–2   PRESTON NORTH END
VENUE: **WEMBLEY STADIUM**
ATTENDANCE: **100,000**

1954–55
NEWCASTLE UNITED   3–1   MANCHESTER CITY
VENUE: **WEMBLEY STADIUM**
ATTENDANCE: **100,000**

of history was now pointing only one way. Another Matthews run saw him dash to the byline in the 91st minute. His attempted cross was this time overhit, but luck was now with Blackpool. The ball fell to Bill Perry to win it. Matthews and Blackpool at last had the cup.

Bolton had become the first finalist to lead by two goals and lose. With that Blackpool comeback, as well as the stoppage-time winner to make it 4–3, this really was the cup Final with everything. It also meant everything. Most of those on the pitch, including two of the Bolton players, immediately went to Matthews. The cheer when he collected his medal from the Queen was one of the loudest Wembley ever heard.

In his own quiet moment afterwards, Matthews held the cup to the sky for his father. He then joined the Blackpool team in parading the cup around the pitch. It was another new tradition created on the day, to go with many of those from the TV broadcast, which of course now has its own standalone slot.

The same TV audience could have seen the "Finney Final" the next season, had events on the day taken a different course. Preston North End's legendary winger, Tom Finney, had never won a major trophy, but he wasn't to enjoy the deliverance his great rival did. Vic Buckingham's West Brom beat Preston 3–2 in another entertaining Final, with Ronnie Allen scoring twice. His second was a penalty to make it 2–2, a moment of such tension that cameras caught West Brom goalkeeper Jim Sanders unable to watch.

Blackpool had meanwhile been eliminated by Port Vale, who became the first third-tier club to reach the Semi-finals. York City

Opposite: West Brom goalkeeper Jimmy Sanders can't watch, as Ronnie Allen scores a crucial penalty against Preston North End in the 1954 Final.

Below: The injured Jimmy Meadows is helped from the pitch in the 1955 Final, a moment that would help Newcastle United beat his Manchester City, and influence the eventual introduction of substitutes as the idea of the "Wembley hoodoo" took hold.

matched that the following year, and even forced Newcastle to a Semi-final replay. The Magpies were never losing that game, though. They were the cup team of the era, as proven by becoming the first club to reach 10 Finals and matching Villa's record of six victories. Manchester City were beaten 3–1, with Milburn even joking before the game that Wembley was like home. He was so comfortable there he scored within 45 seconds, the quickest goal in a Final to date. City had been one of the first English teams to be influenced by Hungary. Manager Les McDowell used the budding Don Revie in the withdrawn forward role made famous by Nandor Hidegkuti in that 1953 win at Wembley. The approach wasn't so successful this time, and City were then scuttled by yet another Final injury, this time to Jimmy Meadows.

Another City injury in the following year's Final remains the most famous in FA Cup history. The Citizens became another club to return to win the cup after a defeat, but Bert Trautmann was afforded a truly unique legacy. The goalkeeper was already a compelling figure, given that he was a former German POW who had developed into a British hero just a decade after the war. His 1956 performance went above and beyond.

With the "Revie plan" working perfectly against Birmingham City, and with Manchester City 3–1 up, Trautmann dived at the feet of Peter Murphy to block an opportunity. That resulted in the forward's knee hitting Trautmann's neck. The pain was instant and obvious.

Manchester City fans sang Trautmann's name as he lay on the ground receiving treatment. He eventually got up, only to incredibly throw himself at the feet of Eddy Brown. Trautmann was in real pain again, to the point he couldn't see properly. The City players managed to shield his goal for the remaining minutes but he was in such discomfort when he picked up his medal that the Duke of Edinburgh told him to see a doctor.

Opposite top: Manchester City's Bert Trautmann saves at the feet of Birmingham City's Peter Murphy in the 1956 Final, in a moment that saw the goalkeeper unknowingly break his neck.

Opposite bottom left: Trautmann struggles with the pain. At one point, his vision went blurry.

Opposite bottom right: Manchester City captain Roy Paul hands the trophy to Trautmann at the club's victory reception at Cafe Royal. At this point, he still hadn't had his neck x-rayed.

Below: Fans heading up Wembley Way for the 1955 Final between Newcastle United and Manchester City, the famous twin towers in sight.

Trautmann didn't do that until after City's civic reception, when an X-ray revealed five broken vertebrae. He could very easily have died. Trautmann was nevertheless determined to play again and did so by Christmas. An OBE was soon added to his Footballer of the Year award. It was a remarkable story but the most affecting was still to come.

Manchester United's Busby Babes were by then bestriding English football, with the manager's evangelising embrace of youth and the newly created European Cup creating a new modernity in the game. The Babes were as illuminating as the floodlights they played under, especially the colossal Duncan Edwards, and came closer to the double than any side since Sunderland 1912–13. It was the last double winners, Aston Villa, who denied Sunderland back then, and it would be Villa who did the same in 1957, but only after another injury.

In the sixth minute, Peter McParland collided with United goalkeeper Ray Wood, accidentally breaking his cheekbone. Wood went out to the right with Jackie Blanchflower in goal. McParland went on to score twice. United could only muster one Tommy Taylor strike in a late siege.

Above: Aston Villa captain Johnny Dixon receives the cup from Queen Elizabeth II, after the 2–0 win over Manchester United in 1957.

Opposite: The lure of the cup, as spectators gather for a Fourth Round tie between Millwall and Newcastle United at The Den in 1956–57.

1956–57
ASTON VILLA 2–1 MANCHESTER UNITED
VENUE: **WEMBLEY STADIUM**
ATTENDANCE: **100,000**

1957–58
BOLTON WANDERERS 2–0 MANCHESTER UNITED
VENUE: **WEMBLEY STADIUM**
ATTENDANCE: **100,000**

The series of Final injuries led to a debate over allowing substitutions, something Busby had long advocated. It was one of many differences he had with football's authorities, among them his team's European adventures. The Football League made it clear they would not make allowances for United's foreign trips, which created pressure to get back home as quickly as possible after every away game.

This led to tragedy on the way back from a European Cup Quarter-final victory over Red Star Belgrade. On 6 February 1958, United's plane attempted to make a third take-off from the icy Munich-Riem airport, only to career off the runway. Eight of Busby's great young team lost their lives: Geoff Bent, Roger Byrne, Eddie Colman, Mark Jones, David Pegg, Tommy Taylor, Billy Whelan and – weeks later – Duncan Edwards. Six had played in the 1957 Final. Jackie Blanchflower and Johnny Berry would never play again. A further 15 passengers died, including Frank Swift. Busby suffered grave injuries.

The club itself looked close to going under but there was a solemn will to keep going. The first game back was just 13 days later, the Fifth Round FA Cup match at home to Sheffield Wednesday. That Wednesday evening was one of the most emotionally charged fixtures football had experienced. The match programme featured a starkly poignant image on the line-up page, with blank spaces where the players' names should have been, a heartbreaking illustration of what had been lost.

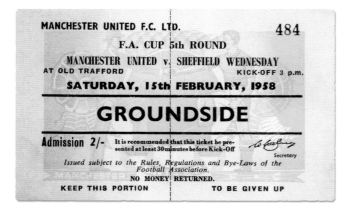

Jimmy Murphy, Busby's assistant, was now in charge and picked a team of reserves, youth players, new signings and two survivors – Harry Gregg and Bill Foulkes. The club just had to keep going. It was the only way. The response as United won 3–0 was an outpouring of support, as thousands stood outside.

The cup run that followed became about something far greater than football. It was about spirit and determination. United's subsequent fixtures became emotional events, almost carrying the players on a wave, as they in turn carried the hopes of a country.

Opposite top left: Bill Foulkes, a survivor of the Munich Air Disaster, captains Manchester United for their FA Cup Fifth Round tie against Sheffield Wednesday at Old Trafford just nine days after the tragedy. A spirit of perseverance ran through the club.

Opposite top right: A ticket for the match, on 15 February 1958, which was United's first after Munich.

Opposite bottom: Matt Busby is helped back to the dressing room after the 1958 Final, as his Manchester United lost to Bolton Wanderers, in what was an emotional first public appearance after Munich. Busby himself had been administered the last rites, twice.

Below: Bolton Wanderers' Nat Lofthouse, who had scored both goals in the 2–0 win over Manchester United, hands the FA Cup to manager Bill Ridding after the 1958 Final.

"I EXTEND MY BEST WISHES TO EVERYONE."

- MATT BUSBY -

United played Bolton in the Final, who again found themselves on the other side of a national story. This time, though, the result was different. It was a game too far for United. As Foulkes was walking out at Wembley, he recalled the memory of the previous season, when he and his friends were "all together". He was then struck by the sight of Busby, walking on a cane, having just returned from his Munich hospital bed. No one expected him to be there. Busby had broken down when trying to give a talk to the team a few days before. It was remarkable perseverance, that was to herald the hope to come. But on the day, there was only hard reality. Lofthouse scored both goals in a 2–0 Bolton win, with the second a barge on Gregg. No allowances had been made. A certain innocence had gone. The FA Cup's golden age was over. A resolve remained, as personified by Busby.

BROADCASTING THE FA CUP

There is nothing like going to a cup tie live, but broadcasting has also given the cup something very special. It has played a huge part in making the competition the distinctive event it is today. For decades, the only live football you were guaranteed to see on English TV was The FA Cup Final, and the same applied to hearing it on the radio before that. The Final's rare ability to reach a mass audience meant it was the fixture that entranced so many people, while the very fact it was on television afforded it a unique glamour.

Many FA Cup heroes have talked about how their first days kicking a ball as children were inspired by television images of the Final, as they looked to recreate what they saw. The relationship, of course, went much further than that. Television deepened the mythology of the competition. When you ask people what their FA Cup Final memories are, many will cite the long build-up on BBC or ITV, the excitement ratcheting up as the main event drew closer. The little segments, like the captains introducing their team, added to the appreciation of the day and its characters.

As much as anything, though, commentary has made so many FA Cup moments. Even for those who attended some of the most famous games, the replaying of exhilarating images means the television coverage becomes part of the memory. The lines that accompanied such pictures are part of the lore. Paul Gascoigne's goal against Arsenal doesn't feel fully Paul Gascoigne's goal against Arsenal without Barry Davies' commentary. There are so many that are similar.

"Is Gascoigne going to have a crack? He is, you know!"

"And Lorimer makes it one each… no! Astonishing!"

"And Smith must score…"

The first-ever broadcasts naturally carried a similar sense of wonder. The first Final afforded that privilege was Cardiff City's 1927 victory over Arsenal, live commentary of which was aired on BBC Radio. The Football League for a long time felt that such broadcasts would detract from attendances, which meant the cup occupied that unique place in the national consciousness. The Final became "event" radio and television before the concept even existed, reflecting how The FA Cup inevitably influenced the history of broadcasting, too.

The 1938 Final between Preston North End and Huddersfield Town was the first on TV, even though there were only 10,000 sets in the country at the time, with the broadcast of the 1946–47 Fifth Round tie between Charlton Athletic and Blackburn Rovers offering a pointer for earlier rounds.

Arsenal's victory over Liverpool in the 1950 Final attracted one million viewers in the two areas covered, London and Birmingham, but it was the 1953 match that was the first to receive a truly mass audience for a sporting event. This was due to a rush on sets with the forthcoming coronation of Queen Elizabeth II, and it proved so popular that it became a fixture. From there, the coverage around the Final became almost as big as the Final itself. The buzz of TV naturally spread into earlier rounds as well, and the very arrival of cameras at lower-league grounds fed into the atmosphere, and the idea an upset might be possible.

Many trappings and traditions developed, from score captions in the 1959 Final – Kenneth Wolstenholme apologising for the use of "Notts Forest" rather than "Nottingham Forest" – to the television build-up beginning before 11am by 1972.

Those involved learned to use it to their advantage, too. Before the 1974 Final, Liverpool's Bill Shankly and Newcastle United's Joe Harvey were interviewed on air, Shankly being overheard conspicuously saying: "Joe's a bag of nerves, isn't he?"

Teams have to get used to the stage they're on now. The FA Cup is shown in over 200 countries, on multiple broadcasters, to a final audience of more than 500 million people. It has certainly come a long way, by being beamed right around the world.

Opposite top left: BBC broadcaster David Coleman interviewing Wolverhampton Wanderers' FA Cup winning captain Bill Slater after the 1960 Final victory over Blackburn Rovers.

Opposite top right: Commentator John Motson, who became another fixture of The FA Cup, shows off his notes on every individual player at the 2000 Final.

Opposite bottom: BT Sport at Damson Park for The FA Cup Second Round match between Solihull Moors and Rotherham United in 2019.

CHAPTER EIGHT

THE RISE OF THE MANAGER

1959–1972

AT THE HEIGHT OF THE 1960S, THE FA CUP WAS SEEN AS THE PINNACLE OF THE CLUB GAME. THE STAR WHO MOST DEFINED THE ERA, GEORGE BEST, DESIRED IT EVEN MORE THAN THE LEAGUE TITLE. BILLY BREMNER, THE LEEDS UNITED STALWART WHO WON A SERIES OF TROPHIES IN THE ERA, SAID HE'D "SWAP THE LOT" FOR AN FA CUP MEDAL.

The two domestic competitions were seen as equal achievements, with the only difference being in the skills they tested. The title measured the ability to sustain a level of quality over a full season, but you could lose your biggest games and still win it. The cup was about rising to the day, and you couldn't afford to lose at all.

Part of the glory that came with The FA Cup was also because it offered the greatest day out in the sporting calendar, and a fixture that was always broadcast live to the nation. The Final was appointment television, affording it an appeal and glamour to go with its prestige.

If the league was a marathon, the cup could almost be a heptathlon: a series of different events, each offering a different challenge. This is perhaps why there wasn't much crossover between league and cup champions for most of English football history. If you split The FA Cup's annals into decades, for example, only two winners from the 1920s also won the title over that period. In the

1950s, only one did. That was despite six different clubs becoming league champions during that golden age.

This distinction changed in the 1960s. Seven of the decade's FA Cup winners also claimed the league title, a return not matched until the big-club dominance of the new millennium. Only Tottenham Hotspur accounted for more than one of those cup victories, winning three. There was a particular sense of achievement and symbolism around Bill Nicholson's great Spurs side becoming the first double winners of the twentieth century, in 1961, a feat then seen as impossible. Rivals Arsenal followed them by winning the league and FA Cup in 1971. You might even call this the age of champions. Aside from those 1960s title-winners, Wolves closed their glory era under Stan Cullis with an FA Cup, before West Ham United's first victory set off a famous sequence of triumph for Bobby Moore. England's most cherished captain won three different trophies at Wembley in successive seasons, culminating in the 1966 World Cup.

If some of this seems to contradict the famous democracy of the cup, it actually points to the greater egalitarianism of English football at the time. No club retained the league title across this period, while eight different clubs became league champions throughout the 1960s.

The FA Cup similarly offered a breadth of winners, each of whom took something different from their triumph. For teams like Manchester United, it was a start. For teams like Leeds United, it was a crowning moment. This might even have been the point when English football achieved a perfect competitive balance, which coincided with the abolition of the maximum wage for footballers.

Just as the 1960s brought a cultural revolution in society, they brought a modernity and evolution to football, as The FA Cup reached its centenary in 1972. Mass communication and floodlights fostered more competitions. England saw the creation of the League Cup. Continental football saw the European Cup and Fairs Cup complemented by the European Championship and Cup Winners' Cup. This expansion and diversification of the game helped spread more ideas, which saw football become more sophisticated, if also more systemic. This was showcased in the 1965 Final, as a modern four-man back line became common

and goal returns fell. Much of this also came down to the most influential factor of the era: the rise of the modern manager.

English football was populated by inspirational visionaries, many of whom had lit up the cup already as players. Matt Busby led a generation of coaches that included Bill Nicholson (Tottenham), Bill Shankly (Liverpool), Don Revie (Leeds United), Harry Catterick (Everton), Ron Greenwood (West Ham United), Joe Mercer and Malcolm Allison (both Manchester City).

The 1958–59 season almost represented an intermission between an age of stars and an age of champions, since its Final featured neither. It did include a semi-famous name in its line-up, however. Roy Dwight's goal set Nottingham Forest on the way to a 2–1 win over Luton Town and their second FA Cup, in the process also

Above: Roy Dwight scores Nottingham Forest's first goal of the 2–1 win over Luton Town in the 1959 Final. He would later go off injured, but that meant his side became the first with ten men to win the showpiece.

Opposite: A series of programmes from FA Cup Finals, a commemoration of the day that has become part of its traditions, as well as a collector's item.

Previous pages: Manchester United's George Best celebrates the first of his six goals against Northampton in the 1970 Fifth Round.

1958–59
NOTTINGHAM FOREST **2–1** LUTON TOWN
VENUE: **WEMBLEY STADIUM**
ATTENDANCE: **100,000**

1959–60
WOLVERHAMPTON WANDERERS **3–0** BLACKBURN ROVERS
VENUE: **WEMBLEY STADIUM**
ATTENDANCE: **100,000**

1960–61
TOTTENHAM HOTSPUR **2–0** LEICESTER CITY
VENUE: **WEMBLEY STADIUM**
ATTENDANCE: **100,000**

becoming the first team to win it with ten men, after Dwight then broke his leg in the 30th minute. Dwight was the cousin of Reg Dwight, better known as Elton John. The pop star would appear at the Final himself 25 years later, as chairman of Watford.

The Wembley hoodoo had by now gone way beyond a quirk to a cause of significant discussion, particularly after what happened the following season. Blackburn Rovers' Dave Whelan suffered a broken leg against Wolves that ended his career. Whelan would return to Wembley as a club chairman himself in 2013, with Wigan Athletic, but this was the worst moment of a miserable afternoon for his club at the time. Blackburn's preparation had already been disrupted by Derek Dougan deciding this was the day to hand in a transfer request.

Despite such advantages, as well as the fact they were second in the league and Blackburn were 17th, Wolves' manager Stan Cullis took nothing for granted. He had been part of the team that had lost to Portsmouth in 1939, at a time when Wolves were overwhelming favourites. Wolves consequently harnessed all their professionalism from successive titles in 1958 and 1959 to easily win 3–0. Norman Deeley, who Whelan had been marking, scored twice. It would have been a hat-trick had Mick McGrath not beaten him to the first effort, only to direct the ball into his own net.

It was an easy win, but not an entertaining one. Cullis' direct football had made Wolves an unpopular side. This 1960 showpiece actually became known as "The Dustbin Final" because of the rubbish pelted at the players after the game. There would have been considerable disgruntlement if a team considered as forgettable as Wolves had secured the immortal feat of the double.

Opposite top: Anguish on the face of Blackburn Rovers' Mick McGrath, right, as he diverts the ball into his own net in the 1960 Final defeat to Wolverhampton Wanderers. Teammates Dave Whelan and goalkeeper Harry Leyland can only look on, as Wolves' Norman Deeley looks to follow up. The moment denied Deeley a hat-trick.

Opposite bottom: Dave Whelan is stretchered off with a broken leg during the 1960 Final, as his manager Dally Duncan holds his hand to try and distract him from the pain.

Right: Tottenham Hotspur's great captain Danny Blanchflower holds up The FA Cup after becoming the first 20th-century team to win the double, in 1961. He is chaired by teammates (left to right) Cliff Jones, Bill Brown, Peter Baker, Terry Dyson, Les Allen, Bobby Smith and John White.

None of this could be said of the side that eventually managed that gold-standard achievement. Tottenham Hotspur in 1960–61 remain one of the most beloved teams of all time. They illuminated stadiums and lit the way for a new era. This really was "the glory game" as articulated by Danny Blanchflower, his side delivered goal after goal. Spurs scored a total of 136 in 49 games that season, with 21 coming in their seven cup fixtures.

Notice had been given in the previous season's Fourth Round, when Spurs pulverised Crewe Alexandra 13–2. That game featured three hat-tricks, with Cliff Jones scoring three, Bobby Smith four and Les Allen five.

It was one of football's little ironies that despite masterminding this joyous side, Nicholson was quite a dour man, but beneath that exterior he had supreme judgement that facilitated a great team spirit and devastatingly beautiful football. Spurs won 22 of their first 25 games to race clear at the top of the table and raise excited talk that "the impossible double" might finally be on. Their comfortable lead in the league meant they could divert all their energy to the cup in a way no one had really been able to do before. Eight sides since Aston Villa in 1896–97 had at least come close to the double. Three of them had won the league but lost the cup Final: Newcastle United in 1905, Sunderland in 1913 and Manchester United in 1957. Another five had won the cup but finished second in the league: Manchester City in 1904, Aston

1961–62
TOTTENHAM HOTSPUR **3–1** BURNLEY
VENUE: **WEMBLEY STADIUM**
ATTENDANCE: **100,000**

Villa in 1913, Manchester United in 1948, West Brom in 1954 and Wolves in 1960.

It was Tottenham who had beaten Wolves late in the season to deny them that 1960 title, and Nicholson's side defeated 1960 champions Burnley 3–0 in the 1961 FA Cup Semi-final. Their credentials couldn't be greater. The only doubt was their recent history. Three Semi-final defeats since the war had cast Spurs as nearly men. Instead they beat a club, Leicester City, who would take on that mantle themselves. This was to be the first of three Final defeats in the space of nine years for the Foxes, making it four overall after 1949.

In 1961, Spurs were simply on another level. Leicester manager Matt Gillies shocked his team by dropping striker Ken Leek for the 21-year-old Hugh McIlmoyle, apparently over a disciplinary issue. They weren't themselves, and soon weren't a full team as right-back Len Chalmers became the latest player injured at Wembley. Spurs didn't even need to be at their best to cruise to victory. Smith scored after 66 minutes and Terry Dyson after 75.

Spurs had, as in their previous two FA Cup victories, won in a year ending in a "one", but this time finished with two trophies. They could even have done a "double double" in 1962, but going for the treble of league, FA Cup and European Cup that year probably cost them. The effort required to reach the European Cup Semi-finals, only to be narrowly beaten by Eusebio's Benfica, saw Spurs slip to third in the league. The title was surprisingly won by Alf Ramsey's Ipswich Town, who had been knocked out of the cup by Norwich City in their first-ever derby in the competition. Spurs' 1962 showpiece against Harry Potts' Burnley was consequently to be a meeting of second against third and was dubbed "the Chessboard Final" due to the high technical level of both sides. Spurs, by then, had become an even better team with the signing of the peerless Jimmy Greaves from AC Milan for £99,999. Nicholson set that price to spare Greaves the pressure of being a six-figure player, but he need not have worried.

With a rate just shy of a goal a game that season, Greaves was so confident that he told the Spurs dressing room he would score in the

Opposite: Burnley's Harry Potts, left, and Tottenham Hotspur's Bill Nicholson lead out their teams ahead of the 1962 Final.

Below: Cliff Jones and Jimmy Greaves parade The FA Cup after Tottenham's win over Burnley in 1962, as they won it for the second successive year, going close to a "double double".

1962–63
MANCHESTER UNITED **3–1** LEICESTER CITY
VENUE: **WEMBLEY STADIUM**
ATTENDANCE: **100,000**

Final after just four minutes. He did so after three. Although Jimmy Robson equalised shortly after half-time with Wembley's 100th Final goal, Spurs just upped the ante. White scored within a minute. Blanchflower then ensured they retained the cup with a late penalty, confirming a place in the following season's Cup Winners' Cup, which they won. That saw Spurs become the first English club to win a European trophy. They then cemented themselves as England's ultimate cup team of the decade, winning a third FA Cup in 1966–67. That year's Final was the first between two London clubs since the gentleman amateur era. A vibrant Chelsea were beaten 2–1. Jimmy Roberston and Frank Saul scored the goals.

The freedom with which Spurs played on the pitch reflected the freedom footballers now enjoyed off it. The early 1960s had brought the end of the maximum wage and the notorious retain-and-transfer system, which allowed clubs to keep players' registrations even after their contracts ran out. This revolutionary shift was initiated by George Eastham's frustration as he attempted to force a move from Newcastle to Arsenal, a dispute that eventually went through the High Court.

The consequences of this decision would transform the game. Players like George Best were able to become stars. Bigger, well-funded clubs could build better teams. The driven Busby had been

constructing a new side in the aftermath of the Munich tragedy, but it hadn't yet come together. His Manchester United were a frustratingly erratic team that came close to relegation in 1962–63.

The cup offered a new spark of life for them that season, however. Like so many other teams before them, United felt released by their cup run, despite a general frustration across the game as that season's icy "big freeze" caused one of the greatest-ever disruptions to the footballing calendar. The FA Cup Third Round took 66 days to complete, with only three of its 32 fixtures played on the scheduled date. One of those was a repeat of the previous year's Final, although Spurs were this time beaten 3–0 by Burnley on a frozen White Hart Lane pitch. United didn't play their Third Round game against Huddersfield Town until 4 March. That forced the Final back by three weeks, by which time the returning Leicester were clear favourites. The Foxes had finished fourth, in contrast to United's 19th.

Above: The Manchester United team line up with manager Matt Busby as they returned to The FA Cup Final in 1963, five years after the Munich Air Disaster.

Above top right: A victorious Bobby Charlton, a survivor of Munich, shows off his FA Cup winner's medal after Manchester United beat Leicester City.

Opposite: A Tottenham Hotspur fan adorned with rosettes and a bobble hat helps sweep snow off the lines ahead of The FA Cup defeat to Burnley during the "big freeze" of 1962–63. The Third Round took 66 days to complete due to postponements from the weather.

"THE PITCH HAD PARTLY FROZEN OVER AGAIN COME THREE O'CLOCK, ESPECIALLY THE END UNDER THE SHADOW OF THE TOWERING DOUBLE-DECKER STAND."

– GORDON BANKS –

1963–64
WEST HAM UNITED **3–2** PRESTON NORTH END
VENUE: **WEMBLEY STADIUM**
ATTENDANCE: **100,000**

Free of relegation pressure, though, Busby's side started to reveal their true quality. Denis Law continued the superb form that had helped save United's First Division status, scoring after 29 minutes. David Herd then hit twice to secure the club's first trophy since the Munich disaster. Many involved believed it was the most important cup win in the club's history. It was certainly a crucial turning point, as well as a tribute to those who'd died just five years prior. Busby's next great United team had started a sequence that would take them to a European Cup win, 10 years after Munich. That triumph was greatly influenced by the team's final piece of the puzzle. In the summer of 1963, a 17-year-old George Best was promoted to the first team.

Best would bewitch English football, but was himself entranced by The FA Cup. He felt he should have won it in 1964, when hubris may have cost United. A week before their Semi-final with West Ham, and with Best, Law and Bobby Charlton rested, United beat Ron Greenwood's Hammers side 2–0 in the league. After the game, United goalkeeper David Gaskell told Bobby Moore: "Don't bother turning up next week." The West Ham captain of course told his teammates. They were fired up on a mucky day at Hillsborough, and won 3–1. One goal came from a Moore pass to Geoff Hurst. West Ham had made their first Final since 1923.

It had been a season with a few surprises. Non-league Bedford Town knocked out Second Division Newcastle United. Two Fourth Division clubs beat top-tier opposition, Aldershot Town eliminating Villa, and

Above: The Oxford United team celebrate in the dressing room after shocking Blackburn Rovers in the Fifth Round of the 1963–64 season.

Opposite: West Ham United captain Bobby Moore holds up The FA Cup after the club's first victory in the Final, over Preston North End in 1964.

1964–65
LIVERPOOL   2–1   LEEDS UNITED
AET
VENUE: **WEMBLEY STADIUM**
ATTENDANCE: **100,000**

Oxford United doing the same to Blackburn. There was no upset in the Final, though, despite Second Division Preston North End making it very difficult for West Ham. Greenwood's side came back from 1–0 and 2–1 down to win 3–2 thanks to Ronnie Boyce's last-minute winner. When Moore went up to receive the trophy from the Queen, he first wiped his hands on his shirt. That, like his pass for Hurst, would be seen again two years later, this time at the World Cup Final.

The FA Cup's true meaning could again be seen, in the huge crowds in East London as West Ham celebrated their first-ever trophy. A similar scene was played out on Merseyside the next season. Liverpool had won a series of leagues by then, including the 1963–64 title, but never the cup. Superstitions had even grown about why the club would never lift it.

That was finally rectified in 1965. In an illustration of the way the league, cup and big clubs had become increasingly intertwined, Liverpool beat Leeds 2–1 in the Final, with Leeds having beaten Manchester United in the Semi-final. Busby's team meanwhile beat both of them to the 1964–65 league.

The tension in that Manchester United–Leeds United Semi-final created one of the most bad-tempered matches the cup had seen. Bremner eventually settled the replay. Don Revie's team were still an inexperienced side but one with a growing reputation. They were already known as "Dirty Leeds", irritating the manager. Early on in the Final that followed, captain Bobby Collins went in on Liverpool's Gerry Byrne. The Liverpool player dislocated his collarbone, and was evidently in immense pain. Remarkably, he persevered.

Liverpool were the better team, but it had been a tight game, really only notable for the fact that Leeds' Albert Johanneson became the first black player to appear in a Final. It then became the first since 1947 to go to extra time, at which point both sides sprang to life. Byrne, of all people, set up Roger Hunt for Liverpool's opening goal. Leeds responded with a half-volley from Bremner before Liverpool raised their game again. Ian St John scored one of Wembley's most distinctive goals with a twisting header.

So Liverpool finally lifted the cup. Wembley was buoyed by renditions of 'You'll Never Walk Alone'. Such was the sense of deliverance that it had the feeling of a religious experience. "I took off my coat and went to our fans because they got the cup for the first time," Shankly wrote in his autobiography. "Grown men were crying and it was the greatest feeling any human being could have to see what we had done."

Revie's post-Final speech was resilient rather than religious. A remarkable 60,000 people had come out to greet Leeds on their return north after they had finished second in both major competitions. It had been the best season in the club's history and a mark of Revie's managerial ability. Leeds had been 19th in the Second Division just three seasons earlier. "To be a big club we have to take setbacks and carry on," Revie said. Leeds would take a lot of knocks over the next few years but they always kept going. That Final was their sixth game in 15 days, the type of fixture pile-up that was to be a feature of the next decade.

Leeds suffered from the unfortunate timing of reaching their peak just as the dense, modern football calendar was created, but before the advent of large squads with the ability to rotate. Their brilliance saw them progress deep into multiple competitions each season, but frequently they ran out of time as much as legs, with a packed schedule of late-season fixtures often proving their undoing. Of the 43 major competitions they entered from their 1964 promotion to the 1975 European Cup Final, Leeds won six, had 11 runners-up finishes and reached a further four Semi-finals. They similarly never finished lower than fourth in the league, other than in that final season. They were very much the team to beat.

"TO BE A BIG CLUB WE HAVE TO TAKE SETBACKS AND CARRY ON."

- DON REVIE -

Top left: Ron Greenwood holds a covered FA Cup, that had been won by his West Ham United team the previous Saturday, as he waits for a train on the London Underground in 1964.

Opposite top: Two managers who typified the visionary figureheads of the era, Liverpool's Bill Shankly on the left and Leeds United's Don Revie with his head in his hands, watch their sides play the 1965 Final.

Opposite bottom: Liverpool's Ian St John twists in mid-air to head in the winner in extra time of the 1965 Final, as the club won their first ever FA Cup.

1965–66
EVERTON **3–2** SHEFFIELD WEDNESDAY
VENUE: **WEMBLEY STADIUM**
ATTENDANCE: **100,000**

Of the trophies Leeds did win, The FA Cup eluded them the longest. The wait was all the more agonising as they kept getting so close. The 1965–66 season ended in a rare Fourth Round exit for Leeds, as Everton responded to Liverpool's victory with success of their own. That 1966 showpiece naturally became known as Wembley's "other final", due to the World Cup that same summer. It would also display the competition's capacity for unexpected heroes.

Called the "Millionairos" due to their expensive signings, Everton had built title-winning sides in 1963 and 1970 under Harry Catterick. Despite that, the star of 1966 was the unheralded Mike Trebilcock. Signed from Plymouth that same season and quickly sold on to Portsmouth after only a handful of appearances, Trebilcock was so little-known he didn't even appear in the Final programme. That soon changed. Trebilcock

scored twice, as Everton came back from 2–0 down against Sheffield Wednesday to win 3–2. Catterick had only picked him over the recently injured Fred Pickering because he wouldn't risk going down to ten men. This, finally, was to be the last FA Cup season without substitutes.

Trebilcock's equaliser brought the so-called "first hooligan," as Eddie Cavanagh ran onto the pitch in jubilation. As a former Everton reserve, who had even played with captain Brian Labone, Cavanagh evaded a number of policemen in a moment that has entered FA Cup lore. It also created another famous image, as Labone put on one of the dropped police helmets. Cavanagh was eventually ejected but claimed he got back in to see Derek Temple's winner.

Everton's next Final, in 1968, was as vibrant in a different way. It was the first to be televised in colour. That meant West Brom's 1–0

Opposite: Liverpool players celebrate winning their first FA Cup, after beating Leeds United 2–1 in the 1965 Final.

Below: Police chase Everton supporter Eddie Kavanagh across the pitch after his team scored the equaliser to make it 2–2 from 2–0 down in the 1966 Final against Sheffield Wednesday. Kavanagh, a former Everton reserve, claimed he got back in to watch his club's eventual winning goal.

victory was seen in all its glory, with Jeff Astle ensuring he'd scored in every round. The Baggies were helped by the fresh legs of Dennis Clarke, who became the Final's first sub, replacing John Kaye.

Subs meant the "Wembley hoodoo" didn't have the same effect, but Leicester's bad luck continued. In 1969, they became the most frequent finalists never to win the cup, losing 1–0 to Manchester City through a Neil Young goal. Worse, they became only the second team to reach the Final and get relegated in the same season, after City themselves in 1926. Joe Mercer and the charismatic Malcolm Allison had a similar effect on City as Revie had at Leeds, taking them up from the Second Division to win the 1968 title, that year's FA Cup and the 1969–70 Cup Winners Cup.

Football's oldest competition was still eluding England's new power, though. Leeds were again denied in the 1970 Final, a defeat made worse by the fact that it came from Chelsea, a team with whom they'd developed a ferocious rivalry. The 1970 showdown was the last of three epic ties between the clubs over five seasons, each stoking the ferocity further, and each won by Chelsea. It was no coincidence that this was the first Final to go to a replay since 1912, with that decider at Old Trafford the only Final played outside Wembley between 1923 and 2000.

The tie is still viewed as one of the most entertaining in FA Cup history. It featured seven goals over three hours of frenetic

1966–67
TOTTENHAM HOTSPUR 2–1 CHELSEA
VENUE: **WEMBLEY STADIUM**
ATTENDANCE: **100,000**

1967–68
WEST BROMWICH ALBION 1–0 EVERTON
AET
VENUE: **WEMBLEY STADIUM**
ATTENDANCE: **100,000**

1968–69
MANCHESTER CITY 1–0 LEICESTER CITY
VENUE: **WEMBLEY STADIUM**
ATTENDANCE: **100,000**

football, including some dramatic Final moments. The chaos wasn't helped by the fact the pitch was still suffering from the staging of the Royal International Horse Show in successive summers before. Jack Charlton said it was the first time he'd ever seen mud there. It appeared that Leeds had overcome the

Opposite: West Brom fans hold distinctive club dolls during their team's 1–0 win over Everton in the 1968 Final.

Below: After beating Chelsea in the 1967 Final, Tottenham Hotspur players (left to right) Terry Venables, Alan Mullery, Dave Mackay and Jimmy Robertson celebrate victory.

"SOME OF OUR GAMES WERE A BIT PHYSICAL TO SAY THE LEAST."

- NORMAN HUNTER -

conditions when Mick Jones put them 2–1 up after 84 minutes, only for Ian Hutchison to equalise two minutes later.

The teams had to wait 18 days for the replay, by which point Chelsea had reflected on a few lessons. Eddie Gray had been brilliant in the first game, so Ron "Chopper" Harris immediately went in hard on him in the opening minutes of the second. It set off a series of bad challenges and retributions that saw Hutchison and Charlton exchange punches and Eddie McCreadie's studs meet Bremner's face. Incredibly, there wasn't a single booking. There was even some good football scattered among the combat. Jones opened the scoring before Peter Osgood's superb diving header levelled it

with just 12 minutes to go, making him the last player to date to score in every round. The decisive goal came from David Webb, in the 104th minute. It was the first time Chelsea had been ahead and ensured that they would lift The FA Cup for the first time. Charlton and Bremner both said it was the most upset they'd been after a game.

At least they weren't bored, as seemed to be the case with everyone involved in the newly introduced third-place play-off. Only 15,000 spectators turned up at Highbury to watch Manchester United beat Watford, the experiment lasting a mere four seasons.

1969–70
CHELSEA 2–2 LEEDS UNITED
AET
VENUE: **WEMBLEY STADIUM**
ATTENDANCE: **100,000**

1969–70 (REPLAY)
CHELSEA 2–1 LEEDS UNITED
AET
VENUE: **OLD TRAFFORD**
ATTENDANCE: **62,078**

Above: Chelsea players embrace Peter Osgood after he scores the equalising goal in the 1970 FA Cup Final replay against Leeds United at Old Trafford.

Opposite: Chelsea goalkeeper Peter Bonetti is helped off the field by a trainer after receiving an injury in the 1970 FA Cup Final replay, watched by captain Ron "Chopper" Harris.

Following pages: One of the game's most memorable celebrations and images, as Charlie George lies on the ground and holds his arms in the air after scoring the winning goal against Liverpool in the 1971 FA Cup Final, a strike that also secured the double.

> "I SCORED THE WINNER NOT JUST FOR THE CLUB BUT FOR THE FANS, BECAUSE I WAS ONE. JUST TO PLAY FOR THE CLUB WAS SPECIAL FOR ME."
>
> – CHARLIE GEORGE –

Left: Colchester United's Dave Simmons, far left, celebrating with teammates after scoring his side's third goal in the momentous victory over Leeds United in the 1970–71 Fifth Round. With Colchester lying in the Fourth Division, it was one of The FA Cup's greatest upsets.

Opposite: Billy Bremner lifts the trophy he wanted most, as Leeds United won their first FA Cup with victory over Arsenal in 1972.

Below: Eddie Kelly comes off the bench to inspire Arsenal in the 1971 Final against Liverpool, although his effort for the opening goal went off George Graham.

Leeds had to content themselves with more second places to come. They lost the 1970 league title to Everton and the 1971 title to Arsenal, meaning The Gunners won their historic double exactly ten years after Tottenham. Arsenal's FA Cup Final against Liverpool was their 64th match of the season, and it went the distance. Steve Heighway gave Liverpool the lead in extra time, but Arsenal manager Bertie Mee had crafted a resilient team. They had already come back from 2–0 down in the Semi-final against Stoke City to win the replay, and at one point in the league were seven points behind Leeds in the title race. Eddie Kelly almost became the first substitute to score in the Final, but future Arsenal manager George Graham got the final touch on the equaliser. Charlie George then offered one of the occasion's great goals, and great images, as he lay on the pitch with his arms raised after a superb winner. To add further edge to the fact they'd matched Spurs' double, Arsenal won the title at White Hart Lane with a 1–0 victory over their rivals.

Leeds finally had their moment the following season, exorcising their many FA Cup ghosts. Some of the players for returning finalists Arsenal even mentioned Leeds' series of failures in the build-up to the showpiece, which only steeled the United players' determination. It was a poor game, hardly befitting of

1970–71
ARSENAL 2–1 LIVERPOOL
AET
VENUE: WEMBLEY STADIUM
ATTENDANCE: 100,000

1971–72
LEEDS UNITED 1–0 ARSENAL
VENUE: WEMBLEY STADIUM
ATTENDANCE: 100,000

the competition's centenary (nine clubs that had competed in the first FA Cup were invited to enter, and flags representing all past winners formed an avenue for the players as they walked out at Wembley). But Leeds finally got their name on the roll of honour, as Arsenal were beaten 1–0 through an Allan Clarke goal.

The long-awaited FA Cup win meant so much that it was raucously celebrated, despite the team again narrowly missing out on the league title. For all that Leeds' standards had typified the age of champions, however, there was a moment in the previous season that signalled what was to come. Leeds, incredibly, had been eliminated by fourth-tier Colchester United in the Fifth Round. The age of the upset was about to begin.

FA CUP FINAL DAY

For so many FA Cup heroes, across so many different seasons, there has been one abiding memory of the Final – the wait to go out of the tunnel at Wembley. All of those who have spoken about it describe a scene that is suitably theatrical. The old Wembley tunnel was dark and quiet, with only the motivational shouts of some players breaking the silence. All that dramatically changed as they got to the entrance. They were hit by a wall of light and sound and colour.

All these players can remember the roar of the crowd, suddenly felt more acutely than at any other point in their careers. It is almost gladiatorial. That was when they knew they were in the game of their lives. The Final can be a paradoxical occasion: a deeply personal experience, played out in front of 80,000-plus fans in the stadium and hundreds of millions more watching from afar, all coming together for English football's national day. That is what The FA Cup Final is, as much as a contest to decide the destination of the trophy. It is a celebration of the country's game, with such a match the most fitting way to recognise that.

Like any national celebration, it is also a collection of traditions and rituals that have been built up over time. Many of these were first set out by former referee and FA secretary, Sir Stanley Rous. After refereeing the 1935 Final, he realised the need for a comprehensive guide for the day, which became known as *From Ball Boys to the King*.

The reconstruction of Wembley has altered some of those traditions, such as the architecture of the tunnel and the walk-out, but all the same feelings remain. There's the coach to the stadium, the awe in the dressing rooms and then the first pre-game steps on to the pitch. All this happens as fans steadily fill the ground from Wembley Way, meanwhile doing the same as everyone else and trying to size up the teams, assess who looks fit, who looks nervous.

Many players have described the final moments before the game as the longest of their careers. The time that the team left the dressing room was something Matt Busby believed had to be timed just right. Some managers felt that they'd said all they could by then, some felt the need for classic motivational speeches, but the last words were usually delivered before the rendition of 'Abide With Me', after which the players were signalled to go out, and prepare themselves for what followed.

Of the match itself, many have said that it can be too intense to really take in. No matter the outcome, however, the players on the pitch are writing themselves into the longest lineage in football. It's a profound feeling, to appear in an FA Cup Final – your name is there forever, etched into history.

The final whistle is when the day diverges, immediately represented by how one end of the ground empties out and the other is overcome with joy. The defeated team generally describe the moments after the final whistle as the most painful of their careers, but Bobby Moore didn't feel like that in 1975. He was content he'd again experienced the day.

For the victors, however, there is no sweeter feeling than soaking in the aftermath of a Wembley win. By then, the players are sharing the cup around, some drinking champagne out of it. The words of a winner like Busby to his Manchester United team appropriately do it justice: "The greatest thrill in soccer is playing at Wembley on cup Final day."

> ## "THE GREATEST THRILL IN SOCCER IS PLAYING AT WEMBLEY ON CUP FINAL DAY."
>
> - MATT BUSBY -

Opposite top: The 2019 Final between Manchester City and Watford gets off to a spectacular start at Wembley.

Opposite right: Manchester United and Leicester City players exit the Wembley tunnel to commence the 1963 FA Cup Final.

Opposite middle right: West Ham United players hold The FA Cup aloft after their 1–0 victory over Arsenal in the 1980 Final.

Opposite bottom right: Chelsea's Dennis Wise cracks open the champagne in the changing room following his side's FA Cup Final victory in 2000.

CHAPTER NINE

THE AGE OF THE UPSET

1973–1989

BEFORE COLCHESTER UNITED FACED LEEDS UNITED IN THE 1970–71 FA CUP FIFTH ROUND, MANAGER DICK GRAHAM REALISED HE NEEDED TO CHANGE HIS TEAM'S MINDSET. IT WOULD DO THEM NO GOOD TO DWELL ON THE SCALE OF THE TASK THAT FACED THEM.

"We must enjoy every minute of it," Graham enthused. "It's going to be something you remember all your lives. No nerves, no tension. And you know what? I think we can win it." This was the attitude that infused most of The FA Cup's famous upsets, so many of them mirroring Colchester's 3–2 win over Leeds at Layer Road. It was far from the first giant-killing but it was the first of an era that stretched to the end of the 1980s, when the folklore of such tales was fully established. When people think of FA Cup upsets, they usually think of this period. It has been imprinted onto the national consciousness by so many memorable TV images.

This was the era when Hereford United, Blyth Spartans, Leatherhead, York City, Ronnie Radford, Chris Kelly, Jim Montgomery and Wimbledon – in two different ways – wrote themselves into FA Cup history. It was also when three different clubs from the Second Division lifted the trophy in the space of eight years. Sunderland, Southampton and West Ham United became the last of just seven sides to manage that feat. That flurry illustrates the spirit of opportunity. A total of seven clubs made their Final debuts, with three winning their first-ever major trophies.

Even the less-surprising victories offered sensations, such as Tommy Docherty's resignation from Manchester United, Arsenal's "five-minute Final" and Ricky Villa's winner for Tottenham Hotspur in 1981. The sporting purity of these moments stood out all the more amid the increasing commercialisation of the game. Clubs started wearing sponsored shirts, there was the first £1 million transfer and FA Cup games began to take place on Sundays. More than anything, though, two decades of broadcasting ensured the cup was the sporting television event of the age. Tens of millions of eyes focusing on the clubs involved only fostered the drama and grandeur of the games.

As to why and how an era dominated by champions gave way to one characterised by shocks, there are a few interlinked influences. This period neatly overlaps with Liverpool's first great dynasty, which was the first of its kind in English football. The club's "Boot Room" culture gave rise to a winning machine, lifting more trophies over a longer sweep of time than any English club had ever done.

The manner in which Liverpool managed those achievements, and the exacting standards which they set, were all the more effective because the league beneath them was so volatile. In the immediate period after the maximum wage was abolished there wasn't yet a substantial difference between the "big" clubs and the rest, as demonstrated by Manchester United's relegation in 1974, and Nottingham Forest getting promoted and immediately winning the league in 1978. So, when Liverpool were eliminated from The FA Cup, it left a vacuum.

Leeds, arguably Liverpool's predecessors as the most dominant team in the country but not as durable, fell victim two of the greatest upsets of the era. That 1971 elimination to Colchester has fair claim to be The FA Cup's most sensational result, up there with Walsall eliminating Arsenal in 1933. Unlike that historic giant-killing however, this time there were cameras present to record the upset. Jack Charlton would later remark that the realisation these moments would be replayed for years to come made the unexpected defeat all the worse.

Leeds were naturally in the midst of another fight on three fronts and would finish the season with victory in the Fairs Cup, but a close second to Arsenal in the league. Colchester, meanwhile, were languishing in the Fourth Division but had generated excitement by eliminating third-tier Rochdale in the previous round. Colchester's Layer Road was filled with 16,000 fans and the Leeds players were on edge. Even before kick-off, they were complaining about the wind, the grass and the uneven surface. Leeds had precisely the wrong attitude going in, while Graham had Colchester primed. He even said he would climb Colchester Castle if they won.

Graham's team would themselves scale the heights. At one point, Colchester were 3–0 up, sensing a vulnerability in Leeds from the off. After 18 minutes, Leeds committed the kind of simple mistake that sets these games up. Goalkeeper Gary Sprake came for a whipped cross that was too quick for him, allowing Ray Crawford to head Colchester ahead. After 28 minutes, the First Division side conceded the kind of freak goal that can convince teams it just isn't their day. Paul Reaney and Crawford went for a loose ball, only for both to fall to the ground. Crawford reacted

quickest, swinging his leg to squeeze the ball inside the post. Finally, there was a moment of uncertainty of the sort that can really unravel bigger sides, as Sprake and Reaney both hesitated on a ball, which Dave Simmons duly nodded in.

The prospect of a proper humiliation in terms of scoreline finally provoked a Leeds response, offering up another classic element of an upset: the nerve-shredding finish. Norman Hunter headed in and John Giles claimed a second, leaving Colchester with 15 minutes to hold out. Goalkeeper Graham Smith somehow held the ball when Mick Jones thundered a shot at goal from just yards out,

and Colchester had done it. Graham did as promised and climbed the castle.

The next season deepened the prospect that there was going to be a sensational FA Cup shock every year, to the delight of broadcasters. Hereford United's 2–1 win over Newcastle was almost as incredible as Colchester's victory, since they were a non-league club, but was more memorable given how telegenic it was.

Earlier in the 1971–72 FA Cup, Ted MacDougall had scored nine goals in Bournemouth's 11–0 First Round win over Margate, and there was talk Newcastle's Malcolm "Supermac" MacDonald would surpass that against Hereford. He later denied reports he'd said as much in the build-up. And it was a long build-up, as the first game was twice postponed due to rain. That alone created a feeling something was building. Hereford had already produced heroics

Above: Hereford fans rush to celebrate with Ronnie Radford, number 11, after his sensational late equaliser against Newcastle United in one of the most famous ever upsets, in 1972.

Previous pages: Tottenham Hotspur's Ricky Villa celebrates with Glenn Hoddle after his wonder goal wins the 1981 FA Cup Final replay, a 3–2 victory over Manchester City.

1972–73
SUNDERLAND 1–0 LEEDS UNITED
VENUE: WEMBLEY STADIUM
ATTENDANCE: 100,000

1973–74
LIVERPOOL 3–0 NEWCASTLE UNITED
VENUE: WEMBLEY STADIUM
ATTENDANCE: 100,000

in the less-remembered first game, taking a 1–0 lead at St James' Park and then coming back for a 2–2 draw. That air of uncertainty remained for the replay at Edgar Street, which was also postponed three times. It meant the fateful game eventually took place on the same day as the Fourth Round, and it still lashed down.

Not that that deterred the crowds, as Edgar Street seemed far busier than the official attendance figure of 14,313. Hereford's attitude was summed up by the display of right-back Roger Griffiths, a local, who played on despite an injury later revealed as a broken leg. His efforts looked to be in vain when MacDonald gave Newcastle the lead on 82 minutes. But the stage was only being set.

Just three minutes after MacDonald's goal, the ball was played back to Hereford's Ronnie Radford and bounced up on the mud about 30yd (27m) from goal. He swung his boot and sent the ball into the top corner. It remains one of the most memorable FA Cup goals ever, and produced brilliant cup scenes. The pitch was immediately invaded by jubilant youngsters in parkas, Radford in the middle with hands in the air. But Hereford still had more to give. Ricky George had been sent on moments before Radford's equaliser and, in extra time, was suddenly played in. The angle wasn't inviting but, as happened with Radford and in so many of these upsets, George just tried his luck. The ball found the corner. The crowd let themselves go.

Hereford had another brush with history in the next round as they were knocked out by West Ham and Geoff Hurst. It was quite a thing for non-league players to say they were undone by the boot that won the World Cup.

Another element of moments like Hereford's heroics is that they are contagious, making everyone else realise what's possible. A grander indication that this era was different arrived the following season, as Sunderland became the first Second Division club to win The FA Cup since West Brom in 1931. Leeds were again the Goliaths felled, this time in the Final, though they were far from the only top side that Sunderland beat. This was one of the great cup runs, as well as one of the great Finals. Bob Stokoe's side knocked out Manchester City and Arsenal en route to Wembley, with every win energising the city more. One local shipbuilders donated £2,000 to cover the team's costs. It was the most uplifting illustration of how the competition brought communities together, but Sunderland also charmed the whole nation. After the Semi-final win over Arsenal, their fans chanted Stokoe's name for 10 minutes. He finally appeared, in tears.

For the Final, this strength of feeling was revved up further by how reviled Leeds had become for their cynical reputation. Stokoe even attempted to play on this, as well as an enmity with Don Revie,

talking in a loaded manner about Leeds' "professionalism", and how Billy Bremner influenced referees.

Bremner had scored one of his customary Semi-final winners in beating Wolves, and Leeds were surely set to trample over Sunderland's dreams. United had so much quality to go with their cynicism, including a team full of internationals. Sunderland had none, and no team without at least one full cap had won the cup since Barnsley in 1912.

All of this made Stokoe's side see the Final as an occasion to enjoy. Leeds were on edge again, creating a thrillingly rare atmosphere of urgency to the game. They were determined to crush any idea of an upset, but that only made it more tense as Sunderland, and especially centre-back Dave Watson, responded with defiance. The game's momentum swept Sunderland into the lead on 32 minutes, as Ian Porterfield lashed the ball into the roof of the Leeds net.

The greatest images from this Final were still to come – and they weren't goals. Midway through the second half, Leeds seemed to get their break. Reaney lofted a fine ball for Trevor Cherry, who threw himself forward with a diving header. Goalkeeper Jimmy Montgomery met it with a brilliant two-handed stretch, only for the parry to go straight to Peter Lorimer. He would usually strike the ball so hard no goalkeeper had a chance to react. This time, Montgomery was already responding, swivelling to somehow touch the ball onto the crossbar and away. Few in the stadium could believe it. All of the commentators thought it was a goal. It was instead one of those moments that ingrains a sense of destiny – perhaps the finest save the Final had witnessed. Leeds knew that was it.

At the final whistle, Stokoe jumped up from the bench and ran across the pitch with his arms waving and coat flapping behind. It was the image Sunderland later chose for his statue. They were commemorating sporting immortality. "There is nothing like the cup," Stokoe later said.

There was to be no repeat of Sunderland's unlikely run the following year, as Liverpool claimed their only FA Cup of the decade. The Reds' 1974 victory was a landmark in English football history for a few reasons, most of all the retirement of the most charismatic of the 1960s' great managers.

Bill Shankly had been the patriarch who created the modern Liverpool but his successor, Bob Paisley, transformed the club in another way. They went from regular winners to relentless winners. From the summer of 1974 to 1990, Liverpool won ten league titles, four European Cups, one UEFA Cup, four League Cups and two FA Cups – an unprecedented run of success.

Much of this was naturally a direct continuation of the Shankly era. Six of the players that started the 1974 FA Cup Final against

Newcastle United also started the 1977 European Cup Final win over Borussia Mönchengladbach. It might have been eight except for injuries to Phil Thompson and John Toshack prior to the latter game. Kevin Keegan was the star in both finals and simply overran a nervous Newcastle.

The Liverpool win was all the more striking because Newcastle had been so dismissive of the Merseysiders in the build-up, but that was another feature of an era in which the theatre of The FA Cup was at its peak. In contrast to the media-trained blandness that often permeates contemporary interviews, many of the period's characters would speak their minds. Malcolm MacDonald had said Liverpool

Above: Liverpool manager Bill Shankly shakes hands with Princess Anne before the start of the 1974 FA Cup Final against Newcastle United. It was to be Shankly's last game as a manager.

Opposite: Sunderland manager Bob Stokoe smiles with his captain, Bobby Kerr, after the shock Final upset against Leeds United in 1973.

Right: The Stoke City coach arrives to protests at Bolton Wanderers' Burnden Park, for one of the first ever big matches held on a Sunday.

1974–75
WEST HAM UNITED 2–0 FULHAM
VENUE: **WEMBLEY STADIUM**
ATTENDANCE: **100,000**

were past it and too slow. It gave Shankly his easiest team talk. He called a meeting the day before the Final and – in classic style – pinned one of the MacDonald articles up on the wall. "There you go, boys… it's all been said."

Liverpool played all the football, Keegan scoring twice and Steve Heighway once in an effervescent 3–0 win. As the players were doing their lap of honour, they noticed Shankly was missing. He was already in the dressing room with a cup of tea, apparently deciding there and then nothing could surpass this, so it was time to retire.

Liverpool's victory had been both a reminder of past glories and a vision of the future, much like that FA Cup season as a whole. Leeds, about to win their last trophy under Revie with a league title, went out to second-tier Bristol City. QPR's Stan Bowles meanwhile showcased the magic of the era's famous mavericks with a floated last-minute free-kick against Coventry City in the Fifth Round. The 1973–74 Third Round featured the first FA Cup game on a Sunday, as Cambridge United drew 2–2 with Oldham Athletic. The Final

itself was meanwhile preceded by more pageantry, as Bruce Forsythe whipped up the Wembley crowd.

A more ominous sign of what was to come was a pitch invasion at St James' Park when Newcastle were 3–1 down to Nottingham Forest. The players were taken off for eight minutes, but referee Gordon Kew was determined to continue. The match had nevertheless changed, Newcastle winning 4–3. Forest lodged a complaint and, in an unprecedented decision, a rematch was ordered. Following a 0–0 draw, Newcastle eventually won a third game 1–0 but a bitterness lingered.

In the 1974–75 campaign, Liverpool were knocked out in the Fourth Round by Ipswich Town, sparking one of the most open editions of The FA Cup to date. Four non-league sides got to the same stage as Liverpool. One was the Isthmian League's Leatherhead, who were fired there by Chris Kelly. He scored the only goal to beat third-tier Brighton at the Goldstone Ground and then predicted

Opposite: Kevin Keegan on the ball during the 1974 FA Cup Final against Newcastle United. The Liverpool star scored twice in a brilliant 3–0 win for his side, and what proved a signature individual performance.

Below: Fulham's Bobby Moore plays the ball in the 1975 FA Cup Final, against his old club, West Ham United. Most of the intrigue around the game was about whether Moore could win one last major trophy, but it wasn't to be.

1975–76
SOUTHAMPTON 1–0 MANCHESTER UNITED
VENUE: **WEMBLEY STADIUM**
ATTENDANCE: **100,000**

Ultimately, it was a step too far, as Alan Taylor scored twice. West Ham became the last FA Cup winners to feature an entirely English squad, although a quintessentially English feature was missing. This was the only Final since 1926 that wasn't preceded by "Abide With Me", but there was so much outcry it was restored.

Both 1975 finalists were knocked out in the Third Round the following season, the first time that had happened since the Second World War. This openness prompted some infamous hubris from Manchester United manager Tommy Docherty, although he was far from alone. In one of the 1975–76 Semi-finals, defending league champions Derby County met Docherty's resurgent Manchester United, reborn after a quick promotion following their 1974 relegation. In the other, Second Division Southampton faced third-tier Crystal Palace, managed by the fedora-wearing Malcolm Allison.

"We're going to win the cup wearing this hat," Allison had stated with his usual bombast, but it was nothing like what Docherty said: "This is the first time a cup Final will be played at Hillsborough," Docherty crowed. "The other Semi-final is a bit of a joke, really."

It would set up quite a punchline. Both United and Southampton won their Semi-finals 2–0, which seemed to set up Docherty's side nicely for their first trophy since 1968. Southampton were aiming for their first major trophy ever, and were in their first FA Cup Final since 1900.

The disparity in the league position of the two finalists, however, belied their squad profiles. While United were quite callow, Southampton featured much more experience in Mick Channon, Peter Osgood and Jim McCalliog. Once again, the spirit of Sunderland prevailed. Bobby Stokes scored the only goal seven minutes from time in a 1–0 Southampton win. Docherty was embarrassed – but not deterred. He immediately told United players and fans they would win the cup the following year. This time he was correct, even dispatching Southampton along the way.

Manchester United were at this point the embodiment of another archetype of the era: the "great cup team". The term applied particularly well to United, Arsenal and Tottenham. All were entertaining, glamorous sides filled with stars, but entirely erratic. That meant they were good enough to rise to any occasion but just weren't consistent enough to regularly challenge Liverpool for the league. The trio exchanged a series of Finals, but weren't always successful. Each of them also suffered at least one big upset.

he'd do the same to Leicester City. That earned him the nickname of "Leatherhead Lip" but Kelly made good on his claim. He scored again as his team went 2–0 up, only to lose 3–2.

Wimbledon, of the Southern League, meanwhile gave notice of sensations to come. They became the first non-league team to win away at a top-tier club in over half a century, as Burnley were beaten 1–0. The goalscorer was Mickey Mahon, who had also been part of the Colchester team that had defeated Leeds. It was Leeds who would subsequently eliminate Wimbledon, but only after a John Giles shot had fortuitously deflected off Wimbledon goalkeeper Dave Bassett.

All of this led to one of the most democratic Finals in modern FA Cup history. West Ham, 13th in the First Division, faced Fulham, ninth in the second. Top quality was replaced by compelling storylines, as Hammers icon Bobby Moore had gone across London to underpin Fulham's run to their first Final. Much of the build-up focused on the potential of one last victory for the England legend, as well as former international teammate Alan Mullery, who were managed by Yeovil's 1949 hero, Alec Stock.

Above: Saints captain Peter Rodrigues holds The FA Cup aloft in 1976.

Opposite top: West Ham United fans celebrate on the Wembley pitch after their team's 2–0 win over Fulham in the 1975 Final.

Opposite bottom: Southampton's Peter Osgood lifts up Bobby Stokes, wearing number 11, as they celebrate the latter's shock match-winning goal in the 83rd minute of the 1976 Final against Manchester United.

"WE'RE GOING TO WIN THE CUP WERING THE CUP WEARING THIS HAT."

- MALCOLM ALLISON -

Manchester United's 1977 victory came at the expense of great rivals Liverpool, who were going for an unprecedented treble. Liverpool had learned to handle multifaceted campaigns in the way that Leeds before them hadn't, however their FA Cup Final strategy was still impacted. With the Merseysiders due to play Mönchengladbach in the European Cup Final four days after their meeting with United at Wembley, The FA announced that any replay couldn't take place until 33 days later. That prompted Paisley to go all out in order to try to win it on the day, in what he described as his "worst-ever tactical decision". A brilliant match worthy of the clubs' status swung on five manic minutes just after half-time. Liverpool's Jimmy Case levelled Stuart Pearce's opener before a Lou Macari shot spun off United midfielder Jimmy Greenhoff's chest and in.

A long-awaited FA Cup victory for United had denied their greatest rivals the treble. It was Docherty's first Final success, but the last meaningful act of his career. He was sacked six weeks later following revelations he was having an affair with physio Laurie Brown's wife, Mary. "I am the first manager to be sacked for falling in love," Docherty lamented.

United were involved in a more climactic "five-minute Final" two years later, although this time it was Arsenal who had the previous season's embarrassment to overcome. Terry Neill's Gunners team were beaten by 18th-place Ipswich Town – managed by Bobby Robson – in the 1978 showpiece. This was the year non-league Blyth Spartans enchanted the nation with a run to the Fifth Round, only suffering a narrow defeat to Wrexham. Ipswich's path had been tumultuous.

Above: Liverpool manager Bob Paisley and his Manchester United counterpart Tommy Docherty lead their teams out at the 1977 Final, with Liverpool fans seen in the background. It was to be Docherty's last game as United boss, due to a scandal over an affair with physio Laurie Brown's wife, Mary.

Opposite: Jimmy Nicholl, Jimmy Greenhoff and Alex Stepney celebrate winning The FA Cup after Manchester United's 2–1 victory over Liverpool, a result that secured the club's first major trophy since 1968 and denied Liverpool a treble.

1977–78
IPSWICH TOWN 1–0 ARSENAL
VENUE: **WEMBLEY STADIUM**
ATTENDANCE: **100,000**

1978–79
ARSENAL 3–2 MANCHESTER UNITED
VENUE: **WEMBLEY STADIUM**
ATTENDANCE: **100,000**

1979–80
WEST HAM UNITED 1–0 ARSENAL
VENUE: **WEMBLEY STADIUM**
ATTENDANCE: **100,000**

Their Sixth Round tie at Millwall had seen fights spilling onto the pitch and 30 arrests made. It also ended in a 6–1 win as referee Bill Gow insisted the game would be completed.

In the Final, local hero Roger Osborne failed to make it to the end of the match for Ipswich, but for a very innocent reason. He passed out due to "nervous exhaustion", after scoring the only goal of the game. In other words, Osborne was overcome with emotion. It was a deserved win for Ipswich, in what was their only poor league season of a fine decade under Robson.

Neill's Arsenal were more rousing than his predecessor Bertie Mee's, but also less reliable. This was signalled in the next two seasons. Arsenal became the first club to reach three successive Wembley Finals, but only won the most difficult of them. Brian Talbot and Frank Stapleton gave Arsenal a 2–0 lead over Dave Sexton's Manchester United in the 1979 Final, which was how it stayed until the 86th minute. Supporters were already leaving when Gordon McQueen pulled one back and then Sammy McIlroy, sensationally, weaved through for an equaliser. It was one of those games that now only seemed to be going one way, but Liam Brady did what great players do and wrenched momentum back the other way. With United still celebrating, the Arsenal winger picked the ball up in his own half and surged through the opposition defence, before slipping the ball to Graham Rix to cross. Alan Sunderland

slid in for the winner. It represented the fixture's best climax since the Matthews Final of 1953.

Arsenal were, by then, so specialised in FA Cup run that they would spend most of their time in the competition. Their 1979 run saw a five-game series against Sheffield Wednesday, their 1980 adventure included a four-match Semi-final against Liverpool. Arsenal won that but lost the Final, which should have been the easier game. The West Ham United they faced were a good Second Division side but couldn't get any kind of consistency for a promotion push. The Hammers had beaten three top-tier clubs en route to the Final but it seemed like cynicism might win out when their winger Paul Allen, the youngest player to appear in the showpiece at 17 years and 256 days, was chopped down by Arsenal defender Willie Young when clean through. There was instead another sensation: a rare Trevor Brooking headed goal. Allen cried on receiving his medal after West Ham's 1–0 win; they remain the last club from outside the top-tier to lift the cup to date.

Top left: Blyth Spartans celebrate their shock win over Stoke City in the 1977–78 season with a dunk in the bath, two-goal hero Terry Johnson in the centre with soap on his head.

Above: Ipswich Town celebrate winning The FA Cup after beating Arsenal in the 1978 Final.

Opposite top left: Arsenal's Frank Stapleton opens the scoring in the famous "five-minute Final" of 1979, heading past Manchester United goalkeeper Gary Bailey.

Opposite top right: Manchester United's Mickey Thomas takes stock, as Arsenal go into a 2–0 lead.

Opposite middle left: The drama really starts in the 86th minute as United's Gordon McQueen gets free between Pat Rice and Sammy Nelson to pull one back and make it 2–1.

Opposite middle right: Sammy McIlroy stuns Arsenal with an equalising goal in the 88th minute, firing past goalkeeper Pat Jennings.

Opposite bottom: A relieved and jubilant Arsenal celebrate Alan Sunderland's remarkable winner, just a minute after McIlroy's equaliser, to complete the "five-minute Final".

Things were to get worse for Arsenal from 1980–81 onwards, as their great rivals Tottenham Hotspur superseded them as the period's FA Cup side.

Keith Burkinshaw's Spurs team was built around the genius of Glenn Hoddle and the allure of Argentinian World Cup winners, Ricky Villa and Ossie Ardiles. The latter lent his name to the title of one of the era's most memorable cup songs, another staple of the time. 'Ossie's Dream' was fulfilled in fantastic fashion in the 1981 Final replay against Manchester City, although it was Villa who conjured the magic on the day.

That showpiece was The FA Cup's 100th Final and it more than lived up to the occasion, opening with a resplendent ceremony, where 30 captains from previous wins were introduced to the crowd. Villa's goal even had some vintage FA Cup plotting, given how subdued he'd been in getting substituted in the initial 1–1 draw. Tottenham had been set for defeat through Tommy Hutchison's 30th-minute strike, only for the City midfielder to score an own goal. Hutchison was the first player to score a goal in the Final for both teams since Bert Turner in 1946, and both players were also the oldest on the pitch.

Spurs weren't going pass up their second opportunity. They'd been ruthless in their run to the Final, eliminating Exeter City after the third-tier side thrashed Newcastle 4–0 and knocked out Leicester. The replay was a far more dynamic affair, with the lead changing three times. Villa scored after eight minutes before Steve MacKenzie responded with one of the great (and most overlooked) FA Cup Final

1980–81
TOTTENHAM HOTSPUR   1–1   MANCHESTER CITY
AET
VENUE: **WEMBLEY STADIUM**
ATTENDANCE: **100,000**

1980–81 (REPLAY)
TOTTENHAM HOTSPUR   3–2   MANCHESTER CITY
VENUE: **WEMBLEY STADIUM**
ATTENDANCE: **92,000**

goals. The forward spun to fire a 25yd (23m) volley into the top corner. Kevin Reeves' penalty then gave City another lead that Garth Crooks cancelled out. The stage was set for Villa to weave his way into the box, leaving Ray Ranson and Tommy Caton flailing before turning the ball past Joe Corrigan in the City goal.

Opposite: West Ham United's Trevor Brooking, wearing number 10, is hugged by Alan Devonshire as Paul Allen lifts his arms, after Brooking had scored a "rare headed goal" to win the 1980 Final against Arsenal. West Ham remain the last club from outside the top tier to win The FA Cup.

Below: Former FA Cup-winning captains line up to mark the 100th Final, in 1981. From left to right are: Tom Parker, Jack Swann, Raich Carter, Don Welsh, Billy Wright, Joe Harvey, Len Millard, Nat Lofthouse, Bill Slater, Bobby Moore, Brian Labone, Frank McLintock, Emlyn Hughes, Mick Mills, Roy Paul and Tony Book.

It was the ultimate way to win a cup Final. It was also Villa's last, as the tumultuous real-world politics of the era began to influence football. The Falklands War meant both Villa and Ardiles missed the 1982 Final out of political sensitivity. That year, Spurs had become the first side to reach both domestic cup Finals in a single

Left: Tottenham Hotspur's Ricky Villa weaves past Manchester City's Tommy Caton to shoot past Joe Corrigan for one of The FA Cup's greatest ever goals, and a fitting winner of the 100th Final.

Opposite: Tottenham Hotspur's Glenn Hoddle scores the penalty that won the 1982 FA Cup Final replay against Queens Park Rangers, as Spurs retained the cup.

Below: Tottenham's Argentine heroes, Ossie Ardiles, left, and Villa, lift up The FA Cup after the latter's heroics secured a 3–2 win over Manchester City.

season, although Liverpool beat them in the League Cup. Their FA Cup Final opponents were Queens Park Rangers, a first showpiece appearance for the then-Second Division club. Many commentators had cited the influence of Rangers' plastic pitch on their cup run, with their Third Round win over Middlesbrough the first FA Cup tie played on an artificial surface.

A fourth all-London Wembley Final had none of the drama of 1981. A dour 1–1 draw was followed five days later by a replay, which Hoddle settled with an early penalty. It was a game only notable for its trivia as Spurs became the first team to retain the cup since their own great side exactly 20 years previously. It also put them on a joint-record seven FA Cup wins with Aston Villa.

Tottenham had maintained their 100 per cent record in FA Cup Finals, but that was to end in their very next showpiece appearance. Coventry City offered another of the era's great surprises, and another iconic goal, spoiling Hoddle's last game for Spurs, in 1987.

Spurs had, by then, signed QPR's free-scoring Clive Allen, whose goal after just two minutes of the 1987 Final was his 49th of the season. Coventry displayed the resilience that had kept them in the First Division for two decades, however, in what was their first trip to Wembley. They came from behind twice, Keith Bennett responding to Allen's goal and Keith Houchen to Gary Mabbutt's. The second equaliser sent them flying – literally. On 63 minutes, Houchen met

1981–82
TOTTENHAM HOTSPUR   1–1   QUEENS PARK RANGERS
AET
VENUE: **WEMBLEY STADIUM**
ATTENDANCE: **100,000**

1981–82 (REPLAY)
TOTTENHAM HOTSPUR   1–0   QUEENS PARK RANGERS
VENUE: **WEMBLEY STADIUM**
ATTENDANCE: **90,000**

Bennett's cross with an exhilarating diving header. It was another glorious cup moment for Houchen, having scored the penalty for York City that eliminated Arsenal in 1985. There was no such follow-up for Mabbutt. He became the third player to score for both teams in a Final, settling this one with an unfortunate own goal off his knee. Coventry had won their first major honour.

Manchester United had, in the meantime, restored a sense of glory under Ron Atkinson as league frustration was tempered by FA Cup success. United's 1983 victory over Brighton and Hove Albion was down to typical cup luck. The Final was 2–2 going into the 119th minute when Brighton's Gordon Smith was put clean through. He'd already scored once and seemed certain to finish again, to earn the

Seagulls their first major trophy. Immortality beckoned. It was instead a line from BBC commentator Peter Jones that remained in the memory: "And Smith must score…" He didn't. United pummelled Brighton 4–0 in the replay, going 3–0 up by half-time. It was the heaviest win at Wembley to date, as Norman Whiteside became the occasion's youngest scorer, at 18 years and 18 days. Brighton, meanwhile, became the third finalist to also be relegated in the same season.

United suffered embarrassment of their own the next season as they went out 2–0 to third-tier Bournemouth in the Third Round. "We don't get many days like this at Bournemouth," their young manager, Harry Redknapp, declared. They would in fact get a day at Old Trafford at the same stage the next season, but this time United

won 3–0 en route to a second FA Cup title in three years. Atkinson's adventurous team beat Liverpool 2–1 in an epic Semi-final replay, and Everton 1–0 in an enthralling Wembley showdown. That match saw Kevin Moran become the first player to be sent off in a Final, for bringing down Everton's Peter Reid as he burst through on goal. Reid, to his credit, protested the decision, but it only invigorated United. In extra time, Whiteside scored another goal in a Final, brilliantly curling the ball round Everton keeper, Neville Southall.

That season's FA Cup was arguably more significant for two other developments, however. One was the way in which crowd trouble was coming to a head. The Sixth Round tie between Millwall and Luton Town was delayed for 25 minutes by a huge riot, all shown on TV. The government demanded the game tackle the issue, but The FA's Ted Croker said it was "society's problem".

The dilapidated state of many stadiums was also a problem, and a factor in several tragedies. That season ended with the Bradford City fire, which killed 56 spectators, and the Heysel Stadium disaster. The latter, in Belgium, happened before the European Cup Final

Above: Gordon Smith's shot is saved by Gary Bailey in the last minute of extra-time in the 1983 Final, and one of The FA Cup's most infamous moments. It denied Brighton and Hove Albion a first ever trophy, and ensured Manchester United won 4–0 in the replay.

Opposite top: Andy Gray fires Everton's second goal past Watford's Steve Sherwood, to secure The FA Cup in 1984.

Opposite middle: Watford chairman Elton John salutes the crowd at the 1984 Final, the club's first appearance in the fixture.

Opposite bottom: Manchester United's Norman Whiteside, the scorer of the only goal in the 1985 Final, celebrates after the 1–0 win over Everton.

when a wall collapsed after a rush by Liverpool fans. A total of 39 people died, mostly Juventus supporters. It was the worst of a series of incidents involving English fans and led to UEFA banning the country's clubs from its competitions until 1990.

The game persevered through all of this. Tragedy and chaos off the pitch so often contrasted with admirable control on it. Liverpool kept on winning. This was another significant trend of the 1984–85 season. It marked the rise of Merseyside in the cup.

For all his success, Bob Paisley never lifted the trophy, but that was not an issue for player-manager Kenny Dalglish. He won it twice, clearly spurred on by the progress of rivals Everton. The 1983–84 FA Cup run had provided a new spark for the Toffees, whose trophy drought at that point stood at 14 years. Former star player Howard Kendall was by then putting together an adept team. That season's Final came against Watford, who had risen from the Fourth Division to the First in five years through the investment of Elton John, the pragmatism of manager Graham Taylor and the genius of winger John Barnes. They were league runners-up to Liverpool in 1983 but were well short of Everton in the 1984 FA Cup Final. Watford's pop star chairman was reduced to tears as Graeme Sharp and Andy Gray scored in a 2–0 win that set off a new glory era for the blue half of Merseyside. United denied Everton a treble in 1985, as they also won the league and Cup Winners' Cup. But Kendall's team couldn't stop Liverpool at last completing their first double in 1985–86. Everton had already finished second to their rivals in the league, which only added to the tension in the first-ever all-Merseyside Final, as well as the first Final in 73 years between the country's top two teams.

A superb match was seen as a positive for the game at a problematic time. Gary Lineker gave Everton the lead by outpacing Alan Hansen

before Ian Rush – so often the tormentor of the Blues – scored twice in a 3–1 win. Dalglish's first season as player-manager ended gloriously.

While the two neighbours continued to play out their local rivalry at the top of the English game, Liverpool were denied another double in 1987–88. That season's Final remains one of the most famous FA Cup upsets, but far from the biggest, because Wimbledon were by then seventh in the First Division, behind champions Liverpool. The real story was in Wimbledon's rise, given it was only 11 years since they were in the fifth-tier Southern League. Alan Cork had played with them through every division of the Football League and burst into tears when they beat Luton Town to reach the Final.

This was the other element that made the occasion: the contrast. Liverpool were going for another double amid a culture of victory. Wimbledon were going for a first major trophy, amid a culture of

Left: Liverpool's Craig Johnston follows in Ian Rush's strike, that opened the scoring in the 3–1 win over Everton in the 1986 Final, the first Merseyside derby on that stage.

Opposite: Lawrie Sanchez beats a stranded Bruce Grobbelaar, the winning goal in Wimbledon's sensational 1–0 win over Liverpool in the 1988 Final.

Below: Coventry City players celebrate the winning moment in the 1987 Final, an own goal by Tottenham Hotspur's Gary Mabbutt.

chaotic defiance. As they came down the tunnel, Wimbledon's John Fashanu let out the team battle cry of "Yidaho!" Liverpool knew they were in a fight when Vinnie Jones cut down Steve McMahon in the opening minutes. On 37 minutes, Wimbledon rose above the champions, Lawrie Sanchez meeting a set piece to head the Dons into the lead. The match had taken on a similar feel to Sunderland's heroic underdog victory in 1973. At half-time, Wimbledon promised themselves they would defend with their lives. Another piece of defiance proved a defining moment. On the hour, Liverpool's John Aldridge went down under a Clive Goodyear challenge to win his side penalty. The striker stepped up – but Dave Beasant saved it. The "Crazy Gang", well, went wild.

Liverpool were back at Wembley for another Merseyside Final the following season but the feeling around it was completely different. That was because of what happened at Hillsborough on 15 April 1989. The FA Cup witnessed the worst disaster in the history of British sport. At Liverpool's Semi-final victory over Nottingham Forest at Sheffield Wednesday's Hillsborough Stadium, The FA Cup witnessed the worst disaster in the history of British sport. In the sixth minute, referee Ray Lewis stopped the match as it became apparent something very grave was happening. A huge crush had been created in the Leppings Lane stand after police match commander

1985–86
LIVERPOOL **1–0** EVERTON
VENUE: **WEMBLEY STADIUM**
ATTENDANCE: **98,000**

1986–87
COVENTRY CITY **3–2** TOTTENHAM HOTSPUR
AET
VENUE: **WEMBLEY STADIUM**
ATTENDANCE: **98,000**

1987–88
WIMBLEDON **1–0** LIVERPOOL
VENUE: **WEMBLEY STADIUM**
ATTENDANCE: **98,203**

1988–89
LIVERPOOL **3–2** EVERTON
AET
VENUE: **WEMBLEY STADIUM**
ATTENDANCE: **82,500**

David Duckenfield ordered an exit gate to be opened to alleviate overcrowding outside the turnstiles. Instead it led to an influx of supporters. Most headed towards a subway entry to two central pens, which were already dangerously packed. A total of 97 Liverpool supporters eventually lost their lives, with 94 dying on the day. The

images were traumatic, with steel twisted under the pressure, and advertising boards used as stretchers.

The initial public enquiry was a whitewash, accompanied by scandalous media reports blaming supporters. It became clear that previous warnings – including a dangerous crush at the 1981 Semi-final between Spurs and Wolves on the same terrace – had not been heeded. Only the landmark Taylor Report, published in January 1990, brought progress. Lord Justice Taylor even lamented how this was the ninth such study into crowd safety since the 1923 FA Cup Final. He found that the main cause was a failure of control by South Yorkshire Police and called for "a totally new approach across the whole field of football". The search for justice from campaigners goes on.

Above: Liverpool manager Kenny Dalglish is comforted by a police offer, as his Nottingham Forest counterpart Brian Clough stands behind. The Semi-final between the two was abandoned due to a crush that caused the deaths of 97 Liverpool supporters.

Above left: Referee Ray Lewis signals to Liverpool captain Ronnie Whelan to get his players off the pitch as he abandons the game.

Left: Anfield became a shrine in the days after the disaster, the stadium filled with flowers and scarves to commemorate those who lost their lives.

Opposite top: Ian Rush beats Everton goalkeeper Neville Southall to make it 3–2 to Liverpool and seal the 1989 FA Cup Final. The game saw a huge outpouring of emotion, coming just weeks after the Hillsborough disaster.

Opposite bottom: Steve McMahon holds up The FA Cup after the 1989 Final, wearing an Everton hat on his head as a symbol of a city united.

At the time, there was the highly sensitive question of whether football should even continue. Dalglish, who displayed incredible fortitude in going to every Hillsborough funeral, summed up the mood of many: "Football is irrelevant now."

Anfield was transformed into a shrine, and a line of scarves linked the stadium to Goodison Park. There was a suggestion that the cup should simply be awarded to Merseyside, especially after Liverpool overcame Forest in a naturally subdued game just three weeks after the initial Semi-final had been abandoned.

The FA nevertheless insisted that it would be a memorial to the victims to carry on to the Final. The only solace was that the occasion allowed Merseyside to come together, in a "requiem cup Final". Wembley saw some of its most moving scenes, as Gerry Marsden led the entire stadium in a rendition of "You'll Never Walk Alone". When the players were coming out, all they could hear was "Merseyside, Merseyside".

It was an emotional and raw occasion for everyone involved, and a strange one for Everton. They naturally wanted to win, but knew all good will was with their neighbours. Liverpool meanwhile felt this was one they had to win. In the event, local boy Aldridge opened the scoring and another Ian Rush double cancelled out Stuart McCall's brace. It was the first Final where two players had scored more than once, but it felt ill-fitting to point out such records.

When Liverpool's Steve McMahon went to lift the cup, he wore an Everton hat. The cup had never mattered less and yet it had never had such emotional impact.

ANATOMY
OF AN UPSET

Each FA Cup upset is unique, and special to those involved for very specific reasons, but all FA Cup upsets are also alike in a few key ways. Every one of them ultimately comes from the same electrifying sense of opportunity, nurtured by certain circumstances.

The vintage picture of an upset is an unsteady top-tier club travelling to a small stadium a few levels below them and getting undone by the disruptive strands of the day. The majority of the most famous examples conform to this pattern: Walsall 2–0 Arsenal, 1933; Gateshead 1–0 Liverpool, 1953; Colchester United 3–2 Leeds United, 1971; Hereford United 2–1 Newcastle United, 1972; Sutton United 2–1 Coventry City, 1989; Wrexham 2–1 Arsenal, 1992; Stevenage 3–1 Newcastle United, 2011, and so on.

It is very much part of the magic of the cup, but it comes from earthier principles. The way these days go is by now enticingly familiar. The bigger club turns up at an unfashionable stadium, and one far removed from the comforts of the top level, amid unsettling weather. This was something that certainly struck Arsenal's players at Walsall in 1933. By the 1970s, the arrival of TV cameras signalled that a fixture had been earmarked as a potential upset, which just watered the seed in the minds of those involved. The crowd is of course raucous, the more enclosed nature of smaller stadiums serving to heighten the atmosphere, and make the bigger team even more uncomfortable. There are then more restricted dressing rooms and – typically – pitches that are someway short of being green carpets. The surfaces tend to give literal meaning to the phrase that is so often used to describe The FA Cup, "the great leveller".

Other disruptions can skew proceedings, including the smaller team's tactics. They might look to really get in the faces of the top-level players. West Ham United's Ron Greenwood once described Port Vale's approach as "diabolical intimidation" in one Third Round tie. But Port Vale were merely following the script. The smaller club turns the game into a battle, every successful tackle getting greater cheers. A hesitation starts to creep into the bigger club's game, influenced by the growing realisation that something embarrassing might be about to happen, almost making it self-fulfilling.

That is what Danny Blanchflower meant when he spoke about "a riot where anything can happen", while "the big fellow is often fighting against himself as well as the upstarts". That's when something gives, and the smaller team senses a moment of immortality. Names like Matthew Hanlan and Ronnie Radford meanwhile become part of cup lore. There's then always a spell in the match that completes the drama, as the bigger club finally gets it together and lays siege to the smaller club's goal. An inspired goalkeeping performance is of course required, such as that from Graham Smith against Leeds United. It all comes together for one glorious event.

There are obvious reasons why these upsets are usually at home, or involve the smaller team taking the lead, since the bigger club will find the going so much easier if the situation is reversed. Precious few upsets have seen small teams come from behind or win after travelling to the bigger stadium, so special mention, then, goes out to Lincoln City at Burnley in 2017, Woking at West Brom in 1991 and Bradford City at Chelsea in 2015.

All upsets come from that same special feeling, though – that sense of opportunity only The FA Cup offers.

Opposite top left: The matchday programme for Walsall's sensational elimination of Arsenal in 1933, arguably the original FA Cup upset that set the template.

Opposite top middle: Colchester United manager Dick Graham celebrates the 3–2 win over Leeds United in 1970–71 by raising a glass of champagne with his players.

Opposite top right: Hereford United enjoy a drink together after one of the most famous upsets of all, over Newcastle United in 1971–72.

Opposite middle left: Sutton United players celebrate in the seconds after Matthew Hanlan's goal to beat Coventry City in 1988–89.

Opposite middle right: Wrexham put David Seaman under the kind of pressure that would ultimately see them shock Arsenal 2–1 in the 1991–92 season.

Opposite bottom left: Stevenage's Stacy Long celebrates with a spot of air guitar after giving his side the lead against Newcastle United in 2010–11.

Opposite bottom right: Chelsea's Petr Cech is beaten by Jonathan Stead's strike for Bradford City in a superb 4–2 comeback in the 2014–15 season.

CHAPTER TEN

DOUBLES
ALL ROUND

1990–2006

1990   2006

WHAT WOULD ASTON VILLA'S 1957 FA CUP WINNERS HAVE MADE OF RESULTS AT THE TURN OF THE MILLENNIUM? BACK IN THAT WEMBLEY APPEARANCE, THE PLAYERS WERE ACUTELY CONSCIOUS OF THE CLUB'S RECORD AS THE LAST TO DO THE DOUBLE, ALL THE WAY BACK IN 1897. THIS KNOWLEDGE STRENGTHENED THEIR RESOLVE TO BEAT THE BUSBY BABES, WHO HAD COME WITHIN ONE GAME OF THE FEAT.

That was towards the end of a long era when the double was seen as an "impossible" achievement. By the mid-1970s, after Tottenham Hotspur and Arsenal had both done it, the double became "historic". By the late 1990s, it was almost an inevitability for certain clubs.

A total of five doubles were won in the nine seasons between 1993 and 2002, all by Manchester United and Arsenal. The two clubs together had four near misses, too: United in 1995; Arsenal in 1999, 2003 and 2005. Arsenal also won a domestic cup double in 1993, with Liverpool following in 2001.

These names and numbers help explain the explosion in what had previously been English football's most elusive feat. Manchester United replaced Liverpool as the country's dominant dynasty, mostly through the sheer will of manager Alex Ferguson. He won five FA Cups in this period, more than anyone else. Another influence was the greatest team rivalry the English game has seen. Arsenal pushed United at every step for seven years, Ferguson and his Gunners counterpart Arsène Wenger trading barbs as the trophies piled up. The FA Cup saw the best of it, peaking in one pulsating match, and ending with one final showdown.

There's a telling fact that illustrates the order of English football at the time, and its effect on the cup. In six of the seven seasons between 1997 and 2004, Chelsea were knocked out by either United or Arsenal. In the one they weren't, Chelsea won it.

Along with Liverpool, no club outside that "big four" won The FA Cup between 1996 and 2007. The rigidity of this order pointed to another reason for this multiplication of doubles. That was the explosion of the game's finances, largely instigated by the

1992 foundation of the Premier League. The influx of additional broadcast revenue meant that the biggest clubs were able to afford stronger squads. This created a virtuous cycle where they became more globally popular, in turn enabling them to draw on superior international talent. The internationalisation of The FA Cup was encapsulated by Ruud Gullit becoming the first foreign manager to win it with Chelsea in 1997, as well as the many star-filled winning sides that would follow. The competition had long been globally famous, but this development put it on another level. By the 2001 Final, with players from 14 different countries involved, the fixture was being broadcast to a global audience of 600 million. The crowd trouble of the 1980s already felt so far away.

This expansion and commercialisation of the game fitted some of the outcomes of the Taylor Report, such as the move to all-seater stadiums. Wembley had its attendance reduced by 17,500, but far bigger changes were to come. The grand old stadium started to look its age, which ultimately resulted in its reconstruction. This age of doubles also saw the Twin Towers disappear into history.

Before the ground was brought into the 21st century, though, the 21st century brought The FA Cup Final outside England for the first time. Six Finals took place in Cardiff's Millennium Stadium between 2001 and 2006. The cup would undergo more changes still – literally – as a new model was cast in 1992, the first since 1911. By 1994, it had its first commercial sponsor.

As one of England's most famous clubs, Manchester United were well placed to capitalise on the changes of the 1990s, though they were still dependent on one of The FA Cup's unique flashes of

"MY FAVOURITE MOMENT HAS TO BE WINNING THE FA CUP [...] I DIDN'T EXPECT IT BUT ALL OF A SUDDEN IT CLICKED, AND IT WAS AN AMAZING TIME.""

- RUUD GULLIT -

fortune. United's rise to prominence could have gone a very different way with a different bounce of the ball. The story has gone down as one of football's great 'what-ifs', as well as a moral sporting lesson in patience and persistence. As Manchester United prepared for their 1989–90 Third Round tie away to Nottingham Forest, Ferguson still hadn't won a trophy in three years. More pressingly, he hadn't won any game in nine matches. The widespread expectation was that United would lose, and Ferguson would lose his job.

Fate had other ideas. The decisive moment at the City Ground summed up so much of what makes The FA Cup: a bit of brilliance, a bit of opportunism, a bit of luck. On 56 minutes, United's Mark Hughes picked the ball up near the Forest box and played an inviting cross with the outside of his foot. Mark Robins showed superb movement but his effort was more of a push than a proper header. It didn't matter because he – and Ferguson – had the good fortune that the Forest defence were caught out. United won 1–0. Ferguson was safe, for now.

So much of modern football history stems from that moment. In the immediate aftermath, United went on a run, though their results were hard fought. They struggled to 13th in the league and were drawn away from home in every round of The FA Cup. Even their 2–1

Semi-final win against a battling Oldham Athletic required extra time, after a brilliant 3–3 draw. Robins scored the clinching goal.

That initial Semi-final afternoon has gone down as one of the great FA Cup days, something mercifully euphoric after the tragedy of the previous year. But the best was yet to come.

Crystal Palace–Liverpool had everything, including upset and revenge. The new league champions had already thrashed Palace 9–0 that season, and the London side were now missing the revelation that was a young Ian Wright, with a broken leg. Another United–Liverpool Final was widely expected. This match at Villa Park was instead gloriously unpredictable, with the lead changing four times.

Palace were leading 2–1 in the 81st minute only for Steve McMahon to strike and John Barnes to score a penalty two minutes later. Liverpool

Above: Mark Robins celebrates scoring one of the most important goals in English football history, as he gave Manchester United a badly-needed 1–0 win over Nottingham Forest in the 1989–90 Third Round. It is seen as a crucial turning point in Alex Ferguson's time as a manager.

Previous pages: Arsène Wenger celebrates with his bench during Arsenal's 1998 Final against Newcastle United, a win which secured the club's second double and the first of the manager's record seven FA Cups.

1989–90
MANCHESTER UNITED 3–3 CRYSTAL PALACE
AET
VENUE: **WEMBLEY STADIUM**
ATTENDANCE: **80,000**

1989–90 (REPLAY)
MANCHESTER UNITED 1–0 CRYSTAL PALACE
VENUE: **WEMBLEY STADIUM**
ATTENDANCE: **80,000**

United were 2–1 up and in control by the 69th minute of the Final, when Coppell decided to bring Wright on. A huge talent who came to professional football late, he more than made up for lost time. Within two minutes, Wright had equalised. Within two minutes of extra-time, he'd put Palace ahead.

Hughes made it 3–3 with seven minutes to play, sending the tie to a replay, which still had one huge twist. Unnerved by Jim Leighton's performance in goal and how he looked "a beaten man" afterwards, Ferguson made the remarkable decision to drop his goalkeeper. Les Sealey, on loan from Luton Town, was in. The decision was simply shocking. Nothing like that had ever been done in the cup before. Ferguson knew it was controversial and that Leighton would be devastated, but ultimately felt logic demanded it. He believed United had a better chance with Sealey. It was the kind of hard decision that would really elevate Ferguson's career. Lee Martin became United's unlikely hero with the only goal.

The result, and the course of history, vindicated Ferguson. It also conditioned perspectives. Both Ferguson and United chairman Martin Edwards have insisted there was no talk of the manager losing his job before the Forest game, but it's possible defeat could have brought a momentum of its own. That was also true of every game up to the Final. This doubtless played into the decision to drop Leighton. Ferguson needed that first trophy, which kick-started the longest spell of success any manager has ever achieved.

For all his single-mindedness, though, United's success wasn't solely about Ferguson's rise. There was also the fall of Liverpool. Few would have thought that possible during the rip-roaring Fifth Round Merseyside derby in February 1991. Everton had set up yet another cup meeting with their rivals after beating the heroes of

would usually close out a match like this with ease, but this was already one of those occasions when the unique atmosphere of the cup brought out something more in the supposedly lesser team. Palace pummelled the league champions, leading to a goalmouth scramble where Andy Gray forced the ball over the line with three minutes left. In extra time, it was Palace who had more, as Alan Pardew headed in from a set-piece in the 109th minute. Those watching were not just witnessing a tie for the ages but perhaps the greatest moment in a club's history.

Palace, whose old stadium had hosted The FA Cup Final from 1895 to 1914, were finally playing in the showpiece fixture for the first time. Manager Steve Coppell, a 1977 cup hero with United, praised their "character, determination, guts and passion". There was more to come.

Above: Alex Ferguson hugs Les Sealey, who he had shockingly picked ahead of first-choice goalkeeper Jim Leighton for the replay of the 1990 Final against Crystal Palace. Manchester United won 1–0 to secure Ferguson's first trophy at the club.

Opposite top: Alan Pardew celebrates an extra-time winner to put Crystal Palace through to their first FA Cup Final, topping off a rip-roaring 4–3 win over Liverpool in the Semi-final.

Opposite bottom: Ian Wright scores his second goal of a brilliant individual performance, to put Crystal Palace into a 3–2 lead in extra time of the first match of their 1990 Final against Manchester United.

Right: One of the great upset stories, as Woking's Tim Buzaglo is congratulated by manager Geoff Chapple, after his hat-trick brought a 4–2 win away to West Bromwich Albion.

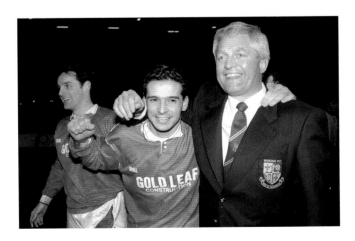

the season, Woking, who had eliminated second-tier West Brom 4–2, with Tim Buzaglo scoring a hat-trick. The non-league club narrowly lost 1–0 to Everton, which was the exact same score by which the Toffees beat Liverpool in a replay. By then, though, so much had changed.

Liverpool had taken the lead four times in the initial game and four times Everton had equalised. Graeme Sharp and Tony Cottee scored twice each for the Blues in a 4–4 draw. It was a match that once more captured everything that was good about the cup, these two clubs and the game. Dalglish just wasn't enjoying it though. Hillsborough had naturally taken a huge emotional toll. A mere 48 hours after the 4–4 draw, he resigned.

It took Liverpool a long time to recover, although there were deeper reasons for that than just Dalglish's departure. The game was moving into a new era, passing by their Boot Room culture. There was still one false dawn, as the 1992 FA Cup was won under former captain Graeme Souness. Ian Rush, of course, scored in a 2–0 win over Sunderland. By 1998, he was the cup's highest post-war goalscorer with 44 goals, only five behind Harry Cursham's all-time record. The other goal was scored by Michael Thomas, who Liverpool had signed after he had scored Arsenal's title-winning goal in the final minute of the final game in 1988–89 – away to Liverpool.

That pointed to another pertinent fact. It was initially Arsenal, not United, that looked the new force. Manager George Graham had built a fine team on a rock-solid defence that would later form the foundation of Wenger's first great team.

The Gunners won the title in 1991 and were going for another double when they faced Spurs in the Semi-final of that year's FA Cup. It was a clash of styles as much as a derby. This was the Spurs of Terry Venables, Gary Lineker and Paul Gascoigne, with the playmaker on another level after a transcendent 1990 World Cup. Gascoigne displayed his genius throughout that cup run, particularly with a match-winner against Notts County, to the point where Italian giants Lazio were offering big money for his services. The FA made a move of their own for that match, such was the demand for tickets, and the Semi-final was switched to Wembley for the first time. There was an outcry about tradition but it proved a fitting venue for what was to follow. Gascoigne, who had been extraordinarily hyped in the dressing room, focused that energy into something fantastic. After just five minutes, he sent a 30yd (27m) free-kick soaring into the top corner. It set Spurs on the way to a 3–1 win and the Final.

That 1991 match had been built up as the Brian Clough Final, since it was the one trophy he hadn't won at Forest. It ended up as the Gascoigne tragedy. This time, he was overhyped for what many felt was going to be his finest hour. Instead it produced his worst moment in football. On 15 minutes, Gascoigne went in recklessly on

Gary Charles, but only ruptured his own cruciate ligaments.

Stuart Pearce immediately scored from the subsequent free-kick, as Gascoigne was helped off. Venables, for his part, expertly rallied and reorganised his team. Spurs came back from 1–0 down and a missed Lineker penalty, first through a Paul Stewart equaliser, and then an own goal, this time from Des Walker, marking a reverse of the 1987 result against Coventry City.

Spurs met Arsenal again in the 1993 Semi-final and the fixture was again played at Wembley. The same privilege was afforded the other Semi-final, a first-ever Sheffield derby at that stage of the competition, in which Wednesday had too much for United. Arsenal, meanwhile, weren't just looking to avenge 1991 but also to bury what had happened in the 1991–92 Third Round, when they were beaten 2–1 by Wrexham, who had just finished bottom of Division Four. It was all the more incredible since Arsenal had gone ahead, but their famous defence was breached by a rocket free-kick from

Opposite: Paul Gascoigne launches the blockbusting free-kick that sent Tottenham Hotspur on the way to a 3–1 win over rivals Arsenal, as a Semi-final was held at Wembley for the first time.

Below: Nottingham Forest manager Brian Clough leads his Tottenham Hotspur counterpart Terry Venables by the hand as they walk out for the 1991 Final. It was all the more emotional for Clough, as he finished his career having never won the FA Cup.

37-year-old Mickey Thomas, who had been part of the Manchester United team that lost to Arsenal in the 1979 Final. There was a similar flurry to that famous "five-minute Final" here, as Steve Watkin scored the winner two minutes after Thomas' strike.

Arsenal were too focused for any slips in 1993. Spurs were dispatched 1–0, to set up another history-making Final – this was the first time the two domestic cup finals had been contested by the same two teams. Arsenal had already beaten Sheffield Wednesday in the League Cup Final but were finding The FA version much tougher.

The replay, following a 1–1 draw, looked set to become the first ever FA Cup Final decided by penalties. Police had the previous year requested there should be a minimum of 10 days between any replay in any round in order to allow for security arrangements to be made, which made the old series of games impossible. Rotherham United's victory over Scunthorpe United in the 1991–92 First Round was the first FA Cup tie to be settled by penalties.

As it turned out, Arsenal and Wednesday didn't have to go through the anxiety of a shoot-out. Andy Linighan instead scored the latest-ever Final winner, in the 119th minute of the replay. Arsenal were the

first winners of the new trophy, made by Toye, Kenning and Spencer at a cost of £12,403. It was to stay in Manchester or North London for most of the decade.

Alex Ferguson had by that point put together his first title winners at Manchester United, ending a 26-year wait in 1992–93. The crucial final piece of his team was the ingenious Eric Cantona. United made such a leap from that title that they immediately surged to the club's first double in 1993–94. Cantona settled a battle against Wimbledon in the Fifth Round, scoring a sumptuous volley. In the 4–0 Final win against Chelsea, he scored two penalties, coolly going for the same spot on both occasions.

Cantona's importance, as well as the other side of his temperament, was fully demonstrated the next season. He was suspended for almost the entirety of United's 1994–95 FA Cup run, after astoundingly launching himself at a spectator in a league game away to Crystal Palace. That created a hostile atmosphere in The FA cup Semi-final between the two clubs, which tragically saw Palace fan Paul Nixon lose his life. A bad-tempered replay saw United progress through goals from Steve Bruce and Gary Pallister.

In the other Semi-final, Spurs were supposedly fated to win, after they had initially been banned from that season's cup over financial

Top left: Wrexham's Mickey Thomas, on the right, celebrates the side's stunning 2–1 win over champions Arsenal, his free-kick having turned the game.

Top right: Ian Rush celebrates the strike that put Liverpool ahead in the 1992 Final against Sunderland. It was one of the striker's 44 goals in the FA Cup, making him the competition's highest post-war goalscorer, just five behind Harry Cursham's all-time record.

Opposite top: Andy Linighan rises above Mark Bright for a 119th-minute winner against Sheffield Wednesday, to prevent the 1993 FA Cup Final becoming the first to go to penalties and ensure Arsenal became the first club to win both domestic cups in the same season.

Opposite bottom: Eric Cantona sends Chelsea's Dmitri Kharine the wrong way to score the first of two penalties in a 4–0 win that brought Manchester United's first domestic double.

1994–95
EVERTON   1–0   MANCHESTER UNITED
VENUE: **WEMBLEY STADIUM**
ATTENDANCE: 79,592

1995–96
MANCHESTER UNITED   1–0   LIVERPOOL
VENUE: **WEMBLEY STADIUM**
ATTENDANCE: 79,007

A 1–1 draw at West Ham United denied Ferguson a third successive title. Paul Rideout took Everton's chance in the Final to claim the club's fifth FA Cup.

Ferguson was so aggravated by the nature of the defeat that he instantly began implementing changes he had been considering for some time. Hughes, Paul Ince and Andrei Kanchelskis were sold. The core of the much-heralded "Class of 92" youth team were fully bedded in, with David Beckham, Nicky Butt and Phil Neville joining Gary Neville, Paul Scholes and Ryan Giggs.

It was another decisive move from Ferguson, but another inspired one. Despite initial criticism, most famously from Alan Hansen, United proved you could win everything with kids. The return of Cantona was integral to that, and the 1995–96 season saw perhaps his best form. The Frenchman scored a series of crucial goals in victorious league and cup campaigns, culminating in the glorious redemption of an 86th-minute FA Cup Final winner against Liverpool.

irregularities. An appeal saw them reinstated but it happened so late that their entry in the Third Round draw read "bye, or Tottenham Hotspur". Jurgen Klinsmann inspired Spurs to the Semi-final but could not get them past a resilient Everton. Joe Royle's side rolled over their more fancied opponents in a 4–1 win. Everton felt primed for the Final, whereas gloom had descended over United, who had lost the league to Blackburn Rovers in the last minute of the last day.

"AN FA CUP GAME IS ALWAYS SPECIAL,
YOU NEVER KNOW. IT'S WHY IT'S SO
INTERESTING AND EXCITING."

– ERIC CANTONA –

Above: Paul Rideout stuns Manchester United to give Everton a 1–0 win in 1995 and their first trophy since 1986.

Opposite top: Liverpool's Robbie Fowler and Jamie Redknapp take in the Wembley pitch ahead of the 1996 Final against Manchester United, wearing their infamous white suits.

Opposite bottom: Manchester United's Eric Cantona celebrates after the late volley against Liverpool that secured the club's second domestic double.

The beauty of that ingenious volley didn't fit the drabness of the game. It had, up to then, only been illuminated by Liverpool's notorious white suits. It was a brash move from a bright young team, but they lacked United's drive. Ferguson had made his club the first to win two doubles, as well as becoming the most successful team in the history of The FA Cup, surpassing Spurs with nine wins.

Mere months after that feat, though, another influential French figure arrived to inspire even greater change. The relatively unheralded Arsène Wenger was initially greeted by headlines like, "Arsène who?" He had been a very successful coach of Monaco, before an interlude in Japan allowed him to hone ideas about the modern game.

One of Ferguson's finest qualities was the ability to adapt but the manner in which Wenger brought together developing trends in sports science, recruitment and tactics saw Arsenal suddenly pull out in front of their northern rivals. His knowledge of France secured the signings of Patrick Vieira and Emmanuel Petit, who drove an exhilarating team. Most symbolically, though, an ageing defence was revitalised. Arsenal surged to the double in 1997–98, easily beating Newcastle United 2–0 in The FA Cup Final, thanks to goals from Marc Overmars and Nicolas Anelka.

Some fiery encounters engendered a personal enmity between Ferguson and Wenger, but a very healthy football rivalry also arose. Ferguson was invigorated by the challenge, again reshaping his team and signing Jaap Stam and Dwight Yorke. There was an emotional intensity to United's 1998–99 season that created a unique momentum and a series of epic matches. Two came in The FA Cup. The first, in the Fourth Round, was a sign of what was to come. Liverpool were 1–0 up at Old Trafford going into the 88th minute, or what was by now known as "Fergie time". United had developed a champion team's reputation for late goals, but not to the extent of this exceptional season, or this amazing tie. Yorke first equalised. Ole Gunnar Solskjaer then hit a stoppage-time winner. The sound at Old Trafford was deafening.

The 1999 FA Cup Semi-final replay between United and Arsenal was a match to equal any in history. The two teams were neck and neck in a title race that became about so much more than just the league. Wenger was going for another double. Ferguson was going for an unprecedented treble. So much of this came together in a spectacular game at Villa Park.

What's remarkable is that it almost never happened. First of all,

Roy Keane scored a legitimate goal in the initial game only for the offside flag to go up. Secondly, The FA had decided that all Semi-finals and Finals would, from 1999–2000 on, be finished on the day. This was to be the last ever FA Cup Semi-final replay. There was some irony to that, given Arsenal had willingly offered a rematch to Sheffield United in that season's Fifth Round. That was because of a curious moment when Overmars didn't follow the protocol of giving the ball back to the opposition after an injury, and scored. Arsenal won 2–1 but Wenger offered to replay the game… where his team won 2–1 again.

Top: Chelsea players celebrate Gianluca Vialli's goal in the 4–2 comeback from 2–0 down against Liverpool in the 1996–97 Fourth Round.

Above: Roberto Di Matteo runs away in jubilation with Gianfranco Zola, after scoring what was then the quickest goal in the history of The FA Cup Final, a long-range strike against Middlesbrough after just 43 seconds.

Opposite top: Marc Overmars, left, and Nicolas Anelka lift The FA Cup after both scored in Arsenal's 2–0 win over Newcastle United, a victory that secured the club's second double.

Opposite bottom left: A delighted Ole Gunnar Solskjaer after his stoppage-time winner completed a remarkable comeback in the final minutes of Manchester United's Fourth Round tie against Liverpool in 1998–99. It wouldn't be the last time he'd score a timely winner that season.

Opposite bottom right: Tottenham Hotspur's David Ginola skips away from Nicky Eaden of Barnsley at Oakwell to score one of the great individual FA Cup goals, in their Sixth Round match in 1998–99.

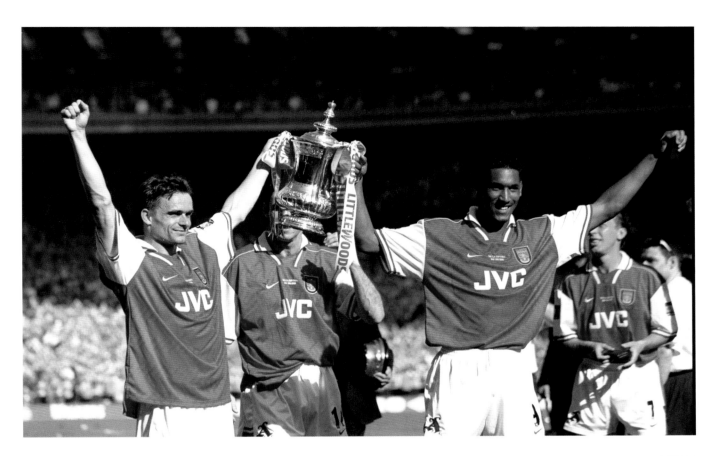

"I GREW UP DREAMING TO PLAY AT
WEMBLEY FOR MANCHESTER UNITED IN
AN FA CUP FINAL."

- DAVID BECKHAM -

The Arsenal manager was applauded for his sportsmanship, but this Semi-final replay would be lauded for its exceptional sporting level. There was a crackle to the atmosphere at Villa Park from the start and it exploded when Beckham curled in the opening goal on 17 minutes. The two teams had been exchanging attack after attack but all this escalated after Dennis Bergkamp's deflected equaliser. Anelka had a goal ruled out, Keane was sent off for a second booking and – in the 90th minute – Phil Neville brought down Ray Parlour for a penalty. A season's tension was built into one kick. Peter Schmeichel saved from Bergkamp. But the best was still to come.

United's ten men had been defiantly digging in through extra time, when one man decided to go it alone. On 108 minutes, Giggs picked up a loose Vieira pass in his own half and began to bob and weave forward. Four Arsenal defenders were beaten before the winger unleashed a ferocious shot into the roof of the net. It was the goal the game deserved.

After an exhaustingly exhilarating 2–1 win, Ferguson was asked whether it might cost United in the run-in. "Look, who's to know what's going to happen in football," Ferguson replied. "It could all blow up in our face at the end of the day, but can you forget moments like this?" United went on to pip Arsenal to the league on the final day of the season before beating Newcastle United 2–0 in The FA Cup Final, and ultimately winning the Champions League through a stoppage-time Solskjaer goal.

It was an historic treble, delivered in an immortal manner. Such an unprecedented feat nevertheless led to an unprecedented situation. United's Champions League success meant they qualified for the inaugural FIFA Club World Cup. That was to be played in Brazil during January, clashing with The FA Cup Fourth Round. With England campaigning to host the 2006 World Cup, it was decided United would go to Brazil, and became the first FA Cup holders to withdraw from the competition, amid huge controversy.

It was all the more poignant since United had played in more Wembley Finals than any other club and 1999–2000 was to be the last season at the old stadium before a total reconstruction – the architectural structure of the Twin Towers meant they could not be preserved.

Opposite top left: David Beckham curls in the opening goal of one of the greatest ever FA Cup games, Manchester United's Semi-final replay against Arsenal in 1998–99.

Opposite top right: Dennis Bergkamp celebrates his deflected equaliser with Lee Dixon, left, as Patrick Vieira runs towards them.

Opposite middle left: Roy Keane commits the foul on Marc Overmars that brings the midfielder's second yellow card, to reduce United to ten.

Opposite middle right: Peter Schmeichel saves Bergkamp's late penalty, to send the game to extra-time.

Opposite bottom: Ryan Giggs reels away in joy after scoring the sensational winning goal.

Below: Arsenal and Sheffield United players argue after a controversial goal by Marc Overmars in the 1998–99 Fifth Round, that went against the usual protocol of giving the ball back to opposition after an injury. In an unprecedented move, Arsène Wenger offered a replay of the match.

It wasn't the only break with tradition. The Third Round was held in December, an idea that was immediately scrapped. There, Darlington became the only club to lose in successive rounds of the cup, as they were drawn out as the "lucky losers" to replace United.

The way was opened for Chelsea to become the last club to win at the old Wembley, and claim a second FA Cup in four seasons. They weren't yet at United or Arsenal's level but had been among the most willing teams to embrace a new sense of internationalism, becoming the most cosmopolitan club in England. Ruud Gullit became the first foreign manager to win the cup in 1996–97, after Gianfranco Zola and Gianluca Villa illuminated that campaign. The pick of Chelsea's cup run wins was a 4–2 Fourth Round comeback against Liverpool, a stage that also saw Trevor Sinclair score one of the great cup goals with a bicycle kick against Barnsley. The crowning moment was the quickest goal ever scored in an FA Cup Final to that point, as Roberto Di Matteo scored a thunderbolt after 43 seconds, putting Chelsea on the path to a 2–0 victory over Middlesbrough.

That result made Middlesbrough the fourth FA Cup finalist to be relegated in the same season, as well as the first club to lose both domestic cup finals in the same year. Their FA Cup run had been somewhat fortuitous, with Boro only coming back from 2–0 down against third-tier Chesterfield after a Jon Howard shot over the line was ruled out for the minnows. Middlesbrough drew 3–3 before winning the replay 3–0. The 2000 Final had no such fireworks, nor a fitting send-off for Wembley. Di Matteo again scored, for a drab 1–0 win over Aston Villa.

1999–2000
CHELSEA 1–0 ASTON VILLA
VENUE: **WEMBLEY STADIUM**
ATTENDANCE: **78,217**

2000–01
LIVERPOOL 2–1 ARSENAL
VENUE: **MILLENNIUM STADIUM**
ATTENDANCE: **72,500**

The Final then relocated to Cardiff for six seasons, but its centre of gravity remained between Old Trafford and Highbury. Arsenal embarked on a run of four Finals in five years, but the first of those was a defeat. Wenger's influence began to spread as much as Ferguson's. Liverpool took Arsenal's lead by appointing Wenger's respected

Opposite: Paul Scholes, Gary Neville and David Beckham celebrate the goal by Teddy Sheringham, far right, that sent Manchester United on the way to a 2–0 win over Newcastle United in the 1999 Final and the second trophy of a historic treble.

Below: Chelsea's Roberto Di Matteo scores the only goal against Aston Villa, to win the last FA Cup Final at the old Wembley, in 2000.

Following pages: Liverpool's Michael Owen scores past David Seaman of Arsenal in the 2001 showpiece – the first held at the Millennium Stadium in Cardiff. A further five Finals would be held in the Welsh capital.

compatriot, Gerard Houllier. He began the long course of correcting the club's direction, building a competitive team spearheaded by Michael Owen and a young Steven Gerrard. The peak of this was the 2000–01 season when the Reds didn't lose a single knock-out game. That led to a unique treble of League Cup, UEFA Cup and FA Cup.

But Liverpool did come very close to losing the last of those, as well as the Semi-final. There they met one of the season's revelations in the last four, third-tier Wycombe Wanderers. They were managed by Wimbledon's 1988 hero, Lawrie Sanchez, who masterminded a victory over his old club in the last 16. He had to resort to some ramshackle "Crazy Gang" resourcefulness for the Quarter-final away to Leicester City. An injury crisis left Wycombe without all six of their strikers, leading to Sanchez putting out an advertisement for any forward not cup-tied. It was seen by Roy Essandoh, whose career peak, up to that point, had been at Finland's VPS Vaasa. Sanchez initially decided to give him a two-week contract, and threw the striker on for the last 15 minutes of the Leicester tie, with the score at 1–1. What happened next felt as inevitable as it did incredible. In the third minute of injury time, Essandoh headed the winner. It was what the cup is all about.

Essandoh came on as a sub in the Semi-final against Liverpool, and there was the threat of another sensation as Wycombe held out for 78 minutes. Eventually, Emile Heskey broke their resistance to set up a 2–1 Reds' win.

The first Final at Cardiff went even closer to the wire. Arsenal were leading through Freddie Ljungberg's 72nd-minute goal, which came as a relief to the Gunners after a host of goal-line clearances from Liverpool – including one off Stephane Henchoz's hand – had fostered the feeling it was going to be one of those days. It was instead a climax like no other. On 83 minutes, the electric Owen

reacted quicker than anyone, firing a loose ball into the corner. On 88 minutes, he was put through for an elusive angled finish. Owen described it as the greatest moment of his career.

Wenger echoed his great rival Ferguson and made big changes after that defeat. Sol Campbell was sensationally signed from rivals Spurs and Arsenal immediately claimed a third club double, this one even more commanding than the last in 1997–98. Chelsea were dismissed in Cardiff by two divine long-range strikes from Ray Parlour and Freddie Ljungberg. The Swede became the first player to score in successive FA Cup Finals since Spurs' Bobby Smith in 1962.

Arsenal then became the first club to retain the trophy since their neighbours in 1982, beating Southampton 1–0 in the 2003 Final through a Robert Pires goal. For the first time the Final was played "indoors", with the Millennium Stadium's roof closed due to heavy rain.

Wenger's side had lost the league to Manchester United in a pulsating title race, but not before beating them 2–0 in the Fifth Round of

Above: Michael Owen scores an equaliser against Arsenal in the 2001 Final, sparking a remarkable late turnaround that won Liverpool The FA Cup and completing a treble that also included the League Cup and UEFA Cup.

Opposite top: Chelsea's Marcel Desailly is unable to stop Ray Parlour firing in the first goal of the 2002 Final, which ended with a 2–0 Arsenal win and the club's third domestic double.

Opposite bottom left: David Seaman makes an acrobatic save against Sheffield United's Paul Peschisolido in the 2003 Semi-final, to send Arsenal through to a third successive Final.

Opposite bottom right: Robert Pires scores Arsenal's winning goal in the 2003 Final as Southampton's Michael Svensson looks on, the London club becoming the first to retain The FA Cup since Tottenham Hotspur in 1982.

The FA Cup. Giggs missed an open goal, but it was a different kind of hit that dominated the headlines. Ferguson was furious following the defeat, and kicked a boot that somehow flew into David Beckham's face, cutting his eyebrow. It was unintentional but the player's conspicuous plaster symbolised their fractured relationship.

Beckham was sold that summer, as Ferguson began another rebuilding job, the number seven shirt taken by a young Portuguese winger named Cristiano Ronaldo. That left United behind Arsenal,

2001–02
ARSENAL 2–0 CHELSEA
VENUE: **MILLENNIUM STADIUM**
ATTENDANCE: **73,963**

2002–03
ARSENAL 1–0 SOUTHAMPTON
VENUE: **MILLENNIUM STADIUM**
ATTENDANCE: **73,726**

who scaled new heights by recording the league's first unbeaten season since Preston North End in 1888–89. There was to be no double, however, as Ferguson made winning The FA Cup his mission. He took great pride in the fact that Arsenal didn't beat United that season, nor were they "invincible" against them.

Ferguson's team had already spoiled neighbours Manchester City's run with a 4–2 win, after the Sky Blues had come from 3–0 down to beat Spurs 4–3 in the Fourth Round. Ferguson had a point to prove in another absorbing Semi-final against Arsenal. Paul Scholes settled it to send United to Cardiff.

There, they met Millwall, who became the first second-tier club to reach the Final since 1992. The constant references to 1973 and 1976 irked United, who focused on the job in hand to record an easy 3–0 win.

Left: A young Cristiano Ronaldo smiling in the Cardiff dressing room with The FA Cup, after scoring in Manchester United's 3–0 win over Millwall.

Opposite: Steven Gerrard scores a blockbusting equaliser in the 91st minute of the 2006 Final, to make it 3–3 against West Ham United, and cap a superb individual display in Liverpool's eventual victory.

Below: A tense Manchester United team look on during their shoot-out with Arsenal at the end of the 2005 Final. It was the first in history to go to penalties.

The next year was quite a contrast, as United at last met Arsenal in a Final, but it was also somewhat different to the contests that had preceded it. It wasn't quite the culmination of an era, since Roman Abramovich's purchase of Chelsea had already dramatically changed the order of English football. Instead, the two great rivals were at their weakest in almost a decade, as illustrated by how United were taken to a replay after a 0–0 with non-league Exeter City at Old Trafford. Their 2–0 victory over Wenger's side in the league had meanwhile sapped Arsenal's edge as it had ended a record 49-game unbeaten run. The aggressive manner of that contest prompted face-offs in the tunnel and, notoriously, a pizza thrown at Ferguson.

The 2005 FA Cup Final showdown was similarly bad-tempered, so much so that José Antonio Reyes became only the second player sent off in a Final. Not an inch was given by either side, however. It became the first Final to finish 0–0 since 1912 and consequently the first to go to penalties. Paul Scholes was the only player to miss. Arsenal were victorious.

The second Final to go to penalties immediately followed, although only after one last great game at Cardiff, this time between Liverpool and West Ham United. This became known as "the Gerrard Final" after the Liverpool midfielder's heroics. Gerrard had already scored a blockbusting strike to make it 2–2 after West Ham had led 2–0, a Paul Konchesky cross then flew into Liverpool goalkeeper Pepe Reina's net.

2003–04
MANCHESTER UNITED   3–0   MILLWALL
VENUE: MILLENNIUM STADIUM
ATTENDANCE: 71,350

2004–05
ARSENAL   0–0   MANCHESTER UNITED
AET
5–4 PENS
VENUE: MILLENNIUM STADIUM
ATTENDANCE: 71,876

2005–06
LIVERPOOL   3–3   WEST HAM UNITED
AET
3–1 PENS
VENUE: MILLENNIUM STADIUM
ATTENDANCE: 71,140

With the score at 3–2 in the 91st minute and West Ham mere moments from a first FA Cup win since 1980, a clearance fell to Gerrard 35yd (32m) from goal. He hit it first time on the half-volley for the ball to fly into the bottom corner.

It was a strike to match any the Final had seen. Gerrard, of course, scored in the eventual shoot-out, while three out of four West Ham players missed. The cup was finally going back to Anfield. The Final itself was about to go home, albeit to a new arena, in a different world.

SPONSORSHIP

If The FA Cup is all about the democracy of the game, sponsorship helps to sustain it. The funds that come in from the current deal with Emirates are spread around the competition, ensuring its benefits to the lower leagues go way beyond cup runs for specific clubs. They are also essential to non-league, amateur and grassroots football. It's another way that The FA Cup is a leveller.

Sponsorship ensures that The FA Cup can deliver a prize fund that currently ranges from £375 for each of the 174 defeated teams in the extra-preliminary round (with £1,125 going to the winners), right up to £1.8 million for the eventual winners of the final. And prize money is just one aspect of the financial support that The FA Cup brings to the game.

Emirates have been working with The FA and its prestige event since 2015, with the agreement extended again in 2020. The Dubai airline are the tournament's fifth main sponsor, after a landmark decision was taken for the future of the game in 1994. That was the year that a deal was struck with Littlewoods, and the competition became known as 'The FA Cup sponsored by Littlewoods'. AXA followed Littlewoods in 1998, with

E.ON signing on in 2006 and Budweiser in 2011. There was a tweak to the title for purposes of clarity with the agreement in 2015, as the competition became known as 'The Emirates FA Cup'. Importantly, however, The FA Cup's full name will always persist.

Working with an airline has also helped the spread of the competition in other ways. Since 2016, The FA Cup trophy has been taken on Emirates aircraft around the world – international tours that started in Ghana and Kenya. These trips reflect a modern acknowledgment of the fact that The FA Cup has always been so popular in so many different corners of the planet.

Sponsorship has also created a breakthrough for other benefits. In 2020, Emirates agreed to a move where its title sponsorship was temporarily altered so the showpiece climax was officially known as the Heads Up FA Cup Final, as part of a campaign around mental health awareness promoted by The FA president, Prince William, Duke of Cambridge. As the partnership continues, expect more initiatives that take advantage of the FA Cup's unique place in football culture, both in England and beyond.

Left: The FA Cup pictured at Marlow Football Club in August 2021 as part of the competition's 150th anniversary celebrations. No side has competed in the cup on more occasions than Marlow.

Opposite top left: The 2020 FA Cup Final was renamed to the Heads Up FA Cup Final, with lead partner Emirates donating their title to the campaign.

Opposite top right: Prince William, Duke of Cambridge and President of The FA, prepares to hand over The FA Cup trophy in 2021.

Opposite middle left: James Ward-Prowse of Southampton prepares to lead his team out of the tunnel during their FA Cup Semi-final at Wembley in 2021.

Opposite bottom left: Sponsorship details extend even to the balls used in FA Cup games.

Opposite bottom right: Becky Hill sings the national anthem prior to the 2021 FA Cup Final, backed by a marching band and a message from Emirates to all supporters of the competition.

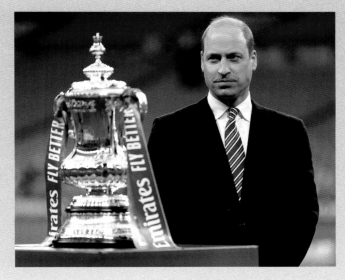

CHAPTER ELEVEN

A NEW WAY

2007-PRESENT

IT IS BY NOW A NEW TRADITION AT EVERY FA CUP FINAL AND SEMI-FINAL. IN THE HOURS BEFORE EACH OCCASION, THOUSANDS OF SUPPORTERS STOP AT THE TOP OF THE STAIRS AT WEMBLEY PARK UNDERGROUND STATION AND TAKE A PHOTO OF THE PATH UP TO THE STADIUM. THAT IS THEIR MEMENTO OF ONE OF FOOTBALL'S MOST FAMOUS WALKS, EVEN IF THE VIEW AT WEMBLEY WAY IS NOW VERY DIFFERENT FROM WHAT WENT BEFORE.

That gleaming arch now dominates the sky rather than the Twin Towers. The ramp has been replaced by steps. There are LED signs showcasing what is to come on a shining facade, but there are also more traditional tributes to that history. The first landmark those same fans walk under is the Bobby Moore Bridge. The picture is one of modernity, imbued with decades of memories.

That is much like the great competition Wembley stages as its prize event. The temptation at times like this is to talk about how the modern FA Cup would be unrecognisable to many of its winners, let alone founding fathers such as Arthur Kinnaird or Charles Alcock.

The clubs that win it now most often resemble multinational corporations more than community institutions. The owners are rarely local businessmen but overseas oligarchs, royals and venture capitalists. The entire competition is on a scale that would have been unimaginable for most of its history. The Final's global audience now stands at over half a billion people. On the pitch, the football is played at a frenetic pace. What would figures like Kinnaird have made of concepts like "counter-pressing"?

And yet, as The FA Cup reaches its 150th anniversary, the last few years have been a truly open era, featuring all of the elements that have enriched that century and a half. There have been new dynasties, as well as great cup teams, while some clubs have ended long waits and others have enjoyed astounding upsets. Figures like Didier Drogba and Arsène Wenger made themselves two of The FA Cup's greatest names, but so did surprise heroes such as Ben Watson, scorer of Wigan's winner in the 2013 Final. The list of finalists has

been more diverse than the concluding years at the old Wembley, as recent showpieces have offered another club from the second tier, three clubs making their debut and two first-time winners.

The 2020–21 campaign meanwhile saw the biggest-ever gap between clubs for a cup tie, as eighth-tier Marine hosted Tottenham Hotspur in the Third Round. That season's Final then offered a timely illustration of what The FA Cup is really about, with supporters were finally able to gather in their thousands as COVID-19 restrictions lifted. It was a celebration of life as much as a celebration of Leicester City's victory.

That was the spirit that fired the competition in its earliest days. The simple beauty of a knock-out tie attracted crowds, and those crowds began to gather to watch their own clubs. It became something more than kicking a ball or healthy exercise. It became about identity, community and tradition.

Much of that history was evoked for that first Final at the new Wembley in May 2007. The wealthiest club in the country were taking on the most famous, as Chelsea faced Manchester United, but they were preceded by a celebration of the occasion that stretched back further than any other.

Guests from 50 previous Finals were invited for the opening ceremony, with 1957 the earliest represented, by Aston Villa's Peter McParland. The marching band of the Royal Engineers, the club that won the cup in 1875, meanwhile performed as the Red Arrows flew over the Wembley arch. The £757m stadium may have looked different to the one that so many of the past winners played in, but players like Michael Carrick and Didier Drogba found the very idea of playing on the same piece of land inspiring. Both remarked on the

"IF YOU GET TO THE FINAL, THAT'S WHEN YOU REALLY KNOW YOU HAVE A CHANCE TO WIN THE TROPHY BECAUSE WHEN YOU COME IN YOU SEE THE CUP. EVERYTHING CHANGES."

- DIDIER DROGBA -

Opposite top: The view of Wembley Way for the 1999 Final, the Two Towers looking down on supporters of Newcastle United and Manchester United.

Opposite bottom: The view of Wembley Way for the 2017 Final, the arch soaring above fans of Arsenal and Chelsea.

Previous pages: Chelsea's Didier Drogba runs in jubilation at the end of the 2010 Final, a 1–0 win over Portsmouth. The Ivorian claimed the only goal, making that the third of a record four Finals that Drogba scored in.

occasion's sense of history, although it gave rise to a tense Final.

This grand return to Wembley naturally marked the beginning of a new era, but also the culmination of another. It was the last of 12 consecutive wins by one of England's so-called "big four", and the first Final since 1986 between the top two in the league. It was also the first-ever Final to involve both the season's champions and the League Cup winners, United having won the title and Chelsea the other domestic cup.

This was a very different Chelsea to the cosmopolitan club that won The FA Cup in 1997 and 2000, though. The drastic growth of the game had not just attracted supporters from all over the world, but also investors. In 2003, Russian oligarch Roman Abramovich bought Chelsea and transformed both the club and the game. His first summer saw a spending spree of a type the sport had never witnessed. Over £110m went out on 12 players. That money made Chelsea mainstays at the top of the game. They won The FA Cup four times in six years between 2006 and 2012, and would later reach four Finals

Top left: Rio Ferdinand was forced into goal in Manchester United's defeat to Portsmouth in the 2007–08 Sixth Round, after Tomasz Kuszczak had been sent off.

Top right: Nwanko Kanu, left, celebrates his winning goal in the 2008 Final against Cardiff City, to give Portsmouth their first FA Cup in 69 years.

Opposite top: The Red Arrows fly overhead during the opening ceremony of the new Wembley, ahead of the 2007 Final between Manchester United and Chelsea.

Opposite bottom: Didier Drogba scores the first goal at the reconstructed stadium, beating Edwin van der Sar.

2006–07
CHELSEA 1–0 MANCHESTER UNITED
AET
VENUE: **WEMBLEY STADIUM (NEW)**
ATTENDANCE: **89,826**

2007–08
PORTSMOUTH 1–0 WALES CARDIFF CITY
VENUE: **WEMBLEY STADIUM (NEW)**
ATTENDANCE: **89,874**

in five years between 2016 and 2021. Such expenditure nevertheless brought exacting standards. Abramovich didn't tolerate what he perceived as failure for long. Those initial four wins under the Russian's ownership involved four different managers. This victory in 2007 was the charismatic José Mourinho's only FA Cup. Even that was driven by resentment at a defeat – Chelsea had lost the league to United just two weeks before the Final. So, Mourinho's side were even more intent on stopping United from achieving what would have been a fourth domestic double.

Drogba scored the first goal at the new Wembley, as his 116th-minute strike secured a 1–0 win. The Ivorian became another mainstay of the competition, scoring in each of those four wins between 2006 and 2012, to become the first player to score in four different Finals. In 2009, his goal was a crucial equaliser against Everton after another record. Louis Saha gave David Moyes' Toffees side the lead with the fastest goal ever scored in a Final, after just 21 seconds. Chelsea had to dig in, but a core of Drogba, Petr Cech, Ashley Cole, John Terry and

2008–09
CHELSEA 2–1 EVERTON
VENUE: **WEMBLEY STADIUM** (NEW)
ATTENDANCE: **89,391**

2009–10
CHELSEA 1–0 PORTSMOUTH
VENUE: **WEMBLEY STADIUM** (NEW)
ATTENDANCE: **88,335**

2010–11
MANCHESTER CITY 2–1 STOKE CITY
VENUE: **WEMBLEY STADIUM** (NEW)
ATTENDANCE: **88,643**

Frank Lampard had developed a real resilience. That season had seen them overcome a mid-season managerial change, as Luiz Felipe Scolari was replaced by Guus Hiddink. The squad responded well to the Dutch strategist, and he joined the list of cup-winning managers after Lampard's 71st-minute winner.

It was testament to that resilience that Chelsea actually made a habit of winning under "interim" managers. The same happened three years later as they beat Liverpool under caretaker Roberto Di Matteo, the match-winner in 1997 and 2000. The Italian only burnished his legend as the 2012 FA Cup was the first of a double success that also brought the Champions League.

That year's Final offered another historical echo, as Liverpool were managed by the incomparable Kenny Dalglish. He had restored an identity to the club on his return and won a first trophy since 2006 with the 2012 League Cup. There was a clear sense of momentum in knock-outs since The FA Cup run saw Liverpool eliminate Manchester United and Everton, both by scores of 2–1.

Chelsea had meanwhile hammered Tottenham Hotspur 5-1 in their Semi-final, although the latter's run involved a moment that put all of this into context. A Sixth Round match at White Hart Lane saw Bolton Wanderers' Fabrice Muamba suffer cardiac arrest on the pitch and collapse. Only the quick actions of paramedics saved his life. Muamba never played again but made a full recovery to become a coach.

The 2012 Final also featured another evolution in the game's traditions. It was the first to be scheduled for 5.15pm rather than the

Opposite top: Leeds United's Jermaine Beckford peels away after scoring the only goal at Manchester United in the 2009–10 Third Round, in what was then a rare meeting between the two fierce rivals.

Opposite bottom: Everton's Louis Saha scores the fastest goal in FA Cup Final history, striking after just 21 seconds in 2009. It couldn't stop Chelsea winning at Wembley yet again.

Below: Chelsea celebrate retaining the FA Cup, while winning the club's first domestic double, after beating Portsmouth in the 2010 Final.

2011–12
CHELSEA **2**–**1** LIVERPOOL
VENUE: **WEMBLEY STADIUM (NEW)**
ATTENDANCE: **89,041**

usual 3pm, to avoid a clash with league fixtures. It still saw Chelsea make a fast start. Ramires scored after 11 minutes before Drogba netted his customary goal shortly after half-time. Andy Carroll pulled one back for Liverpool, and then thought he'd claimed a dramatic equaliser late on, when Cech just got to a header. There was considerable debate over whether the ball crossed the line. Replays, in the period before goal-line technology, were inconclusive. Referee Phil Dowd ruled it wasn't a goal.

The result saw a series of records broken. As well as Drogba's feat, Cole became The FA Cup's most successful ever player with seven wins – three with Arsenal and four with Chelsea. It was the penultimate of those that represented the peak of this team, as Chelsea won their first double in 2010. Carlo Ancelotti's free-scoring side hit 103 goals in the league and averaged more than three per game in the cup. That figure could have been even higher, had they not hit the frame of the goal five times in the first half of the Final against Portsmouth.

That streak encouraged the belief that Portsmouth's luck might be in. It ended up representing more of the cup's notorious capriciousness, to go with a calamitous season for Portsmouth. Kevin-Prince Boateng had a penalty saved by Cech in the 54th minute. Drogba inevitably scored the only goal in the 58th. Lampard then missed a penalty later on, but it didn't matter. Ancelotti had beaten another former Chelsea boss in Avram Grant.

Portsmouth had shown character in getting that far, since they had already become the fourth club to reach The FA Cup Final and get relegated the same season. It was a fate that came thanks to a 10-point deduction, as a financial implosion saw Portsmouth become the first Premier League to go into administration.

The club was over £100m in debt, and many felt such a nadir was the deeper cost of one of the greatest moments in their history. Two

years before, in 2008, Portsmouth won The FA Cup for the first time in 69 years. Only four players got on the pitch in both Finals, illustrating the scale of change. One of them, Nwankwo Kanu, was the cup-winning hero against Cardiff City.

The Welsh club were in their first Final in 81 years and remain only the second club from below the top tier to reach the showpiece in the new millennium. Cardiff embodied the fresh feeling surrounding the cup that season, as the hold of the big four was broken. Barnsley did a lot of the breaking. The club who would eventually finish 18th in the second tier knocked out Liverpool and holders Chelsea in successive rounds, before being beaten by Cardiff in the Semi-final. Harry Redknapp meanwhile claimed a third cup upset against Manchester United in his career, as his Portsmouth won an epic Quarter-final. It saw United's Rio Ferdinand forced to go in goal after a Tomasz Kuszczak red card, but they still threw everything forward to try and level Sulley Muntari's penalty. Portsmouth held on, to deny Alex Ferguson another treble, but his team still won both the league and Champions League.

It's possible that atmospheres were amplified by an added motivation for second-tier clubs in that Sixth Round. The 2007–08 season was the first where it was decided Semi-finals would also be played at Wembley. It was also the first since 1908 when only one club from the top tier reached the last four. They won out, as Portsmouth defeated West Brom and then Cardiff. Kanu described his opportunistic strike in the Final as the best moment of his life. Redknapp gushed about a "dream come true". It arrived 24 years after his first game in the cup, that shock win over Manchester

Top left: Tottenham Hotspur and Bolton Wanderers players stand with concern as Fabrice Muamba receives medical attention after collapsing in a 2011–12 Sixth Round match. The Bolton midfielder thankfully made a full recovery, although never played again.

Top right: An elated Roberto Di Matteo is thrown into the air by Chelsea players after guiding the club to another FA Cup in 2012, with Liverpool this time beaten in the Final.

Opposite: Yaya Touré celebrates after scoring the only goal of the 2011 Final, against Stoke City, to give Manchester City their first trophy in 35 years.

United with Bournemouth in 1984. Around 200,000 people turned up for the victory parade.

The innocent joy Portsmouth took from the victory was invigorating, but was maybe even surpassed by what happened in 2013. Wigan Athletic's Final victory over Manchester City has a claim to be up there with Sunderland's in 1973, or any other from history. A number of elements elevated the day. Owned by Dave Whelan, whose career was ended by that broken leg in the 1960 Final, Wigan had never reached the Final. They had never won a trophy at all, and were on the brink of relegation going into the game.

More daunting was the scale of the challenge. Wigan took on Manchester City. Much like Chelsea in 2003, City had been transformed by the Abu Dhabi Group's 2008 takeover. Stars like David Silva and Yaya Touré were brought in, and became totems of a new era of success. They first had to break a psychological complex. By 2011, City still hadn't won a trophy in 35 years. The phrase that had grown in that time was "typical City", for the myriad ways they seemed to find a way to lose. This was especially true in Manchester derbies. Ferguson's United side had scored predictably late winners in four of their last six meetings with City before the clubs were drawn together in the 2010–11 Semi-final. Many at City cite this as the match that changed the mindset of the

team. Touré scored the only goal of the game, and the club never looked back. There was never a sense that they were going to lose the 2011 Final, especially since it was opponents Stoke City's debut appearance in the fixture. Touré again scored. City kept going. They followed that FA Cup with a first league title in 44 years, Sergio Aguero scoring a sensational winner in the very last seconds of the 2011–12 season.

Such success, and such expenditure, nevertheless brought the same levels of expectation at City as they did at Chelsea. City finished a distant second in the league in 2012–13 and the morning of the cup Final brought headlines that Roberto Mancini was to be replaced with Manuel Pellegrini as manager, regardless of the result.

There was a sense of vulnerability that Wigan seized on. It was another of those seasons that had that air of possibility. Millwall again reached the Semi-final, to be beaten by Wigan, but the biggest shock came from one of the clubs Millwall eliminated. In the Fourth Round, Luton Town won 1–0 at Norwich City, becoming the first non-league club to knock out a top-tier team since Sutton United in 1989.

The story of Whelan's broken leg dominated the build-up to the Final, to the point the players started to make light-hearted fun over how often they heard it. Match-winner Watson himself had suffered

Top left: Scott Rendell celebrates his goal over Norwich City in the 2012–13 Fourth Round at Carrow Road, as Luton Town became the first non-league club to knock out top-tier opposition since 1989.

Top right: Ben Watson, right, celebrates his shock late winner for Wigan Athletic in the 2013 Final against Manchester City, giving Wigan Athletic the first major trophy of their history.

Opposite top: Arsène Wenger lifts what he describes as his most important trophy, as a 3–2 win over Hull City in the 2014 Final brings Arsenal's first silverware in nine years.

Opposite bottom: Matthew Fryatt scores in the 2013–14 Semi-final against Sheffield United at Wembley, to send Hull to their first ever Final.

a serious leg break just six months beforehand, and had only just returned to action. The longer City went without scoring in the Final, the more it felt like a number of strands were coming together. That familiar anxiety on such days was creeping into City's play. The first give was on 84 minutes with Pablo Zabaleta's second booking for taking down Wigan's Callum McManaman as he surged through. Seven minutes later, with the game into stoppage time, Wigan won a corner. Shaun Maloney swung it out, Watson flashed in a header.

It was Wigan's only effort on target.

As the players went up to collect the trophy with manager Roberto Martinez, Emmerson Boyce joked with Whelan that this was now the story to tell people. "It's closure," Whelan said. "It was the first time I had been back on that turf since I was carried off… it floods through your memories."

The season ended up bittersweet for Wigan. Just a few days later, they became the first club to win The FA Cup and get relegated in the same year, after defeat at Arsenal. By then, debate had grown over whether it was time for Gunners manager Arsène Wenger to stand aside. The retirement of his great rival Alex Ferguson, in that same month, only fuelled this. Wenger hadn't won a trophy in eight years and, worse, silverware seemed to come so easily to the club's rivals.

The wait would extend to nine years, but from 2014, FA Cups would now flow like they had in the 1930s. The first of those trophies didn't come easily or logically, however. Wenger's team had an easier time beating Tottenham Hotspur, Liverpool and Everton in their run than they did against Wigan in the Semi-final or Hull City in the Final.

The holders had eliminated Manchester City again, this time a 2–1 win away from home in the Sixth Round. To add more edge, former City hero Uwe Rosler was Wigan's new manager. They then pushed Arsenal all the way in the Semi-final, leading through Jordi Gomez's penalty with eight minutes left, only for Per Mertesacker to divert in an equaliser. Lukasz Fabianski saved the first two penalties

> ## "THIS WAS MORE IMPORTANT THAN ALL THE OTHERS."
> – ARSÈNE WENGER –

of the shoot-out and Arsenal had reached their 18th FA Cup Final, matching Manchester United's record. Hull City were meanwhile in their first, after beating third-tier Sheffield United in the Semi-final. Steve Bruce's team took to Wembley straight away, with James Chester scoring after four minutes and Curtis Davies after eight.

It seemed as though Arsenal's capacity for calamity was becoming more acute the closer they got to glory. Instead, they showed their character, as it all made for the new Wembley's best Final so far. Santi Cazorla thundered in a superb free-kick on 17 minutes to make the next hour tense. Laurent Koscielny eventually turned in an equaliser before Aaron Ramsey stabbed in an extra-time winner. Wenger lifted his first trophy

for nine years, which also happened to be a new FA Cup. A third version of this model had been made by Thomas Lyte Silver, with the weight increased to 13.9lb (6.3kg) to make it more durable.

Wenger, on the other hand, felt that bit lighter. "This was more important than all the others," he said after the comeback. "We have twice won the double but were not under pressure then like we were today. "We waited a long time for this and the happiness is linked sometimes with the suffering, and the time that you have to wait."

They wouldn't have to wait at all for the next triumph, and this time it didn't involve much suffering. Arsenal cruised to a 4–0 victory over Aston Villa in the 2015 Final. Alexis Sanchez electrified the game with a brilliant swerving strike. Arsenal's only real challenge in their run was a 2–1 win over Louis van Gaal's Manchester United, who had earlier been held 0–0 by Cambridge United. Even the 3–0 replay defeat made a huge difference to the fourth-tier club's finances.

The biggest sensation of the 2014–15 season was still Chelsea's elimination at home to third-tier Bradford City. Even more remarkable than the result was its nature. This was no narrow win over a team off form. José Mourinho's side were on their way to another league title, and were 2–0 up at Stamford Bridge by the 38th minute. A speculative strike from Jon Stead ensured the gap was respectable but it probably should have become wider when Cesc Fàbregas and Eden Hazard were brought on. Chelsea were instead unbalanced. Bradford realised they had a chance. Within five minutes, Filipe Morais equalised. Seven minutes later, Andy Halliday edged Bradford in front with an incredible strike, before putting his head in his hands as if he couldn't believe it. There was still more to come. For the game's finale, Stead flicked Mark Yeates through for a winner that was almost casual. The travelling support behind the goal were in raptures.

Mourinho graciously went into the visiting dressing room afterwards to shake everyone's hands, later describing the 4–2 win as exactly what makes The FA Cup so special. He added that it was a "disgrace" by his own team. Mourinho had the previous season described Wenger as a "specialist in failure". The Arsenal manager instead equalled George Ramsay's managerial record of six FA Cups, and his club also surpassed United's 11 wins, with 12 in all.

United immediately responded the next season, coming from behind against Crystal Palace. Alan Pardew offered one of the images of the game with a touchline dance following Jason Puncheon's opening goal, before Juan Mata equalised for United and Jesse Lingard won it in extra-time with a fine volley. While the 1990 meeting between the two clubs was the first of so many trophies for

Ferguson, this first one since his retirement was also Van Gaal's last. Celebrations were soured by news he was to be replaced by Mourinho, who had by then left Chelsea after a cataclysmic title defence that saw them hover above the relegation zone.

Antonio Conte suffered a similar fate at Stamford Bridge in 2018, despite beating Mourinho's United in that season's cup Final through a Hazard penalty. Tension had grown between the Italian and the board over signings after the 2017 Final, when Chelsea just lost out on another double.

The Blues had already won the league and seemed set for The FA Cup against an Arsenal side that were now ailing under Wenger. That 2016–17 campaign marked the first season where the Frenchman didn't finish in the league's top four. He stood alone in the cup, though. A resolute 2–1 win over Chelsea, Ramsey again scoring a late winner, gave Wenger a record seventh

Top: Bradford City's Felipe Morais celebrates a shock equaliser against Chelsea in the 2014–15 Fourth Round, the third-tier side coming back from 2–0 down to win 4–2.

Above: Jamie Mackie brings Bradford back down to earth, as Reading won 3–0 in the Sixth Round.

Opposite top: Alexis Sanchez electrifies the 2015 Final, and another Arsenal victory, with his side's sensational second goal in a 4–0 win over Aston Villa.

Opposite bottom: Michael Carrick stands in delight, after Manchester United come from behind to beat Crystal Palace in the 2016 Final.

victory. Arsenal meanwhile became the cup's most successful club on their own again, with 13 wins.

Arsenal's victory had been aided by Victor Moses' red card, and their run to the Final had involved one element of farce. The Fifth Round victory over Sutton United had seen the non-league side's substitute goalkeeper Wayne Shaw receive much attention for eating a pasty on the bench. It later emerged he was motivated by odds of 8–1 that he would do that, and was later banned for two months for breaching betting rules.

The unlikely heroes of that season's cup were Arsenal's opponents in the next round. Lincoln City became the first non-league club since 1914 to reach the Quarter-finals and did so by becoming the last

Opposite top left: Louis van Gaal lifts the FA Cup in 2016, in what was his last act as Manchester United manager. He was swiftly replaced by Jose Mourinho.

Opposite top right: A defiant Arsène Wenger proudly holds what was to end up his last trophy at Arsenal, a record seventh FA Cup, secured with a 2–1 win over Chelsea in 2017.

Opposite bottom: Manager Antonio Conte sprays champagne over his Chelsea squad after they beat Manchester United 1–0 in the 2018 Final.

Below: Lincoln City celebrate in the Turf Moor changing room after beating Burnley in the 2016–17 Fifth Round, a victory that made them the last non-league side to eliminate Premier League opposition.

2016–17
ARSENAL 2–1 CHELSEA
VENUE: **WEMBLEY STADIUM**
ATTENDANCE: **89,472**

2017–18
CHELSEA 1–0 MANCHESTER UNITED
VENUE: **WEMBLEY STADIUM (NEW)**
ATTENDANCE: **87,647**

non-league club to eliminate Premier League opposition. Burnley were beaten at Turf Moor by an 89th-minute goal from centre-half Sean Raggett, which was his side's only shot on target. It was only confirmed through goal-line technology, with Lincoln manager Danny Cowley describing it all as a "football miracle". His side were beaten 5–0 by Arsenal, but had made their mark.

Wenger ended the 2017 Final revelling in the glory of a third FA Cup in four years. Summing up his situation at the time, though, much of the post-match discussion was on his future rather than his place in history. Wenger was due to meet the board the following week. "The best presentation?" he wondered aloud. "Watch the game… and there can be no doubt."

Football as a whole was looking to the future in another way. Continuing The FA Cup's tradition as a pioneering event for changes

to the game, it became the first English competition to feature a Video Assistant Referee – commonly named VAR – in 2017–18. Leicester City's Kelechi Iheanacho became the first player to have a goal awarded by the system, when he was adjudged to be onside for a strike that secured a 2–0 win over Fleetwood Town in a Third Round replay. Leicester were humbled 2–1 by fourth-tier Newport County at the same stage the next season, perpetuating their miserable record in the cup.

The way the 2018–19 season panned out was the very opposite of an upset. It was instead the most devastating display of power The FA Cup has seen. Under their visionary manager Pep Guardiola, Manchester City became the first team to win a domestic treble. The manner of the victory matched the manner of the achievement. City destroyed Watford 6–0, in what was the joint-biggest FA Cup Final win, along with Bury's victory over Derby County in 1903. "It was an incredible Final for us and we have finished an incredible year," Guardiola said. "I love the Champions League but to do that is more difficult than to win the Champions League."

It didn't feel like it on the day. It was all the more painful for Watford given this was their first Final since 1984, and how they'd got there. Javi Gracia's team had come from 2–0 down against Wolves in their Semi-final to win 3–2, Troy Deeney scoring an equalising penalty four minutes into stoppage time.

2018–19
MANCHESTER CITY 6–0 WATFORD
VENUE: **WEMBLEY STADIUM (NEW)**
ATTENDANCE: **85,854**

2019–20
ARSENAL 2–1 CHELSEA
VENUE: **WEMBLEY STADIUM (NEW)**
ATTENDANCE: **0**

Opposite top left: Padraig Amond races away after scoring the clinching goal in Newport County's shock victory over Leicester City at Rodney Parade in the 2018–19 Third Round.

Opposite top right: Troy Deeney celebrates after scoring Watford's late second goal from the penalty spot during the 2019 Semi-final against Wolverhampton Wanderers at Wembley.

Opposite bottom: Raheem Sterling celebrates with the trophy during the 2019 FA Cup Final between Manchester City and Watford at Wembley.

Below: Norwich City and Manchester United take the knee against racial inequality, ahead of the first FA Cup game behind closed doors, after the long disruption caused by the COVID-19 crisis in 2020.

By the time of the next Final, the world had changed. The COVID-19 crisis forced the longest disruption to the game since the Second World War. The FA Cup had just completed the Fifth Round when the sport was suspended for three months, as football, and so many other bodies, worked out what to do next and how they could play safely. The game's authorities had to go through a series of trials, until it was eventually agreed televised football could resume behind closed doors.

The first-ever FA Cup match played in such circumstances was at Carrow Road on 27 June 2020, as Manchester United beat Norwich City 2–1 after extra-time. The empty stands weren't the only sign of a changed world. The death of George Floyd in the USA had prompted a wave of activism around football, with players deciding to "take the knee" as a gesture against racial inequality.

The image preceded every match and was propelled around the world. Amid such global upheaval, that season's showpiece was officially named the Heads Up FA Cup Final as part of a mental health awareness campaign. The occasion, taking place on 1 August rather than 23 May, still had 'Abide With Me'. It was just with singer Emeli Sandé offering a virtual performance, projected onto the roof of Wembley on television.

Arsenal again made the Final, proving themselves the cup team of the era, capable of adapting regardless of the circumstances. They had changed manager mid-season, Unai Emery replaced by the influential midfielder of the 2014 and 2015 wins, Mikel Arteta. He faced another former midfielder, as Frank Lampard now managed Chelsea. It was the third time the two clubs had met in the Final, making it the third-most common pairing in the fixture, along with Aston Villa–West Brom, Chelsea–Manchester United, Arsenal–Newcastle United and Arsenal–Liverpool. Pierre-Emerick Aubameyang followed his brace in the Semi-final against Manchester City with another brace in the

Final, as Arsenal won 2–1. The circumstances forced another break with tradition, as the trophy was lifted on the pitch.

Restrictions continued into the next season, diluting what would have been exhilarating moments for some clubs. Fourth-tier Crawley Town thrashed Leeds United 3–0, while non-league Chorley beat Derby County 2–0. In the case of one cup tie, though, the restrictions brought out something greater. Marine, of the Northern Premier League Division One North West, were denied the grandest home game in their history as they drew Mourinho's Tottenham Hotspur. The FA Cup had never seen a gap like it, as 161 places separated the two clubs. Marine were only the second eighth-tier club to ever reach the third round, and their size was reflected in how Rossett Park could only hold just over 3,000 people. Instead, 30,000 "virtual" tickets were sold. Many were Spurs fans or just general football supporters. Tottenham's eventual 5–0 win was very much the secondary story.

That sense of community was just as keenly felt for the Final. Restrictions had sufficiently lifted by then so 4,000 fans could attend Leicester's Semi-final win over Southampton and 20,000 saw their eventual meeting with Chelsea in the showpiece. Many of those Leicester fans surely weren't expecting victory. This was Chelsea, who almost always won these occasions. This was Leicester, who were the club to have reached the most Finals without ever actually winning the cup. This was the ultimate "hoodoo", especially for those who had witnessed their three defeats in the 1960s.

This was also a different Leicester, though. The club had already offered a once-in-a-lifetime achievement with their astounding Premier League title victory in 2016. They now offered a moment for which so many of their supporters had waited a lifetime. On 63 minutes, Youri Tielemans took a pass just inside the Chelsea half and drove forward. In what almost felt like one flowing movement, the midfielder strode towards the Chelsea goal and then unleashed a stunning drive into the top corner. The reduced crowd had already been making as much noise as a full stadium. The goal produced a roar that went beyond even that. It was a Wembley strike for the ages.

Tielemans' goal was a moment that the football world had been waiting so long for, too. It saw people come together again, united by a shared love of the game and reflecting the ideas and the passion that drove Charles Alcock to create this competition more than a century and a half ago.

Above: Tottenham Hotspur's Moussa Sissoko controls the ball during their 2020–21 Third Round tie with Marine at Rossett Park, a match which represented the biggest ever gap between clubs in the FA Cup, with 161 places between them.

Top left: Crawley Town's Jordan Tunnicliffe celebrates scoring his side's third goal with Tony Craig, to round off a shock elimination of Leeds United at The People's Pension Stadium in the 2020–21 Third Round.

Opposite bottom: Pierre-Emerick Aubameyang lifts Arsenal's record 14th FA Cup, in an empty Wembley, after Chelsea are beaten 2–1 in the 2020 Final. It was the first time the fixture was played in front of empty stands, due to the COVID-19 pandemic.

Following pages: Fans return to Wembley for the 2021 FA Cup Final, a year after the showpiece had to be played behind closed doors.

Below: Leicester City players celebrate with the Emirates FA Cup trophy following their win against Chelsea at Wembley, 2021.

INDEX

BIBLIOGRAPHY

Bagchi, Rob; *The Biography of Leeds United: The Story of the Whites*; 2020

Banks, Gordon; *Banksy*; 2003

Barclay, Patrick; *The Life and Times of Herbert Chapman*; 2014

Butler, Bryon; *The Official Illustrated History of the FA Cup*; 1996

Carragher, Jamie; *The Greatest Games*; 2020

Carrick, Michael; *Michael Carrick; Between the Lines*; 2018

Charlton, Jack; *Jack Charlton: The Autobiography*; 2020

Collett, Mike; *The Complete Record of the FA Cup*; 2003

Dewhurst, Keith; *Underdogs*; 2012

Dickinson, Matt; *Bobby Moore*; 2014

Drogba, Didier; *Commitment: My Autobiography*; 2015

Dunphy, Eamon; *A Strange Kind of Glory: Sir Matt Busby and Manchester United*; 1991

Edwards, Martin; *Red Glory*; 2017

Ferguson, Alex; *Alex Ferguson: My Autobiography*; 2013

Ferguson, Alex; *Managing My Life*; 1999

Fowler, Robbie; *Fowler: My Autobiography*; 2009

Giggs Ryan; *Giggs: The Autobiography*; 2005

Gillan, Don; *The First FA Cup*; 2017

Goldblatt, David: *The Game of Our Lives*; 2014

Green, Geoffrey; *The Official History of the FA Cup*; 1949

Hamilton, Duncan; *Immortal*; 2013

Henshaw, Philip; *Showdown at the Palace: The 1898 FA Cup Final*; 2021

Herbert, Ian; *Quiet Genius*; 2017

Holt, Nick and Lloyd, Guy; *The FA Cup – The Complete Story*; 2005

Hughes, Simon; *Ring of Fire*; 2016

Keane, Roy; *Keane: The Autobiography*; 2002

Keane, Roy; *The Second Half*; 2014

Keegan, Kevin; *My Life in Football*; 2019

Lampard, Frank; *Totally Frank: The Autobiography*; 2006

McIlvanney, Hugh: *McIlvanney On Football*; 1994

McKinstrey, Leo; *Jack and Bobby: A Story of Brothers in Conflict*; 2003

Mitchell, Andy; *Arthur Kinnaird: First Lord of Football*; 2020

Mitten, Andy; *Glory Glory!*; 2009

Neville, Gary; *Red: My Autobiography*; 2011

Saffer, David; *Match of My Life – FA Cup Finals 1953–69*; 2006

Southall, Neville; *Neville Southall: The Binman Chronicles*; 2015

Tossell, David; *Alan Ball: The Man in White Boots*; 2017

Tossell, David; *All Crazee Now – English Football and Footballers in the 1970s*; 2021

Tossell, David: *The Great English Final: 1953: Cup, Coronation and Stanley Matthews*; 2013

Tossell, David; *Natural: The Jimmy Greaves Story*; 2019

Venables, Terry; *Born to Manage*; 2014

Wenger, Arsène; *My Life in Red and White*; 2020

Wilson, Jonathon; *Inverting the Pyramid: The History of Football Tactics*; 2008

Wise, Denis; *Dennis Wise: The Autobiography*; 2000

The Guardian
The Independent
The Daily Mail
The Daily Mirror
The Daily Telegraph
The Observer
The Sun
The Times
British Pathé
ESPN

CREDITS